the
promised land of
recovery

the promised land of recovery

Brad Bertelsen

Millennial Press

Millennial Press, Inc.
P.O. Box 1741
Orem, UT 84059

ISBN: 1-932597-64-6

Cover design and typesetting by Adam Riggs

dedication

Darlene,
Nate,
Bekkah,
Mom, Dad,
and the addict who still suffers

contents

foreword

Having struggled with alcoholism for seventeen years, including seven years without a sober day, and having now gone over 19 years without alcohol, Brad Bertelsen is in a position to be a tremendous help and encouragement to those who struggle with addiction. In addition, this book will be invaluable in helping those whose loved ones and friends struggle with addiction to understand what they are going through and be better able to help and support them.

Brad has done a masterful and inspired job of integrating the Twelve Step program with the scriptures, ancient and modern, which illuminate the true power of the Atonement of Jesus Christ, which is the only power through which complete healing and newness of life can come.

I have known Brad for over thirty years and have watched and marveled gratefully at his own recovery and at the great wisdom and skill he exhibits as he helps others overcome addiction. He has taught in the Twelve Step program now for many years and is highly respected and appreciated by recovering addicts and their family and friends.

In this book, Brad Bertelsen employs wisdom, inspiration, humor, and a pleasant conversational and personal writing style to teach, encourage, reason, warn about traps, and guide along the road to recovery. Once started, it is hard to put the book down. Above all, the Atonement of Christ is interwoven such that it prepares the way for the Holy Ghost to give individual instruction and provide private insights and testimony to the reader as to how the Atonement's power to cleanse and heal can work its miracle.

This book is a must read for those who struggle with addiction and for those who endeavor to help them.

—David J. Ridges

introduction

My name is Brad. I am a grateful alcoholic and addict in recovery. As I reflect on my many blessings and try to express feelings of gratitude, which are difficult to express in words, I realize I am truly rich. In my personal prayers I try to thank my Heavenly Father for bounteous blessings, such as my dear wife, our temple marriage, our wonderful children, my family, having the gospel as a meaningful part of my life today, and feeling God's love and an outpouring of His Spirit. The list goes on and on. I know today that those things that matter most would be absent from my life if it were not for my sobriety. As I have approached the undertaking of addressing some aspects of addiction recovery, I have been impressed with a feeling of intense love that the Lord has for every suffering alcoholic and addict and their families, who also feel their affliction and suffering.

I remember the feelings of hopelessness and despair. I remember one night about twenty years ago. As I looked at one of my empty liquor bottles, I could somehow imagine a little, shrunken down man trapped inside it, kicking and screaming to get out. I knew that man was me! Today, I also know that without Alcoholics Anonymous, its Twelve Steps, and the Atonement of Jesus Christ, I would either be dead or still trapped in that bottle.

But on July 31, 1989, after struggling with alcoholism for seventeen years and not having a sober day in seven, I kneeled down and pleaded with my Maker for one sober day. I was suddenly filled with a peace beyond my understanding.

Forty days later, I found myself in a hotel room in Washington D.C. As I searched the dresser drawers for a phone book to call Alcoholics Anonymous, I found instead about fifty full mini bottles of liquor. Later that evening, after an AA meeting and as I returned to that room, I felt almost overpowered by the "enemy to all righteousness," and the compulsion to drink seemed unbearable (see Alma 34:23).

With a racing mind and a pounding heart, I fell to my knees again and breathed a desperate plea for help. The storm in my heart was suddenly calmed, my strength was sapped, and I collapsed harmlessly on the bed and fell asleep. I know today the same God who parted the Red Sea and delivered the children of Israel on dry ground came to my aid. By the grace of that same God, I am on dry ground too. I have been sober from alcohol and drugs ever since that July day in 1989.

Today, one of my favorite things to do is study the scriptures. I love "feasting on the words of Christ" (see 2 Nephi 32:3). Almost every day I find something in the scriptures, particularly in the Book of Mormon, relating directly to the Twelve Steps of Alcoholics Anonymous. One day I noticed several of the steps in Alma chapter 39, and upon a closer examination of this chapter, I found all Twelve Steps at least touched upon in this great chapter. This is just one of many examples of how the Twelve Steps are illuminated and expounded upon by the scriptures.

If you are one who struggles with addictions, I write to you, knowing that these Twelve Steps can and will lead you to Christ if you sincerely work them and that through Him and His Atonement, you can find true healing, peace, joy, happiness, and recovery. To the still-suffering alcoholic or addict, I echo the invitation of the First Presidency, "Come back and feast at the table of the Lord, and taste again the sweet and satisfying fruits of fellowship with the saints" (The First Presidency, "An Invitation to Come Back," *Church News*, Dec. 22, 1985, 3).

alma's twelve-step program

The following is a comparison between the original Twelve Steps of Alcoholics Anonymous (AA) and the principles of recovery and repentance as taught by Alma to his son Corianton in Alma, chapter 39.

AA Step 1:

"We admitted we were powerless over alcohol [or drugs, gambling, pornography, etc.]—that our lives had become unmanageable."

This step is probably the hardest to recognize in this chapter, but if we take the opposite of this step, it would sound like this: "I have such marvelous self-control and willpower that I can manage my own life without any help from anyone else!" or "I can handle it." Wouldn't this sound a little boastful? It is the philosophy that just one time, or one drink, or a little bit of sin won't hurt. Alma said to his son, "Now this is what I have against thee; thou didst go on unto boasting in thy strength and thy wisdom" (Alma 39:2). It is not likely that Corianton boasted that he had committed one of the "most abominable sins" (see v. 5), but rather he probably boasted that he could handle a little sin and not be ensnared by the bigger ones.

The Apostle Paul warned against such attitudes. In writing to the Corinthian Saints, he reminded them of "what [they] used to be like, what happened, and what [they] are like now" (*Big Book of Alcoholics Anonymous*, p. 58). While speaking of adulterers, abusers, drunkards, revilers, and so forth, he said, "And such were some of you: but ye are washed"—cleansed by baptism and the Atonement. Then he stated further, speaking of these sins, "All these things are *not* lawful unto me. . . . Therefore I will not be brought under the power of any" (see 1 Corinthians 6:9–12, particularly the JST in v. 12).

Even Paul, an Apostle, who possessed great spiritual strength, realized he could become powerless if he yielded to such temptations. Corianton, however, learned this principle the hard way. He succumbed to the harlot Isabel.

Alma's language provides a critical warning: "And this is not all, my son. Thou didst do that which was grievous unto me; for thou didst *forsake* the ministry, and did *go* over into the land of Siron among the borders of the Lamanites, *after* the harlot Isabel" (v. 3, emphasis added). Anytime we "forsake" the Lord to "go after" something else, we are in extreme spiritual danger!

AA Step 2:
"Came to believe that a Power greater than ourselves could restore us to sanity."

Practicing alcoholics and addicts living in denial seldom, if ever, see the real connection between their behavior and its consequences, choosing instead to blame other people, places, and things. *The Big Book of Alcoholics Anonymous* (referred to as the *Big Book*) talks about "the persistence of this illusion" that we "pursue . . . into the gates of insanity or death" (p. 30). The most common form of insanity for the practicing addict is to believe that somehow he or she can continue with the same actions and expect different or better results.

Alma addressed the issue of insane and unsound ideas by exposing the fallacies of Corianton's thinking. Alma said, "Ye cannot hide your crimes from God" (v. 8) and "Suffer not yourself to be led away by any vain or foolish thing; suffer not the devil to lead away your heart" (v. 11). He continued, "Seek not after riches nor the *vain* things of this world; for behold, you cannot carry them with you" (v. 14, emphasis added).

How often do addicts chase after vain, useless, or imaginary things in pursuit of an escape from reality or that illusionary, ultimate "high?" Only the Lord can restore sound thinking and proper priorities. The Savior's words to the woman with an issue of blood were: "Daughter, be of good comfort: thy *faith* hath made thee *whole*; go in peace" (Luke 8:48, emphasis added). To be made *whole* is to be *restored*.

There is a clear connection between faith, as the term is used in a gospel context, and the phrase "came to believe" as it is used in this step. Faith involves a proper understanding of God, His true nature, and what He will really do if He is sought. It is always the process of faith, or "coming to believe," that precedes being "made whole." It replaces insanity with peace, just as He promises!

AA Step 3:
"Made a decision to turn our will and our lives over to the care of God as we understood Him."

This is a giant, pivotal step in the life of the recovering addict. Alma's language is very similar: "*Turn* to the Lord with *all* your mind, might, and strength" (v. 13, emphasis added). This is a "decision" or "make up your mind" step. In AA's twelve-step program, we call it "turning it over." As Alma says, it will take *all* of our mental power and strength. Then, the rest of it will involve trust and faith in the Lord to leave the outcome in His loving and capable hands. This is a total surrender step—surrendering our will to God's, using the Savior's great example as our model: "The will of the Son being swallowed up in the will of the Father" (Mosiah 15:7).

Alma teaches another lesson that parallels the greatest commandment as taught by our Lord in Matthew 22:37 (emphasis added): "Thou shalt love the Lord thy God with *all* thy heart, and with *all* thy soul, and with *all* thy mind." The phrase "all your (or thy) mind" is included in both verses. Note the difference, however. Alma omits the phrase "all thy heart." There are things we can do to work each step, and there are things we must leave to the Lord. We may be able to change our mind and exert our best effort, might, and strength, but in recovery we must leave our hearts in the hands of God and truly trust Him to change both our hearts and our very natures.

There is also a balance or connection between grace and works. Those who have been successful in working these steps and staying clean and sober realize they really didn't do it. A common saying in the program is "But for the grace of God, there go I." This expression is often used in reference to all the misfortune seen in the world that is caused by addictions—broken homes, lost jobs, jail sentences, deaths, overdoses, wayward children, etc. The *Big Book* states, "Remember that we deal with alcohol [or other addictions]—cunning, baffling, powerful! Without help it is too much for us. But there is One who has all power—that One is God. May you find Him now!" (pp. 58–59). Compare this statement with one of Mormon's: "Know ye not that ye are in the hands of God? Know ye not that he hath *all power?*" (Mormon 5:23).

Steps Two and Three compliment each other. As we turn our will and our lives over to the care of God, we develop greater faith and trust in Him. He makes of us "new creatures" (see Mosiah 27:26), and we become able to "walk in newness of life" (Romans 6:4). Addicts particularly begin to see that life with the Lord as a partner in recovery becomes rich and rewarding, especially in comparison with their old life and its inherent, unmanageable nature.

In the Book of Mormon, the blessings of "turning it over" are enumerated: "Nevertheless they did fast and pray oft, and did wax stronger and stronger in their humility, and firmer and firmer in the faith of Christ, unto the filling their souls with joy and consolation, yea, even to the purifying and the sanctification of their hearts, which sanctification cometh because of their *yielding their hearts unto God*" (Helaman 3:35, emphasis added). Turning our lives over to God increases our humility and faith as we work the ABCs of the program. The ABCs are outlined in chapter 5 of the *Big Book* as "(a) That we were alcoholic [or addicted] and could not manage our own lives. (b) That probably no human power could have relieved our alcoholism. (c) That God could and would if He were sought" (p. 60).

An AA bumper sticker says it well with the adage, "Don't quit—surrender."

AA Step 4:
"Made a searching and fearless moral inventory of ourselves."

Alma stated, "Acknowledge your faults and that wrong which ye have done" (v. 13).

This list is not so much what we did under the influence of alcohol or drugs, or simply that we drank too much. Instead, it gets at the underlying causes of our behaviors.

An excellent example of a moral inventory is given in Helaman 4:12:

> And it was because of the pride of their hearts . . . yea it was because of their oppression to the poor, withholding their food from the hungry, withholding their clothing from the naked, and smiting their humble brethren upon the cheek, making a mock of that which was sacred, denying the spirit of prophecy and revelation, murdering, plundering, lying, stealing, committing adultery, rising up in great contentions, and *deserting away into the land of* . . . (fill in the blank for whatever addiction you are struggling with; emphasis added).

There are eight significant parts in this inventory as it is so well expounded in this verse. Notice how they almost go in order.

Pride

According to President Ezra Taft Benson, "The central feature of pride is enmity—enmity toward God and enmity toward our fellow men. Enmity means 'hatred toward, hostility to, or a state of opposition'" ("Beware of Pride," *Ensign* [May 1989]: p. 4). It is an attitude of "self-will run riot" (*Big Book*, p. 62).

Don't confuse the terms "beaten down" and humility. I thought I was humble because I had been thoroughly defeated in the game of life, yet I wouldn't surrender anything. Sometimes the things I surrender to God have claw marks in them by the time He gets them.

Selfishness

The *Big Book* calls it "Selfishness—self-centeredness! . . . Above everything, we alcoholics must be rid of this selfishness. We must, or it kills us! God makes that possible" (p. 62). Notice how many of the behaviors listed in this verse of Helaman are directly related to selfishness—oppression to the poor, withholding food from the hungry, withholding clothing from the naked, and smiting a brother on the cheek.

Irreverence

"Making a mock of that which (is) sacred" is displayed by not keeping the Sabbath day holy, by mocking others who are trying to be righteous, by demonstrating a lack of respect for ordinances such as the Sacrament, by disregarding commandments and temple covenants, etc.

Loss of testimony

Revelation 19:10 states, "For the testimony of Jesus is the spirit of prophecy." Therefore, "denying the spirit of prophecy" could mean either not being "valiant in the testimony of Jesus" (D&C 76:79) or losing one's testimony. Denying the spirit of revelation can be manifested in things such as being critical of Church leaders or not following promptings of the Holy Ghost. Notice the introduction of the word "denial"—one of the roots of addiction.

Dishonesty

The verse calls it "plundering, lying, stealing." Practicing alcoholics and addicts learn to lie, cheat, and steal in order to manipulate others and stay in their addictions. Don't confuse "cash register" honesty with "rigorous honesty." When I entered the rooms of Alcoholics Anonymous, I considered myself honest since I cannot remember a time when I stole anyone's money or property. However, a more "searching inventory" revealed that I was living in denial and lying to myself by saying, "I can quit anytime I want" or better yet "I'm not hurting anyone else." I was still a thief, stealing peace of mind and sleep from my parents who had to stay up all night and worry whether I would come home.

Sexual immorality

This verse calls it "committing adultery," but it includes all forms of sexual immorality. These sins are an extension of the "natural man" (see Mosiah 3:19) and the desire for immediate self-gratification. Pornography and sexual addictions are addictions in and of themselves, but all alcoholics and drug addicts are affected too since they do not make good moral decisions under the influence of alcohol or drugs.

Resentments

The phrase "rising up in great contentions" speaks of conflict and resulting resentment. Resentments are like poison to the addict. Again, the *Big Book* gives a profound warning: "Resentment is the number one offender. It destroys more alcoholics than anything else" (p. 64). At this stage, relationships are damaged or destroyed.

Escape

It is the running away or "deserting away" to wherever addicts' "vain imagination" takes them. This is the only part of their moral inventory that many outsiders see. It is their "drug of choice"—sexual addictions included. Ironically, after chasing vanity for many years, the tables of perception are turned. The world of escape starts to appear real and meaningful, and the real world of promised gospel blessings starts to look like a fantasy world. This is a particularly real danger of pornography.

AA Step 5:
"Admitted to God, to ourselves, and to another human being the exact nature of our wrongs."

There are three groups or audiences that addicts need to admit to or "come clean with"—God, themselves, and other human beings, including sponsors, bishops, and priesthood leaders. Alma addresses all three groups. Concerning the Lord, he said, "Ye cannot hide your crimes from God; and except ye repent they will stand as a testimony against you at the last day" (v. 8). In other words, "You better repent and confess your sins to God and stop living in denial!"

Second, he addresses honesty to ourselves in Alma 42:30, which is part of the same set of commandments to his son Corianton (see the heading before chapter 39), exhorting, "Do not endeavor to excuse *yourself* in the least point because of your sins, by denying the justice of God." This is an honesty step. It is time to quit making excuses (or living in denial) and time to start admitting. Many recovering alcoholics carry sobriety chips in their pockets. Mine reads, "To thine own self be true."

Third, he instructed Corianton by saying, "I command you to take it upon you to counsel with your elder brothers in your undertakings; for behold, thou art in thy youth, and ye stand in need to be nourished by your brothers" (v. 10). "Take it upon you" means to take the initiative to call your sponsor, your bishop, or another alcoholic (or addict).

There is an AA adage that says, "You are only as sick as your secrets." Is Alma suggesting addicts get a sponsor and solicit his or her help? He asks, "Have ye not observed the steadiness of thy brother, his faithfulness, and his diligence in keeping the commandments of God? Behold, has he not set a good example for thee?" (v. 1).

For full forgiveness in cases of serious sin, it is also necessary for addicts to confess their sins to their respective bishops and to "give heed to their counsel" (see v. 10). Bishops are a real key to recovery. As one of my bishops told me, it is the only place where the Savior can fully heal someone.

When we do a Step Five, it is a carryover from Step Four, because it reveals the "exact nature of our wrongs." "Because of the fall our natures have become evil continually" (Ether 3:2), thus a "mighty change of heart" must be "experienced" (see Alma 5:14) to effect real change of our natures. Otherwise, we end up "white knuckling it" in an unsuccessful attempt to stay clean and sober.

AA Step 6:
"Were entirely ready to have God remove all these defects of character."

This is a willingness step. Alma sums it up succinctly: "Refrain from your iniquities," and "forsake your sins" (vv. 12, 9). This sense of willingness is well said by King Lamoni's father with the plea, "O God . . . and if there is a God, and if thou art God, wilt thou make thyself known unto me, and I will give away *all* my sins to know thee" (Alma 22:18; see also John 17:3). If addicts are to know God and receive the grace necessary to change their lives, they must be willing to "lay aside every sin" (Alma 7:15) and put them all on the altar of sacrifice. It doesn't mean they instantly achieve perfection, but there needs to be a willingness. This becomes a "make it or break it" step.

AA Step 7:
"Humbly asked Him to remove our shortcomings."

Alma had already addressed the issue of pride and "boasting in thy strength" (v. 2). "Turning it over" or "giving away our sins" requires real humility and faith in the Lord Jesus Christ and His Atonement. Alma gives a powerful promise in connection with this step: "And now, *my son,* I would say somewhat unto you concerning the coming of Christ. Behold, I say unto you, that it is he that *surely* shall come to *take away the sins* of the world" (v. 15, emphasis added; see also John 1:29). This promises that if we give our all, our prayers will not be in vain. He "surely" will remove (or take away) our sins and shortcomings.

Paul said, "For all have sinned, and *come short* of the glory of God; Being justified freely by his grace through the redemption that is in Christ Jesus" (Romans 3:23–24, emphasis added). The promise is sure, when the Lord says, "My grace is sufficient." (Ether 12:27, also Moroni

10:32). These four words are the best news ever exclaimed for the suffering alcoholic or addict!

There is a big list of things the Lord did for the Anti-Nephi-Lehies after they demonstrated their sincere repentance by "working a program" and after "they did bury [their swords and weapons] *deep* in the earth" (Alma 24:17, emphasis added). Note the parallel between their commitment and a phrase in the *Big Book*, which states we must be "willing to go to any length" (p. 58) to get clean and sober and stay clean. After they worked the steps and buried their swords, the Lord softened their hearts, took away the guilt from their hearts, took away their stain, washed their swords bright with His own blood, and made them clean! (See Alma 24:8–17.)

AA Step 8:
"Made a list of all persons we had harmed, and became willing to make amends to them all."

Alma helps Corianton start on his list right away by saying, "Behold, O my son, how great iniquity ye brought upon the Zoramites; for when they saw your conduct they would not believe in my words" (v. 11). Corianton has a pretty good list already, consisting of Alma, Corianton, the Lord, and the Zoramites, among many others.

When we are active in our addictions, we rationalize that we aren't hurting anyone else, but in recovery, as we begin to see the "wreckage of [the] past" (*Big Book*, p. 164), we see that many innocent people, such as family members, friends, employers, fellow Church members, etc., have been deeply hurt. In Corianton's case, the Church was hindered as were Alma's missionary efforts—not to mention Alma's personal embarrassment, disappointment, and sadness, which were certainly felt by the rest of Alma's family.

AA Step 9:
"Made direct amends to such people wherever possible, except when to do so would injure them or others."

Alma admonishes Corianton to "Return unto them, and acknowledge your faults and *that* wrong which ye have done" (v. 13, emphasis added). The phrase, "return unto *them*," implies there was a target audience to be addressed. Corianton must "return" to them and directly make amends, face to face "wherever possible."

Alma had had much experience with this step, as he and the sons of Mosiah had "traveled throughout all the land of Zarahemla, and among all the people . . . zealously striving to repair all the injuries which they had done to the church" (Mosiah 27:35). This is a step of making amends and expressing true sorrow for harming another person.

Now, a word of caution. There are rare instances when addicts will attempt to make amends and their efforts will be rejected. They need to work the step anyway for true healing and the blessings of the Atonement to take place. This is part of "turning it over."

It is truly a miracle how often addicts in recovery will stumble across old acquaintances and people from their past and how the Lord will open doors for them to work this step. It also includes making amends with and frankly forgiving themselves, which is often the most difficult part of this step.

I am always impressed upon hearing real stories of fellow alcoholics and addicts who have labored diligently to make amends. In my line of work I have seen other alcoholics pay back financial debts from the past. I have also seen some voluntarily go to jail after going to the authorities and confessing their crimes.

AA Step 10:
"Continued to take personal inventory and when we were wrong promptly admitted it."

This is a maintenance step, but addicts are not trying to simply maintain the status quo. It is a growth step involving "spiritual progress" (p. 60), as the *Big Book* mentions. It is an ongoing effort to work Steps Four, Five, Eight, and Nine. These basic principles have already been outlined, however, Alma provides some real keys to make this a true growth step.

He counsels Corianton with these words: "Do not endeavor to excuse yourself in the *least point* because of your sins." He continues by saying, "And now, my son, go thy way, declare the word with truth and *soberness*" (Alma 42:30–31, emphasis added). In fact, it is interesting that he ends all three discourses to his three sons with a message of being "sober." He says the same thing to Helaman and Shiblon (see Alma 37:47; 38:15), yet there is no clue of either Helaman or Shiblon having any kind of problem with addictions. Alma compliments both of them on their righteousness. Helaman is entrusted with the sacred record, and Alma describes the joy he has in Shiblon because of his "steadiness and faithfulness" (see Alma 39:1). So what is Alma saying? This was also a common theme of Peter, who held the keys of presidency in the Church in the previous dispensation. He uses the phrase "be sober" three times in his first general epistle (see 1 Peter 1:13; 4:7; and 5:8). According to *Strong's Exhaustive Concordance of the Bible*, the word *sober* means to be watchful (see *Strong's Exhaustive Concordance of the Bible* #3525).

We all need the grace and power of the Savior's Atonement, and in order to activate it and make it a reality in our lives, we must be watchful in our minds and our very thoughts. Recovering addicts need to be watchful to identify warning signs and triggers, which could spur a relapse. They need to stay away from "slippery places," such as bars and inappropriate Internet sites. Peter gives this sobering warning, "Be sober, be vigilant; because your adversary the devil, as a roaring lion, walketh about, seeking whom he may devour" (1 Peter 5:8). Many recovering addicts do a daily personal mini inventory, often before retiring to bed, to assess individual progress. This also allows them to consider deficiencies and "nip them in the bud."

Alma gives Corianton a caution, alerting him of a dangerous trigger. "Go no more after the lusts of your eyes, but cross yourself in all these things" (v. 9). Lust chokes the word of God, drives away the Spirit, and poisons programs (see Mark 4:19; D&C 42:23; and Mosiah 7:30).

AA Step 11:

"Sought through prayer and meditation to improve our conscious contact with God as we understood Him, praying only for knowledge of His will for us and the power to carry that out."

This is my favorite step because there is no greater blessing of sobriety than to have a "conscious contact with God" through the Holy Ghost.

"Ye stand in need to be nourished by . . . the good *word* of God, to keep [you] in the *right way,* to keep [you] *continually watchful* unto *prayer,* relying alone upon the merits of Christ, who was the author and the *finisher* of [your] faith" (Alma 39:10 and Moroni 6:4). These two verses are tied with the phrase "nourished by." We all need spiritual nourishment from God. Alma teaches about the means by which we communicate with God. He ranks this sin of Corianton's third in seriousness behind denying the Holy Ghost and the shedding of innocent blood (v. 5). Logic would suggest that if the blasphemy against the Holy Ghost carries the biggest penalty, then obedience to the Spirit and "conscious contact with God" through the Holy Ghost would yield the greatest blessings. Alma states, "If ye deny the Holy Ghost when it once has *had place in you,* and *ye know that ye deny it,* behold, this is a sin which is unpardonable" (v. 6, emphasis added). If we can be consciously aware of the Holy Ghost and know it has place in us, then we can be certain we are experiencing a "conscious contact with God."

Alma gives a personal example of how one can identify the Holy Ghost and His influence as he says, "And now the Spirit of the Lord doth say unto me: Command thy children to do good, lest they lead away the hearts of many people to destruction" (v. 12).

Another key principle of this step is the relationship between knowledge and power—the two things we pray for in Step Eleven. Let us look at three examples.

Example One

Before the Prophet Joseph Smith went into the Sacred Grove to ask God which church was true, he asked himself the following: "What is to be done? Who of all these parties are right; or, are they all wrong together? If any one of them be right, which is it, and how shall I *know* it?" He concludes, "If any person needed wisdom from God, I did; for how to act I did not *know*, and unless I could get more wisdom than I then had, I would never *know*."

Obviously, Joseph was seeking *knowledge*. In the grove came the answer to his question: "They teach for doctrines the commandments of men, having a form of godliness [so far, it doesn't sound too bad since there is a form of godliness present, but you know there is a major disclaimer coming], *but* they deny the *power* thereof" (see Joseph Smith—History 1:10, 12, 19; emphasis added). So while Joseph was seeking *knowledge*, he found that *power* was also missing.

Example Two

In the book of Revelation, John sees four beasts. Each had "six wings about him; and they were full of eyes within" (Revelation 4:8). The Prophet Joseph Smith explains that these four beasts are "figurative expressions, used by the Revelator, John, in describing heaven, the paradise of God, the happiness of man, and of beasts" (D&C 77:2). The Prophet explains the symbolism of the eyes and the wings of the beasts. "Their eyes are a representation of light and *knowledge*, that is, they are full of *knowledge*; and their wings are a representation of *power*, to move, to act, etc" (D&C 77:4, emphasis added).

Example Three

In the Word of Wisdom, a latter-day revelation, we are commanded to abstain from alcohol, tobacco, coffee, tea, and harmful drugs—the very substances many addicts are trying to recover from. Those who follow this counsel, "walking in obedience to the commandments, shall receive health in their navel and marrow to their bones; And shall find wisdom and great treasures of *knowledge*, even hidden treasures; And shall run and not be weary, and shall walk and not faint" (D&C 89:18–20, emphasis added).

We are promised both *knowledge* and *power*, allowing us to run and not be weary and to walk and not faint. This promise, conditional upon obedience, is both physical and spiritual in nature. Spiritual power helps addicts conquer addiction. They have spiritual endurance, and they don't quit trying. *Fainting*, in this context, is not passing out. *Faint* means to withdraw, abandon, relax, or forsake (see *Strong's*, #7503). In other words, we continue to have the strength and divine power to overcome temptation and addiction.

Just as we need physical food to be able to "run and not be weary," we also need daily spiritual nourishment, such as prayer and scripture study, to keep up and improve our spiritual strength. In the Book of Mormon, those who were baptized and received into the Church "were wrought upon and cleansed by the power of the Holy Ghost." They were "nourished by the good word of God, to keep them in the right way, to keep them continually *watchful* unto *prayer*" (Moroni 6:4, emphasis added).

AA Step 12:

"Having had a spiritual awakening as the result of these steps, we tried to carry this message to alcoholics [or addicts], and to practice these principles in all our affairs."

Alma suspects that Corianton will have a spiritual awakening as a result of the Twelve Steps and the Atonement of Jesus Christ. Alma lets Corianton know he is called again to the ministry—to "carry this message" to others. Alma says, "And now, my son, this was the ministry unto which ye were called, to *declare these glad tidings* [or "carry this message"] unto this people, to prepare their minds; or rather that salvation might come unto them" (v. 16).

> And now, O my son, ye are called of God to preach the word [carry this message] unto this people. And now, my son, go thy way, declare the word [carry this message] with truth and *soberness*, that thou mayest bring souls unto repentance, that the great plan of mercy may have claim upon them. And

may God grant unto you even according to my words. Amen.
(Alma 42:31)

Alma speaks of Jesus Christ and His message of "glad tidings" (vv.
15, 16, and 19). The gospel of Jesus Christ and the Twelve Steps are
good news for the suffering addict. The Savior said, "Wherefore by
their fruits ye shall know them" (Matthew 7:20), and the gospel and the
Twelve Steps bring forth wonderful fruit. It is exciting to go to meetings, eat birthday cake, and celebrate years and years of sobriety!

Those of us who enjoy recovery have a responsibility to "carry the
message." It is truly a blessing to witness miracles in the lives of others. We are privileged to "stand as witnesses" for the God of Abraham,
Isaac, and Jacob (see Mosiah 24:14). It's a simple program, and it's not
always easy, but it's worth it!

Alma tells Corianton to let this message and the mercy of God have
"full sway" in his heart (see Alma 42:30). The *Big Book* states, "Those
who do not recover are people who cannot or will not completely give
themselves to this simple program" (p. 58). If you are new to this program of recovery, I plead with you to give it your all! Let it have "full
sway" in your heart! In other words, "Practice these principles in all
[your] affairs." Immerse yourself in the gospel of Jesus Christ and become embraced in the "arms of his love" (2 Nephi 1:15).

On July 17, 1989, I attended my first AA meeting. At the end of
the meeting, we all stood and held hands and recited in unison what
is termed "The Serenity Prayer"—"God, grant me the serenity to accept the things I cannot change, courage to change the things I can, and
the wisdom to know the difference." Then we recited, "Keep coming
back—it works!" My understanding of a higher power, or God, was so
diminished and messed up because of seventeen years of hardcore addiction. Oh yes, I had a testimony of God. Academically I remembered
spiritual experiences of years gone by. I had seen miracles in the mission
field. I *knew* God was out there somewhere, but why should He help me
after all the terrible things I had done? I could only hope as we stood
and recited, "Keep coming back—it works!" I looked around the circle
and saw smiles on faces and a glimmer of light in others' eyes. It was the

only hope I had and the only way I could get myself to a second meeting the next day.

Today, I know it really does work! And better yet, I can feel God's influence in my heart and a burning desire to be closer to Him, to do His will, and to be a better disciple.

Dr. Bob and Bill W.

An article appearing in the February 2000 edition of *Time*, an edition honoring the top 100 heroes and icons of the twentieth century, had this to say about AA co-founder Bill W.:

> Second Lieut. Bill W. didn't think twice when the first butler he had ever seen offered him a drink. The 22-year-old soldier didn't think about how alcohol had destroyed his family. He didn't think about the Yankee temperance movement of his childhood or his loving fiancé Lois Burham or his emerging talent for leadership. He didn't think about anything at all. 'I had found the elixir of life,' he wrote. Wilson's last drink, 17 years later, when alcohol had destroyed his health and his career, precipitated an epiphany that would change his life and the lives of millions of other alcoholics. Incarcerated for the fourth time at Manhattan's Towns Hospital in 1934, Wilson had a spiritual awakening—a flash of white light, a liberating awareness of God—that led to the founding of Alcoholics Anonymous and Wilson's revolutionary 12-step program, the successful remedy for alcoholism. The 12 steps have also generated successful programs for eating disorders, gambling, narcotics, debting, sex addiction and people affected by others' addictions. Aldous Huxley called him 'the greatest social architect of our century.'

The article goes on to say:

> Five sober months later, Wilson went to Akron, Ohio, on business. The deal fell through, and he wanted a drink. He stood in the lobby of the Mayflower Hotel, entranced by the sounds of the bar across the hall. Suddenly he became convinced that by helping another alcoholic, he could save himself.

Through a series of desperate telephone calls, he found
Dr. Robert Smith, a skeptical drunk whose family persuaded him to give Wilson 15 minutes. Their meeting lasted for
hours. A month later, Dr. Bob had his last drink, and that
date, June 10, 1935, is the official birth date of A.A., which
is based on the idea that only an alcoholic can help another
alcoholic. 'Because of our kinship in suffering,' Bill wrote, 'our
channels of contact have always been charged with the language of the heart.' ("Bill Wilson," *Time* [February 2000])

A Happy Ending

In conclusion, the true story of Corianton has a wonderful, happy
ending—typical of a good Twelve-Step personal program. Corianton is
called back to the ministry. There is "continual peace" and "great prosperity" in the Church because of the "heed and diligence" given to the
word of God. Only four missionaries are named as those who delivered
the word of God. They are Helaman, Shiblon, Ammon, and Corianton!
(See Alma 49:30.) But if you pay close attention to Mormon's editorial
comments, you may find an even greater compliment. One could argue
that if Mormon had a hero, it was Captain Moroni. He even named his
son Moroni. Mormon relates:

> Yea, verily, verily I say unto you, if all men had been, and
> were, and ever would be, like unto Moroni, behold, the very
> powers of hell would have been shaken forever; yea, the devil
> would never have power over the hearts of the children of
> men.
>
> Behold, he was a man like unto Ammon, the son of Mo-
> siah, yea, and even the other sons of Mosiah, yea, and also
> Alma and *his sons*, for they were *all men of God*. (Alma 48:
> 17–18)

If Corianton can be likened to Moroni, I call that an awesome recovery.

Jesus descended below all things (see D&C 122:8), and we all, no
matter our struggles, really can "be of good cheer" because of our Sav-

ior's declaration, "I have overcome the world" (see John 16:33). Thus even the "vilest of sinners" (Mosiah 28:4) can be transformed into "men [and women] of God" through His loving and infinite Atonement.

the great and spacious building and the denial suite

In Lehi's vision of the tree of life, he sees a "great and spacious build-ing." He tells us, "It stood as it were in the air, high above the earth" (1 Nephi 8:26). His curious wording, "as it were," in the subjunctive case, reveals that this is not a real building. It stands in the air. It has no foun-dation. It has no basis in reality. It doesn't have to because it is merely a "vain imagination" (see 1 Nephi 12:18).

Unlike the pathway to the tree of life, which represents the love of God, this is Easy Street—the "easier, softer way!" You can tell because the people are "feeling their way towards that great and spacious build-ing." It takes real effort to get to the tree of life. You must keep "press-ing forward" (see 1 Nephi 8:24, 30, 31; 11:25). Many opt for the easier road.

On the top floor is the "denial suite" (or sweet denial for those just starting out). You can believe anything you like with vain imagination. The shoptalk is, "I can quit anytime I want" or "I'm not hurting anyone" or "One drink won't hurt me" or "Just one more time." I should know. I took up residence there for seventeen years!

The great and spacious building is the birthplace of false hopes and false gods. One of its counterparts in the Bible is found in Revelation, chapter 13. John sees a beast rise up out of the sea. We can be grateful we have the Joseph Smith Translation to correct the false idea that it is John who stands upon the sand of the sea. The JST of Revelation 13:1 reads, "And I saw another sign, in the likeness of the kingdoms of the earth; a beast rise up out of the sea, and he stood upon the *sand of the sea,* having seven heads and ten horns, and upon his horns ten crowns, and upon his heads the name of blasphemy" (emphasis added).

The chapter heading tells us that this beast and the other beast described in the same chapter represent "degenerate earthly kingdoms controlled by Satan." You will notice that the beast stands upon sand—reminiscent of the foolish man who built his house upon the sand (see Matthew 7:26–27). This is certainly not a good foundation, as the sand shifts and will not provide a solid foundation like a rock would (see Helaman 5:12). Sand that is near the water, as in this case, also becomes like quicksand.

Thus, the beast and the great and spacious building are both standing upon faulty foundations. Both will eventually fall. John describes the fall of Babylon, and one verse is of special significance for the addict. Spiritual Babylon (the world with its degenerate kingdoms) becomes a "cage of every unclean and hateful bird" (see Revelation 18:2). Unclean in this context can mean defiled, contaminated by drugs and alcohol, or unclean due to sexual immorality or the effects of pornography.

Hateful is synonymous with resentful. Remember, in the *Big Book of Alcoholics Anonymous,* "Resentment is the 'number one' offender. It destroys more alcoholics than anything else. From it stem all forms of spiritual disease, for we have been not only mentally and physically ill, we have been spiritually sick" (p. 64). Whether a man lives in the great and spacious building or in Babylon, life as a practicing addict becomes like a bird in a cage, and the cage shrinks as time goes by.

The final lot of the beast is described as follows: "And the devil that deceived them was cast into the lake of fire and brimstone, where the *beast* and the false prophet are, and shall be tormented day and night for ever and ever" (Revelation 20:10, emphasis added).

Like the addict who will not find God, there is no respite from the torment. As for the great and spacious building, its final doom is told in the Book of Mormon: "And it came to pass that I saw and bear record, that the great and spacious building was the pride of the world; and it fell, and the fall thereof was exceedingly great. And the angel of the Lord spake unto me again, saying: Thus shall be the destruction of all nations, kindreds, tongues, and people, that shall fight against the twelve apostles of the Lamb" (1 Nephi 11:36). Without divine help, our addictions will eventually destroy us.

Let's look next at the first beast in Revelation 13. He is described as "having seven heads and ten horns, and upon his horns ten crowns, and upon his heads the name of blasphemy" (Revelation 13:1). The great and spacious building, the beast, and the image of the beast (introduced in verse 14) are all types of the same thing. The seven heads are symbolic of deception and illusion. The number seven in scripture is symbolic of perfection. Thus, the seven heads represent Satan's counterfeit world and his attempts to imitate God's perfection. For every good thing that God gives us, Satan throws out a counterfeit—for love, Satan offers lust; for peace, he offers sedation; for dedication and consecration, he uses force and compulsion; and for service, he offers bondage. I am sure when Lehi and Nephi saw the great and spacious building, it looked like a perfect, very beautifully built building—all except the foundation.

The ten horns are symbolic of power. If two beasts go to battle, usually the one with the most horns will win. The number ten means numerical perfection or well organized. Our individual programs of recovery must be well-fortified because we have to battle some pretty well-organized forces in the world that seem to have an almost unlimited supply of money to fund them. We have to be able to stand against Hollywood, the advertising media, the brewery companies, and the drug cartels. That's the bad news. The good news is that in the Joseph Smith Translation of Revelation 5:6, John sees "a Lamb as it had been slain, having *twelve horns* and *twelve eyes*, which are the twelve servants of God, sent forth into all the earth" (emphasis added). So even though we battle a most formidable foe, Christ and His Twelve Apostles are still more powerful because the Lamb has more horns! Thus, we have nothing to fear if we follow the brethren and are in a partnership or a covenant relationship with Jesus Christ.

The number *twelve* represents divine government or God's organization. Note that with His divine government comes power and knowledge—the two things we pray for in Step Eleven. The twelve horns represent divine power, and the twelve eyes represent divine knowledge (see D&C 77:4).

The ten horns are not only powerful by themselves, but they also have ten crowns. The crowns are symbolic of authority and dominion. Paul admonishes us to "Put on the whole armour of God, that ye may be able to stand against the *wiles* of the devil. For we wrestle not against flesh and blood, but against *principalities*, against *powers*, against the *rulers* of the darkness of this world, against spiritual wickedness in *high places*" (Ephesians 6:11–12, emphasis added).

Upon the heads of the beast is the name of blasphemy. We live in an age when there is often little reverence for God in society at large. The words "under God" are now being challenged in the Pledge of Allegiance, yet it is still legal to use the Lord's name in vain on TV or in the movies. For many it is perfectly acceptable to use God's name in a blasphemous manner, but not in a worshipful, respectful manner. Taking God out of the Pledge of Allegiance would fulfill the prophecy of "vain imagination" characterized by the great and spacious building (see 1 Nephi 12:18). The Lord said, "I, the Lord God, make you *free*, therefore ye are *free* indeed" (D&C 98:8, emphasis added). The Book of Mormon prophet Jacob teaches us that justice is a characteristic of God and comes from Him. "O the greatness and the *justice* of our God!" (2 Nephi 9:17). If we delete God from the Pledge of Allegiance, we might as well delete the rest of it, which says, "with *liberty* and *justice* for all."

The mouth of the beast is "as the mouth of a lion," suggesting that some of these kingdoms and organizations have enough force to tear us apart and destroy us, much like alcohol, drugs, and pornography. "And the dragon [Satan] gave him his power, and his seat, and great authority" (v. 2). Some of these wicked entities will even have great clout and legal authority.

Then Satan's program of denial is introduced into the picture. One of the heads of the beast is "wounded to death; and his deadly wound was healed: and all the world wondered after the beast" (v. 3). This has many symbolic implications, but let's look at just one of them.

Everyone has now become increasingly aware of the health dangers of alcohol, drugs, and sexual immorality with its accompanying HIV and other sexually transmitted diseases. How many addicts and alcoholics went into denial with a rationalization sounding something like this: "Well, I'm a beast with seven heads and ten horns, and if I lose a head and a couple of horns, then I am still pretty macho and cool. Besides, I'll still have six heads and eight horns, and I'll be able to function okay"? Or maybe they said, "I may lose a little of my brain capacity or endurance, but I can still get by alright" or maybe "I might be scathed a little, but it won't really hurt me. I can survive it. I've seen other people drink (or use) longer than I have. And look at those guys in the movies and beer commercials. They look strong, healthy, and happy."

They start believing these rationalizations, and soon they believe it is highly likely that medical science will be able to heal any deadly wound. They marvel at medical science and all of its power and capability and start to have full faith in "the arm of flesh" (see 2 Nephi 4:34). Thus they enter into the denial suite on the top floor of the great and spacious building, telling themselves that everything is okay, and they can always quit drinking, using, or smoking before any serious negative consequences occur. They are "lull[ed] away into carnal security . . . [and] say: All is well . . . and thus the devil cheateth their souls, and leadeth them away carefully down to hell" (2 Nephi 28:21, emphasis added). Please observe that when they get careless or go into denial, Satan gets very careful.

The degenerate earthly kingdoms portrayed in this chapter by these beasts are laden with powerful tools used by Satan to attempt to bring us all into captivity. One of his most powerful forces is addiction. You will observe that the beast is allowed to "make war with the saints, and to overcome them: and power was given him over all kindreds, and tongues, and nations" (v. 7). Addictions, including pornography, are running rampant both inside and outside the Church. It is a malicious monster that can overcome us and leave us powerless.

Then the Lord issues a wake up call: "If any man have an ear, let him hear." This usually means there is a major spiritual message just around the corner. Here is the message: "He that *leadeth into captivity* shall *go into captivity*" (vv. 9–10, emphasis added). Here we find an interesting translation origin. The Greek word for *leadeth* is "sunago," which has multiple meanings, including to entertain, resort, or take in (see *Strong's Exhaustive Concordance of the Bible* #4863). Even if we intend to use alcohol and drugs or to view pornography on a recreational basis only, we are heading for deep trouble and likely addiction if we do so. The word *resort* is also interesting. A vacation resort is a place we visit once in a while for recreation or escape from the daily world. Our addictions become the places and things we run to instead of turning to God.

I can remember, when I was a practicing alcoholic, firmly believing that I was a recreational, social drinker—even when I drank alone every day. I believed I could quit whenever I wanted to—just like a traveler on vacation, who could go home whenever he or she tired of travel. Alcoholics and addicts have the mistaken notion that they can dabble in these potentially addictive substances, and then turn around and walk away—just as if they were walking in and out of a revolving door. The reality is that when we walk into or lead ourselves into enticing, addictive situations, there is no revolving door. It is more like the sound of an iron bar door—like those you would hear close behind you in jail cells. Addicts find themselves in it for the long haul, not just a recreational visit once in a while.

Continuing with the discussion of Revelation 13, next we see "another beast coming up out of the earth" (v. 11). This beast has the ability to counterfeit and deceive, just like Satan. Notice that he has "two horns like a lamb, and he spake as a dragon." In other words, he appears to be like the Lamb (Christ), but he gives the rhetoric of the dragon, which is defined as the devil, or Satan, in Revelation 12:9. Then the second beast "deceiveth them that dwell on the earth by the means of those miracles which he had power to do" (v. 14). This beast then proposes that an image should be made to the first beast. Once again, the underlying principle is that we are led to chase after vain images or imagination rather than reality.

There are many things in today's society that would fit the description of these beasts and the image of the beast. Certainly those things that have power to addict and take us captive would qualify as a beast. The world in general with its shifting and decaying moral values could be another beast. What about Hollywood and the advertising media? Do they "give life to the image of the beast?" (v. 15). Are there factions in the media and entertainment industry that "give life" or create credibility for false ideas or immoral lifestyles? Sometimes even lifestyles of heavy alcohol or drug use are glamorized by TV shows and movies. Movie stars and entertainers who are in a position to be role models are often almost glamorized or put in the spotlight to promote lifestyles that can lead to addiction or immorality.

This chapter in Revelation gets sadder and scarier as you read on. For a revelation that was received almost two thousand years ago, it is remarkably telling and fitting for our day and has powerful and scary implications for the addict of any kind. As the chapter winds down, the language is insightful and powerful. "And he causeth *all*, both *small* and *great*, *rich* and *poor*, *free* and *bond*, to receive a mark in their *right hand*, or in their *foreheads*" (v. 16, emphasis added).

There are many symbolic implications of the beast and lots of speculation on meanings of symbols in this chapter. My purpose here is to address those that have implications dealing with addiction and recovery. That is one of the beauties of scripture—it has different symbolic meanings. You may read a certain passage of scripture one time and have a distinct feeling or impression. On another occasion you may have another idea or impression. I have found that scripture study is most rewarding and rich when the scriptures come to life through the workings of the Spirit. One of my favorite verses describes the role of the Comforter and how He "quickeneth all things" and "maketh *alive* all things" (Moses 6:61, emphasis added).

Revelation 13:16 has some very scary implications and lessons for the practicing addict. This "mark of the beast" as it is called, is received in the right hand. In scripture, the right hand is symbolic of covenants. It is the covenant hand. Here are a couple of examples.

In Alma 5:58 the Lord states, "For the names of the righteous shall be written in the book of life, and unto them will I grant an *inheritance* at my *right hand*" (emphasis added). Another one is found in Mosiah 5:9: "And it shall come to pass that whosoever doeth this shall be found at the *right hand* of God, for he shall know the name by which he is called; for he shall be called by the name of Christ." King Benjamin makes it clear he is speaking to those who have "entered into the *covenant* with God" (Mosiah 5:8, emphasis added). The dictionary defines the word *covenant* as "a formal binding agreement." Thus, something that binds us or brings us into subjection is a type of covenant, even if it is merely an unconscious agreement we make with ourselves. It becomes a code of living or something we swear by.

The forehead symbolizes total dedication or loyalty. Our loyalties to alcohol, drugs, immorality, or other addictions become more entrenched over time as the addiction grows within us. I can remember my parents and others talking about those they called "bad alcoholics," meaning they were in bad shape or in a bad way. I have shared in Twelve Step and AA meetings that I consider myself to be a "good alcoholic." I was once a dedicated alcoholic. I gave seventeen years of my life to alcohol. I sacrificed family vacations, relationships with others, my own peace of mind, all of my leisure time, and just about everything else in life all for the cause of alcoholism. I arrived at the liquor store faithfully before every Sunday or holiday when it might have been closed. I went on a seven-year stint wherein I drank every day. I was willing to lie and make up stories to support my alcoholism. I did whatever my disease told me to, and what did it give me in return? When I hit bottom, I had nothing left. I hated myself. On July 17, 1989, I woke up with the stark realization that I had been cheated big time. I had carefully followed every step of Satan's program of addiction and bondage, but when I hit bottom and needed some help and support, where was he? I was left abandoned just like Korihor (see Alma 30:60). I had been a dedicated, loyal follower of the plan of the devil. I never would have admitted it. I never intended it to be that way, and yet I had done everything required to stay in my addiction.

One time in the summer of 1982, I was on vacation with some family members. Against my own will, I was required to practice some "white knuckle" sobriety for about three days. I was with family members and could not just run off to the liquor store like I had done every other day. It was awful. Each day was agony, and I spent them thinking about how

I could get away to drink by myself. I vowed to myself that I would never let that happen to me again.

The bottom line of Revelation 13:16 is that whether addicts like it, whether they ever intended it to be that way, and whether they are rich or poor, small or great, bond or free, or anything else—they end up absolutely loyal to their individual addictions of choice, and it becomes their number one priority in life.

THE BIRTH OF A FALSE GOD

The great and spacious building could probably be appropriately re-named the house of vain imagination (see 1 Nephi 12:18). One of the hazards of living there is that addicts have a tendency to create false gods. A descriptive story illustrating how we do this is contained in the 44th chapter of Isaiah, which gives an enlightening description of the vanity behind false gods or idols, of how they come to be a part of our lives, and of how we can easily build up a system of denial because of them.

Verse 9 gives us this insight: "They that make a graven image are all of them *vanity*; and their delectable things [beloved things, see footnote b] shall *not profit*; and they are their own witnesses; they see not, nor know; that they may be *ashamed*" (emphasis added). In other words, it is vain or useless to chase after idols or false gods, including alcohol, drugs, or pornography, none of which see or know us. They obviously cannot deliver us, help us, or save us from anything. It says that those who pursue this course will end up "ashamed." In Hebrew the word *ashamed* means to be disappointed (see *Strong's* #954). Thus, chasing after such vain, useless things or relying on them can bring us only disappointment.

Verse 12 reads as follows: "The smith with the tongs both worketh in the coals, and fashioneth it with hammers, and worketh it with the strength of his arms: yea, he is *hungry*, and his *strength faileth*: he drinketh no water, and is *faint*." Unlike the Lord Omnipotent, who has all power (see Mosiah 3:5, Mormon 5:23, and *Big Book*, p. 59; emphasis added), the maker of this idol gets hungry, tired, and thirsty, and has very limited power. He can't even save himself. How is he going to save anyone else? Better yet, how is this idol, which was created by this very limited, mortal maker, going to save anyone?

The story continues in verses 14–17:

> He heweth him down cedars, and taketh the cypress and the oak, which he strengtheneth for himself among the trees of the forest: he planteth an ash, and *the rain doth nourish it.*
>
> Then shall it be for a man to burn: for he will take thereof, and *warm himself;* yea, he kindleth it, and baketh *bread;* yea, he *maketh a god,* and *worshippeth it;* he maketh a *graven image,* and falleth down thereto.
>
> He burneth part thereof in the fire; with part thereof he *eateth flesh; he roasteth roast, and is satisfied:* yea, he *warmeth himself,* and saith, Aha, I am warm, I have seen the fire:
>
> And the residue thereof he *maketh* a god, even his graven image: he falleth down unto it, and worshippeth it, and *prayeth* unto it, and saith, Deliver me; for thou art my god (emphasis added).

The idol worshipper in this allegory plants a tree, yet he did not create the seed from whence it sprang forth. It is nourished by the rain that God sends forth. After years the tree has grown and has been fed and nourished by the elements in the soil, which were prepared by the Lord, and it is large enough to be cut down and used for fuel for a fire. This man still has to kindle a fire. He cannot do it without the atmosphere and oxygen created by Deity. He did not create the materials used to make a spark either. He gets the fire going and makes bread. He is dependent upon God for the grain, the leaven, and every ingredient in the bread. He uses the fire to cook his food and to warm himself. Because the wood of this tree temporarily rescued him from hunger and cold, he is ready to fall down and worship the stump of the tree. He is oblivious to God's role in the creative process—every step of the way!

How often do we worship the creation instead of the Creator? And just like this man, who took from the creations of "the God of nature" (1 Nephi 19:12), burned the ash tree, made a lifeless idol, consumed the bread, and killed an animal, so do we take the elements and resources over which God has given us a stewardship and misuse them to sap the life out of our own bodies—temples that He created in His image. Others misuse the procreative powers and make a mockery of His plan and the Abrahamic Covenant, which allows for "all the families of the earth (to) be blessed" through "the literal seed, or the seed of the body" (see Abraham 2:11).

Addicts and alcoholics are like the man in this story. Their drug of choice gets them through some temporary crisis. It numbs their feelings when relationships turn sour. It seems to calm them down, relieve their stress, make them feel like they can socialize, or give them a false sense of euphoria. As addicts become more dependent on the drug, it seems like they cannot get by without it—like it has rescued them time after time. If it doesn't really solve the problem, it at least provides a temporary escape. I remember cold winter nights when I sat in my car with my beverage of choice, drinking away and feeling "warm and satisfied," much like the man in this story, yet I always needed one more drink. I was never really filled or satisfied, but somehow in my vain imagination, the artificial escape had come through for me one more time.

The rest of Isaiah 44 is very telling about our patterns of denial. In verse 18, we have "shut [our] eyes, that [we] cannot see." We are now in big-time denial, yet we don't think too deeply about our attitudes and behaviors. Our moral inventory doesn't go far enough to ask the question: "Shall I fall down to the stock of a tree?" (Isaiah 44:19). Shall I literally fall down to CH_3CH_2OH (the chemical formula for alcohol)? I have! Does it make any more sense to worship these three atoms of carbon, hydrogen, and oxygen, than it does to worship the stump of a tree? I don't think so.

The big lie continues in verse 20. "He feedeth on *ashes: a deceived* heart hath turned him aside, that he *cannot deliver his soul,* nor say, Is there not a *lie in my right hand?"* (emphasis added). In denial, how often do we feed ourselves lies, while we watch everything around us turn to "ashes?" We are not honest enough to admit that we really need help. We will not admit that we cannot deliver ourselves. Remember, the right hand is the covenant hand. Are we living up to covenants we have made? Are we being "rigorously honest" with ourselves and with the Lord?

Page 58 of the *Big Book* confirms this idea of "rigorous honesty." We read:

> Rarely have we seen a person fail who has thoroughly followed our path. Those who do not recover are people who cannot or will not completely give themselves to this simple program, usually men and women who are constitutionally incapable of being *honest* with themselves. There are such unfortunates. They are not at fault; they seem to have been born that way. They are naturally incapable of grasping and developing a manner of living which demands *rigorous honesty*. Their chances are less than average. There are those, too, who suffer from grave emotional and mental disorders, but many of them do recover if they have the capacity to be *honest*.

From the chapter titled, "How It Works," we see the word *honest* repeated three times for emphasis in the opening paragraph. The bottom line is this: Denial and dishonesty keep us in our addictions, and "rigorous honesty" is the first, and maybe the biggest, step in our recovery. It simply does not work without honesty.

FALSE GODS LEAVE YOU H.A.L.T

Another lesson from Isaiah 44 has close ties with a famous AA slogan: "HALT—Don't get too Hungry, Angry, Lonely, or Tired." The acronym, HALT, stands for these dangerous conditions, which are direct threats to a program of recovery and can be triggers for relapses. Isaiah says the same thing. Let's examine a little closer.

Hungry

"The smith with the tongs both worketh in the coals, and fashioneth it with hammers, and worketh it with the strength of his arms: yea, he is *hungry*, and his *strength faileth*: he drinketh no water, and is *faint*" (Isaiah 44:12, emphasis added).

Angry

"That *frustrateth* the tokens of the liars, and maketh diviners mad" (Isaiah 44:25, emphasis added). Anger often follows frustration.

Lonely

"Behold, all his fellows shall be ashamed" (Isaiah 44:11). In other words, his friends and associates become ashamed of him, and he is left alone in his pursuits.

Tired

"The smith with the tongs both worketh in the coals, and fashioneth it with hammers, and worketh it with the strength of his arms: yea, he is hungry, and his *strength faileth*: he drinketh no water, and is *faint*" (Isaiah 44:12, emphasis added).

Each of these physical characteristics has its likeness in the spiritual realm. If we live our lives void of spiritual experiences such as prayer, scripture study, and the companionship of the Holy Ghost, we can become spiritually starved. If we chase after the vain things of the world, we can become angry, resentful, and frustrated. If we retreat to our addictions, we push others away and out of our lives. We can become lonely as relationships suffer. We can become heavy laden, downtrodden, and simply worn out from the effects of sin. Nephi, the son of Helaman, became "weary" because of the iniquity of his people (Helaman 5:4). There's no getting around it—sin wears you down.

"HAVE YE ANY THAT ARE . . . HALT?"

The good news of the gospel is that there is a spiritual cure for each of these maladies. After the Savior's Resurrection and during His visit to the people of Nephi, He asks this question: "Have ye any that are sick among you? Bring them hither. Have ye any that are lame, or blind, or halt, or maimed, or leprous, or that are withered, or that are deaf, or that are afflicted in any manner? Bring them hither and I will heal them, for I have compassion upon you; my bowels are filled with mercy" (3 Nephi 17:7).

The good news is that there is still hope for the addict! Just as the

Savior is able to heal those who suffer from physical diseases and infirmities, He is every bit as able and willing to heal all forms of spiritual sickness as well. In fact, as Jesus was victorious over both the grave and spiritual death, it follows that "death and hell *must* deliver up their dead, and hell *must* deliver up its captive spirits, and the grave *must* deliver up its captive bodies" (2 Nephi 9:12, emphasis added). This promise is contingent upon a proper program of repentance and recovery, but it is a sure promise.

THERE IS A CURE FOR HALT

The Lord has an answer and a cure for the hungry, the angry, the lonely, and the tired.

Cure for the Hungry

For the hungry and the thirsty He proclaims, "I am the bread of life: he that cometh to me shall never hunger; and he that believeth on me shall never thirst" (John 6:35). Jesus answers the woman at Jacob's well with the promise: "Whosoever drinketh of the water that I shall give him shall never thirst; but the water that I shall give him shall be in him a well of water springing up into everlasting life" (John 4:14).

Finally, there is a wonderful promise that has direct implications to covenants, which states, "He that eateth this bread eateth of my body to his soul; and he that drinketh of this wine drinketh of my blood to his soul; and his soul shall never hunger nor thirst, but shall be *filled*" (3 Nephi 20:8). In the physical realm, we eat food and hunger again soon after. In the world of addictions, addicts chase after the "vain things of the world" and are left unsatisfied and empty. They always want just one more drink, or one more drug, or one more indulgence in instant gratification, yet it is never enough. On the other hand, the Lord's promise is that everyone will be "filled" up and made whole as they partake of the wonderful things of the Spirit and as they "feast upon the words of Christ" (see 2 Nephi 32:3).

Cure for the Angry

The Savior offers peace—*real* peace. Peace is more than absence of war and contention. The "peaceable things of immortal glory" encompass "the truth of all things; that which quickeneth all things; which maketh alive all things; that which *knoweth* all things, and hath all *power*" (Moses 6:61, emphasis added). Notice again the combination of knowledge and power—the two things we pray for in Step Eleven. If you read this verse in its entirety, you will see that true peace is conveyed through the Comforter or the Holy Ghost—that member of the Godhead who gives us "conscious contact" with, and who testifies of, the Father and the Son (see Step Eleven). Jesus promised His disciples that His Father would send the Comforter in His name, and then gives them and us this promise: "Peace I leave with you, my peace I give unto you: not as the world giveth, give I unto you. Let not your heart be troubled, neither let it be afraid" (John 14:26–27).

In more modern times the Lord has said, "The hour is not yet, but is nigh at hand, when peace shall be taken from the earth, and the devil shall have power over his own dominion" (D&C 1:35). As this prophecy becomes more and more fulfilled, peace becomes harder to see and recognize. What is clear and recognizable is that Satan is gaining more control and "power over his own dominion" and that his ability to lure many away into sin and addictions and to tighten his grip on those who become ensnared is increasing. Remember, just as the *Big Book* so clearly teaches us, "resentment (or anger) is the 'number one' offender" (p. 64). It is one of the biggest, if not *the* biggest, of all triggers that allow Satan to destroy through addiction.

Cure for the Lonely

There is strength in numbers. In the Book of Mormon, as Alma is organizing and establishing the Church of Christ, he says unto his people, "Behold, here are the waters of Mormon (for thus were they called) and now, as ye are *desirous to come into the fold of God*, and to be called his people, and are willing to bear one another's burdens, that they may be light; Yea, and are willing to mourn with those that mourn; yea, and comfort those that stand in need of comfort . . . what have you against being baptized in the name of the Lord?" (Mosiah 18:8–10, emphasis added). This became part of their baptismal covenants—to help each other, to comfort each other, and to strengthen each other.

One of the great blessings of activity in the Church of Jesus Christ of Latter-day Saints is the fellowship with the Saints. It is truly marvelous to go to Church and share experiences. It is uplifting and satisfying to give service in the kingdom. My family has been blessed by wonderful friends, neighbors, and ward members who served us in difficult times and in times of sickness.

Cure for the Tired

The Lord emphasizes in numerous passages the importance of enduring to the end. In Twelve-Step meetings we measure our individual endurance in days, months, and years of sobriety. Just as the quality of sobriety is vastly important, so is the length of sobriety. It is very interesting that one of the Lord's best answers to the tired and weary comes in Doctrine and Covenants 89:18–20. This revelation, Doctrine and Covenants 89, is known as the Word of Wisdom. It is a modern-day revelation addressing some of the addictions of our day. It is highly prophetic and telling of the world in which we now live. In the preface to this revelation, the Lord states, "Behold, verily, thus saith the Lord unto you: In consequence of evils and designs which do and *will* exist in the hearts of conspiring men in the last days, I have warned you, and *forewarn* you, by giving unto you this word of wisdom by revelation" (D&C 89:4, emphasis added). This revelation then warns about the partaking of addictive substances, including alcohol, tobacco, coffee, and tea. In later years, harmful drugs were also added to the list.

The idea of "designs" of "conspiring men" is very interesting. Joseph Smith did not live in an age of television and radio advertising. Most of today's forms of media were unheard-of in Joseph's time. There was no Internet. It would be another eighty years before Hollywood would make its first film. There were no movies to glamorize drinking or immorality. The idea that there would be a conspiracy to sell evil was probably pretty absurd for the time in which this revelation was given, yet it sadly describes our day perfectly.

The Word of Wisdom was given as a "principle with promise," and the promises of sobriety are amazingly powerful. The promises come at the end of the revelation and are stated as follows: "And all saints who remember to keep and do these sayings, walking in obedience to the commandments, shall receive *health* in their navel and marrow to their bones; And shall find wisdom and great treasures of knowledge, even hidden treasures; And shall run and *not be weary*, and shall walk and *not faint*" (D&C 89:18–20, emphasis added).

A similar promise is given in Isaiah 40:31: "But they that wait upon the Lord [meaning those who trust the Lord and have faith in Him] shall *renew their strength*; they shall mount up with wings as eagles; they shall run, and *not be weary*; and they shall walk, and *not faint*" (emphasis added). The phrase, "mount up" implies that we can fly higher and higher as we learn to trust in God and be obedient to His commandments.

One of the reasons addicts don't have to be so tired in recovery stems from the concept of complete and total surrender to God's will. They just don't have to fight everything, anymore. Elder Neal A. Maxwell summed it up so well in addressing the blessings of complete surrender and consecration: "Consecration thus constitutes the only unconditional surrender which is also a total victory!" (Neal A. Maxwell, "Swallowed Up in the Will of the Father," *Ensign* [November 1995]: 22). Imagine that—addicts don't have to constantly fight alcohol or their addiction of choice any longer. They can be victorious over it through the grace of God.

In conclusion, addiction is a spiritual disease, and the cure has to be a spiritual cure. The world may come up with 1001 physical cures and remedies for each addiction out there, but only a spiritual awakening will be of any lasting effect for the suffering addict. The disease of HALT (hungry, angry, lonely, and tired) is both physical and spiritual in its symptoms, and the blessings of recovery from HALT are also physical and spiritual, with a disproportionate quantity and quality weighing in on the spiritual side. If you have been chasing after false gods, and your belief, hope, and trust lie in a pill or in a bottle or on some dark, secret Internet site; if your life has been taken over by vain imagination and illusion, and you cannot go on living a lie—or living in denial—then you are ready for recovery!

"if you have decided you want what we have"

If you are teetering on the fence, or unsure about your potential success in this Twelve-Step recovery program, then let me help you weigh the pros and cons. I can give you two guarantees. Here is the first one.

A MISERY-BACK GUARANTEE

When I attended my second AA meeting, the man who became my first sponsor reasoned with me in this manner. He said, "What have you got to lose? Here's the deal. Try it for ninety days. Go to a meeting at least every day and don't drink between meetings. Then, in ninety days, take a look at your life and what you have. If you don't like it, we'll refund your misery."

That put it all in perspective. My sponsor was right. It took one hundred and four days from that point to get ninety days of sobriety, but at the end of ninety days, I was so much happier being sober! The fog was starting to lift, and I was on the pink cloud of sobriety! Indeed, I had "newness of life" (Romans 6:4).

"HOW IT WORKS"

Chapter 5 of the *Big Book of Alcoholics Anonymous* is titled, "How It Works." It is an invitation and a testimonial addressed to the newcomer. The text begins, "Rarely have we seen a person fail who has thoroughly followed our path." The story is often told in AA groups of how Bill W., when asked what he might have changed in the *Big Book*, said he would only change one word—the first word of chapter 5—*rarely*. He said he would change that word to *never*. Thus the chapter would begin, "Never have we seen a person fail who has thoroughly followed our path." There you have the second guarantee—right from Bill W.

There are a few absolutely crucial principles that are vital to recovery. The principle of honesty, particularly honesty with ourselves, is mentioned three times in the opening paragraph of chapter 5. Another basic concept is that of thoroughly following a path or a specific program of recovery. Then there is something of paramount importance: the addict in recovery must completely give himself or herself to this simple program. "Half measures availed us nothing. We stood at the turning point. We asked His protection and care with *complete abandon*" (p. 59, emphasis added).

The Lord says, "I would thou wert cold or hot. So then because thou art lukewarm, and neither cold nor hot, I will spue thee out of my mouth" (Revelation 3:15–16). Let's look at this verse in context, and take a look at what follows in verse 17 of Revelation 3. "Because thou *sayest*, I am rich, and increased with goods, and have need of nothing; and knowest not that thou art wretched, and miserable, and poor, and blind, and naked" (emphasis added). What a great statement about denial from the Savior himself! As long as we can lie to ourselves, and not see that we are wretched and miserable on the inside, then we can never see our need for the Savior, His gospel, and His brand of healing and recovery. No wonder honesty is mentioned three times in the first paragraph of chapter 5 of the *Big Book*.

ALMA 36—A CHAPTER JOSEPH SMITH
COULD NOT HAVE WRITTEN

Step Four states that each addict must take his or her own inventory and not someone else's. The scriptures describe Alma as "a very wicked and an idolatrous man" before his conversion (see Mosiah 27:8). I do not pretend to know what his idols were or how compulsive he was with his behaviors. I do find it interesting, however, that he was able to teach the concepts of the Twelve Steps so effectively to his son Corianton when Corianton got into trouble. Alma had special insight into recovery. I will venture to say that what Alma experienced immediately before his conversion has strong similarities to the feelings of an addict who hits rock bottom. Every addict who has hit that awful, yet wonderful, bittersweet turning point knows exactly what Alma experienced. His memory of the event, as he recounts it at least nineteen years later, is as vivid as yesterday. It is the same for me and countless other addicts.

Certainly all of those in recovery who have read the Book of Mormon have had their testimonies strengthened by Alma, chapter 36. I know of addicts in recovery who came back into the gospel and are active in the Church today in part because of this chapter. This is a chapter that Joseph Smith could not have written; it truly is the word of the Lord to us in the latter days. Like the rest of the Book of Mormon and other latter-day scripture, it stands as a witness that Joseph Smith, a true prophet of God, was the translator of the book and not the author. This chapter is a firsthand account of the awful hell and hopelessness of hitting rock bottom.

I believe that Joseph was thoroughly acquainted with the powers of hell and darkness. He had to deal with them firsthand in the Sacred Grove before he saw the Father and the Son, and when the Prophet was told that "if the very jaws of hell shall gape open the mouth wide after thee, know thou, my son, that all these things shall give thee experience, and shall be for thy good" (D&C 122:7), it was probably more prophetic than it was hyperbolic, but I do not believe he experienced "the pains of a damned soul" (Alma 36:16) that Alma did.

Alma says, "I was *racked* with eternal torment, for my soul was *harrowed up* to the greatest degree and *racked* with all my sins" (Alma

36:12). Elder Boyd K. Packer clarified this imagery in a general conference address: "Anciently a rack was a framework on which the victim was laid with each ankle and wrist tied to a spindle which could then be turned to cause unbearable pain. A harrow is a frame with spikes through it. When pulled across the ground, it rips and tears into the soil. The scriptures frequently speak of souls and minds being 'harrowed up' with guilt" (Boyd K. Packer, "The Touch of the Master's Hand," *Ensign* [May 2001]: 22).

I have thought much on this imagery as it relates to the addict. The victim on the rack is having his body pulled and twisted in different directions at the same time. The addict is also being pulled in different, opposing directions. His spirit is yearning to be free, wanting to go back home where his roots lie. Notice how Alma talks about seeing "God sitting upon his throne, surrounded with numberless concourses of angels, in the attitude of singing and praising their God; yea, and my soul did long to be there" (Alma 36:22).

Deep down inside, I imagine Alma had wanted this for a long time, but the body of an addict is chained to addiction and the captive spirit is bound up inside. The soul yearns for fulfillment and enrichment, but the physical body is never satisfied and can think of only getting one more drink, one more drug, or one more cheap thrill.

Sometimes in Twelve-Step meetings you hear both addicts and the family members who live with them share how addicts have a tendency to repress or "stuff" the feelings of guilt and shame associated with their addictive behaviors. When they reflect seriously on these things, those old feelings of guilt and shame are "harrowed up" and brought to the surface of their emotions. This is especially true as they work through Step Four—a searching and fearless moral inventory.

Using the symbolism of the harrow and the soil, addicts must get out the hard, jagged rocks so their soil can be cultivated and prepared for a seed to be planted. Alma likens the planting of this seed to planting the word of God in our hearts (see Alma 32). The word of God can grow into a tree of life, bearing the fruit of the love of God (see Alma 32:41–43 and 1 Nephi 11:21–25). The seed needs to be planted in good soil and nourished daily. Recovery also requires much care, hard work, and spiritual nourishment if it is to become fruitful and rewarding. If they do not get the jagged rocks out of the soil before they plant the seed, then it is not likely that they will experience quality recovery or long-term sobriety. If they try to plant the seed in "stony ground," then their program of recovery may "endure but for a time: afterward, when affliction or persecution ariseth . . . immediately they are offended" (Mark 4:16–17). The resentments return, and many of us go back out.

Now returning to Alma's suffering and miraculous conversion, he recalls: "So great had been my iniquities, that the very thought of coming into the presence of my God did rack my soul with inexpressible horror. Oh, thought I, that I could be banished and become extinct both soul and body, that I might not be brought to stand in the presence of my God, to be judged of my deeds" (Alma 36:14–15). This reveals the breadth of Alma's suffering. He sought relief from the severe anguish of the spirit and the body. Perhaps he wanted to be extinct so he didn't have to feel anymore. In the early days of addiction, addicts often go for the feeling of exhilaration, but as they approach the bottom, they want to become numb, so they do not have to feel anything.

Alma's feeling about going into the presence of the Lord also underwent a mighty change. This is vivid language, describing an incomprehensible fear of God. Later, Alma would describe his feelings about coming into the presence of God by asking himself and others the following:

> Do you look forward with an eye of faith, and view this mortal body raised in immortality, and this corruption raised in incorruption, to stand before God to be judged according to the deeds which have been done in the mortal body? I say unto you, can you imagine to yourselves that ye hear the voice of the Lord, saying unto you, in that day: Come unto me ye blessed, for behold, your works have been the works of righteousness upon the face of the earth? (Alma 5:15–16)

In this same chapter, Alma returns to his present feelings and states, "And I have been supported under trials and troubles of every kind, yea, and in all manner of afflictions; yea, God has delivered me from prison, and from bonds, and from death; yea, and I do put my trust in him, and he will still deliver me. And I know that he will raise me up at the last day, to dwell with him in glory" (Alma 36:27–28).

This turning point is always bittersweet. Alma says he was "in the gall of bitterness" and was "encircled about by the everlasting chains of death" (Alma 36:18). *Gall* means something extremely bitter. In the scriptures it can also mean venomous or poisonous (see *Strong's Exhaustive Concordance of the Bible* #7219). Alcohol and drugs are literal poisons. Pornography pollutes and poisons the mind and spirit. This is a profound insight given to us by Alma. He realizes he has been poisoned and brought into bondage.

There is another side to this turning point. He said to Helaman, "Yea, I say unto you, my son, that there could be nothing so exquisite and so bitter as were my pains. Yea, and again I say unto you, my son, that on the other hand, there can be nothing so exquisite and sweet as was my joy" (Alma 36:21). The word exquisite seems to be reserved in scripture to describe the ultimate suffering or the ultimate joy.

It was the Atonement that changed Alma's life. He suddenly remembered hearing his father, "prophesy unto the people concerning the coming of one Jesus Christ, a Son of God, to atone for the sins of the world. Now, as my mind caught hold upon this thought, I cried within my heart: O Jesus, thou Son of God, have mercy on me, who am in the gall of bitterness, and am encircled about by the everlasting chains of death" (Alma 36:17–18). Alma says he "cried within [his] heart." Do you get the impression that he was almost too afraid to cry out loud? He saw a glimmer of hope, but was it too much to hope for? To bring this down to the personal level, an addict might say, "I have a desire deep in my heart, but do I really dare to ask God for a miracle?" He is the one who "could and would" rescue you and me "if He were sought."

"May you find Him now!"

"willing to go to any length"

The *Big Book of Alcoholics Anonymous* states,

> Our stories disclose in a general way what we used to be like, what happened, and what we are like now. If you have decided you want what we have and are willing to go to *any length* to get it—then you are ready to take certain steps.
>
> At some of these we balked. We thought we could find an easier, softer way. But we could not. With all the earnestness at our command, we beg of you to be fearless and thorough from the very start. Some of us have tried to hold on to our old ideas and the result was nil until we let go absolutely.
>
> Remember that we deal with alcohol [or other addictions]—cunning, baffling, powerful! Without help it is too much for us. But there is One who has all power—that One is God. May you find Him now!

Half measures availed us nothing. We stood at the turning point. We asked His protection and care with complete
abandon. (pp. 58–59)

There are several key phrases in these paragraphs that are absolutely crucial to recovery. These phrases are listed below. We will examine
each one separately.
1. Willing to go to any length.
2. Fearless and thorough from the very start.
3. Let go absolutely.
4. Half measures availed us nothing.
5. Complete abandon.

THE JOURNEY BEGINS

We will take a look at each phrase and the concepts relating to it.
To help us in this analysis, we will follow the excellent advice given by
Nephi—"For I did liken all scriptures unto us, that it might be for our
profit and learning" (1 Nephi 19:23)—and liken these five concepts to a
powerful, true story selected from the Book of Mormon—the story of
Lehi and his journey into the wilderness.

When Lehi took his family and embarked on this new adventure, he
probably had no idea what to expect. He was in a situation addicts can
liken to recovery. He is charting new waters as he starts out. He is going
into the wilderness and away from the masses in Jerusalem. As addicts
begin their own recovery, they are also going out into a strange wilderness. After years of drinking and using, this is all strange, new territory
for them. They begin to experience new emotions and have the opportunity to learn how to deal with life's emotions without numbing their
feelings. They may have to "flee into the wilderness" (2 Nephi 5:5) to get
away from old friends and old haunts. There is a new life to learn as they
are now faced with living life on life's terms. In the wilderness they are
not able to just run to the nearest bar when life gets tough. They may
wonder what they will do with those hours they spent drinking or using
and whether they will ever have fun again after leaving Jerusalem—or
comfort zones and addictions of choice. There are many questions and
worries at the beginning, and it is lonely out in the "wilderness."

Lehi had a Liahona to guide him and his family in the wilderness, and addicts can rest assured, knowing the Lord will not leave them alone in the wilderness either. Addicts have a particular version of the Liahona—the Twelve Steps. They will also have the guidance of the Spirit—a precious gift some never dreamed possible. They will also have friends in the fellowship—real friends who care about them and don't disappear when the booze and the drugs run out.

Another good reason for using this likeness is because it provides us with great role models like Nephi, Lehi, and Sam. It also provides an excellent example of a program of "half measures" appearing in the form of Laman and Lemuel.

"Willing to go to any length"

When Lehi started out, he knew some things, but there were probably many uncertainties. How would they get to the promised land? How would they find their way in the wilderness? And where was this promised land anyway? But Lehi and Nephi were willing to do whatever the Lord required, even if it meant returning to Jerusalem twice, risking their lives to obtain the plates of brass, building a ship from scratch, finding and digging ore to make tools, eating raw meat, or sojourning in the wilderness for eight years. It never mattered to Nephi how tough the assignment was because of his faithful attitude. "I will go and do the things which the Lord hath commanded, for I know that the Lord giveth no commandments unto the children of men, save he shall prepare a way for them that they may accomplish the thing which he commandeth them" (1 Nephi 3:7).

This brings us to another caution. Sometimes we don't want to work the steps because they seem too difficult. Other times we don't want to work the steps because they seem too easy, or maybe we do not see the relationship between the steps and our sobriety. I remember the fourth AA meeting I attended. I sat and stared at the Twelve Steps, trying to decide which ones, if any, I would have to work to get sober. I looked at Step Seven: "Humbly asked Him to remove our shortcomings." I thought that sounded easy. It was just a simple prayer, but why should I do it? It wouldn't do me any good. God wouldn't listen to me anyway, I thought. When I finally got around to working Step Seven in earnest several months later, I discovered that it wasn't nearly as easy as I had imagined. In fact, it was extremely difficult.

I looked at Step Four and thought about making a moral inventory of myself. How would that help me get sober? "I am here to get sober— not to make a bunch of silly lists," I thought to myself. I could not see the connection. I guess I was something like the children of Israel when Moses put a fiery serpent on the pole and told the people that those who had been bitten by poisonous serpents had only to look upon the fiery serpent, and they would live and be healed. Many would not look "because they did not believe that it would heal them" (see Numbers 21:6–9; Alma 33:19–20). It is just as foolish for addicts to ignore the steps because they think those steps will not get them sober.

The steps can also be intimidating because of their difficulty. When Laman and Lemuel were asked to go back to Jerusalem and retrieve the brass plates, they murmured and said it was a "hard thing" (see 1 Nephi 3:4–5). As I sat in that AA meeting and scanned over the steps, I looked at Step Three: "Made a decision to turn our will and our lives over to the care of God as we understood Him." I counted the cost. Would I have to surrender my whole life? Would I have to surrender my whole will and give it to God, just to get sober? It was staggering!

Addicts wishing to recover must be "willing to go to any length" for their sobriety. Sobriety in this context means much more than just not drinking or using. I am talking about the kind of sobriety that will bring real "spiritual progress." The kind that "God wants" for them. The kind that will make them "happy, joyous, and free" (*Big Book*, p. 133). When Lehi and Nephi started out on their journey, they were "willing to go to any length" to be obedient to the Lord and to arrive safely in the promised land. Laman and Lemuel, on the other hand, were not willing to go to any length, and whenever the going got tough, they wanted to turn around and go back to Jerusalem. Addicts cannot afford to go back on their recovery! The *Big Book* correctly teaches, "And with us, to drink is to die" (p. 66). Laman and Lemuel had the same option (see 1 Nephi 7:15).

"Fearless and thorough from the very start"

After Lehi had traveled in the wilderness for three days, he pitched his tent in a valley near a river. He called the river Laman (see 1 Nephi 2:6, 8). Then he called his two oldest sons together and said to Laman: "O that thou mightest be like unto this river, continually running into the fountain of all righteousness!" (1 Nephi 2:9). In modern language he might have said, "Oh that you might be thorough and complete in your program of recovery—that you might be continually running and pursuing righteousness and good works!" Addicts can't afford to let their program of recovery dry up! If you follow a river down a canyon, you will notice that it is continuous and complete. It doesn't run for a mile, end, and resume again a mile or two down the canyon. It is continuous from start to finish.

Our individual programs need to be just as complete and thorough. A good program involves daily prayer, daily scripture study, and regular attendance of Twelve-Step meetings. It is recommended that an addict do ninety meetings for the first ninety days. I was once a facilitator for one of the LDS Substance Abuse Recovery meetings. There is nothing sadder for me to witness than people who attend meetings for a while and then seem to disappear from off the face of the earth. Many of them disappear for months and even years. Some of them reappear at meetings. Those who make it back (and it isn't all of them) then share about the intervening time when they had gone back out and done things like revisit jail and other undesirable places.

Everyone needs to take time for the daily necessities, but addicts can't afford to get too busy to work a daily program. It is critical that recovery takes a top priority; sobriety has to come first. I know there are ultimately things in life that are probably more important than just not drinking or using. But not for the addict! Today I have a wife, a son, a daughter, a temple recommend, and joy in gospel activity as a direct result of my sobriety. If I took one drink, I know I would probably lose everything. Remember this AA slogan: "SLIP stands for Sobriety Lost Its Priority."

The Savior teaches, "If any man will come after me, let him deny himself, and take up his cross daily, and follow me" (Luke 9:23). This kind of daily program of surrendering our will over to the Lord, and being willing to "deny [ourselves] of all ungodliness" (Moroni 10:32) is the kind of program that qualifies as being a thorough program. We need to be careful and complete—following the Twelve Steps and the words of God with "exactness" (see Alma 57:21).

After speaking to Laman, Lehi turned to Lemuel and said, "O that thou mightest be like unto this valley, firm and steadfast, and immovable in keeping the commandments of the Lord!" (1 Nephi 2:10). There are very few things that are as constant or immovable as a valley. However, one absolute constant is truth. The Twelve Steps and the principles of the gospel are just as firm and unchanging. They are true principles regardless of their acceptance or popularity by the world's standards. The Twelve Steps and the corresponding principles of the gospel have been tested and proven effective. They will work in any set of circumstances or any situation. The Twelve Steps have been adapted for use in recovering from drugs; gambling; sexual addictions, including pornography; eating disorders; codependency; and numerous other addictions, yet they remain constant and unchanging as the Twelve Steps. We may substitute words like *drugs, sex, overeating,* and *gambling* in place of the word *alcohol* but the steps remain the same for all programs. The same thing applies to principles and ordinances of the gospel. They worked in the days of Adam, Abraham, Moses, Nephi, and Joseph Smith, and they will work for addicts too.

In an individual program of recovery, addicts need to be just as firm and immovable as a valley. A valley does not slide, waver, shift, fall away, or give up. A valley is "down to earth" as opposed to being theoretical. One of the main components of being immovable is to have faith. The valley does not run away from the mountain because of its intimidating stature. The opposite of fear is faith, so if they are fearless like the *Big Book* begs them to be, then they are full of faith or faithful. Recovering addicts do not shrink in the face of adversity. They do not give up or change their values when the heat of temptation is turned up. They work a solid program even when it is not convenient or easy. "Drinking (or using) is just not an option for me today," is a phrase often heard in AA meetings. Addicts must never back down or give up on their sobriety! Sobriety is everything, and it must come first and foremost!

To summarize, the words *fearless, immovable, firm,* and *steadfast* all mean the same thing in your program of recovery. Lehi thought it was important enough that he urged his sons Laman and Lemuel to be steadfast right at the very begining of their eight-year sojourn in the wilderness.

Notice that the *Big Book* admonishes addicts to be "fearless and thorough from the very start." The Lord thought it was important enough in a program of recovery that He put this counsel in the second chapter of the Book of Mormon. He also placed Lehi's vision of the tree of life, where people are "clinging to the rod of iron" (1 Nephi 8:24), in the eighth chapter of the Book of Mormon. The rod of iron represents the word of God (see 1 Nephi 11:25). Addicts need to be constantly "clinging" to the word of God, and the Twelve Steps I might add, if they are going to make it through the "mists of darkness," which represent the "temptations of the devil" (1 Nephi 12:17). Clinging to the rod is far different than periodically reaching out to make sure it is still there. They need to be firm, fearless, immovable, and steadfast, as they work the steps, and as they begin and progress in their journey of recovery.

"Let go absolutely"

The *Big Book* says, "Some of us have tried to hold on to our old ideas and the result was nil until we *let go absolutely.*" Isn't that just like an alcoholic? Wanting to hang on to some of their ideas, habits, and "stinking thinking," and still have full recovery? I learn these kinds of things at the speed of pain. When it gets painful enough and unmanageable enough, then I surrender, but I must confess that everything I surrender has claw marks in it, because I cling onto it as long as I can.

After Lehi and his family had traveled in the wilderness for three days, Lehi stopped, pitched his tent, "built an altar of stones, and made an offering unto the Lord, and gave thanks unto the Lord our God" (1 Nephi 2:7). He was willing to make a sacrifice—a surrender—right at the start of his journey. I cannot think of a more graphic example the Lord could give us. Beginning at the time of Adam and continuing until the Savior's Atonement, men were commanded to "offer the firstlings of their flocks" (see Moses 5:5) as a sacrifice to the Lord. It required great faith to take of the first and the best of the flocks, put the animals on the altar, and burn them in a sacrifice. What are you willing to lie down on the altar of sacrifice and turn over to God? It is an excellent Fourth Step inventory question. This kind of sacrifice of the first and the best one possesses is a leap of faith. It is not a half measure. It is not a "wait and see" sacrifice, where we wait and see what the harvest brings, and if there is enough left over, we will give the Lord his share. No, there may not be a "secondling" (my Spell Check tells me there is no such word) or a second flock or batch of the harvest, after we have offered the firstlings to the Lord. We must trust Him that He will somehow see us through to the end. We must trust Him unequivocally with our own individual recoveries.

The supreme image of "letting go and letting God" is portrayed in the sacrifice of the animal upon the altar. The animal represents the physical body—fallible enough to succumb to any addiction. It seeks only two things: pleasure and the relief from pain. As the animal is consumed on the altar, the smoke and ashes ascend heavenward, typifying a letting go. But there is something even greater. As Elder Neal A. Maxwell so beautifully illustrated, "So it is that real, personal sacrifice never was placing an animal on the altar. Instead, it is a willingness to put the animal in us upon the altar and letting it be consumed! Such is the 'sacrifice unto the Lord . . . of a broken heart and a contrite spirit'" (Neal A. Maxwell, "Deny Yourselves of All Ungodliness," *Ensign* [May 1995]: 66; ellipses in original).

"Half measures availed us nothing"

The story of Lehi and his family and their journey to the promised land provides such a contrast in examples that it is a priceless model for addicts to look at as they mold a personal program of recovery. There is the excellent example of total obedience and submission to the Lord, which is demonstrated so well by Nephi, and then there is the program of half measures and excuses, which is demonstrated by Laman and Lemuel.

Example #1. The Lord commanded Nephi and his brothers to return to Jerusalem to obtain the brass plates, which contained the genealogy of Lehi's family and also the scriptures. Laman and Lemuel murmured from the beginning, but they eventually agree to go. Upon their arrival in Jerusalem, they cast lots to see who should go to the house of Laban, the man who had the records. The lot fell upon Laman, and he went in and made an attempt to get the plates. Laban was angry and threw him out of the house. "Laman fled out of [Laban's] presence" (1 Nephi 3:14) and returned to his brothers to give a report of what had happened. At this point Laman and Lemuel wanted to give up and return to their father without the records. Had they carried out their desire, they would have completed a half measure, returning to their father with nothing even though they did make an attempt.

There are two other spiritual messages in this story. It eventually took three attempts to obtain the records. The first attempt was left to chance. They merely cast lots to see who should complete the assignment. The second attempt consisted of a plan to return to the place of their father's inheritance and gather up all of their gold, silver, and precious things and return to Laban's house and make a trade for the plates. When Laban saw their property, he lusted after it, and instead of making a trade he planned a way to keep his brass plates and obtain their property as well. He sent his servants to kill Nephi and his brothers, and they were forced to run for their lives and leave the property behind. On the third attempt, Nephi left his brothers behind and went back to the city alone. He said, "I was led by the Spirit, not knowing beforehand the things which I should do" (1 Nephi 4:6).

One of the main themes of the Book of Mormon is deliverance from bondage. I do not know of a better book on the subject of deliverance. Only four chapters into the Book of Mormon, there is a story about a drunken man being overcome by a sober man. Isn't it interesting that the Lord places this story right at the beginning of the Book of Mormon—a story with a major message for the alcoholic?

When Nephi arrives at the house of Laban, Laban has already "fallen to the earth" (1 Nephi 4:7). In a symbolic sense, he has fallen to the realm of the earthy, sensual, and carnal. He is powerless (see Step One). The Lord required Laban's life because he had refused to surrender the records, he had stolen Nephi's family's property, and he had sought the lives of Nephi and his brothers. The Lord could have sent a bolt of lightning out of the heavens to strike him. He could have caused Laban to have a heart attack; or Laban could have just fallen dead like someone else will do in a much later chapter (see Alma 19:22).

The reality is that the Lord did not have to do any of these things because Laban had already rendered himself powerless by choosing to get drunk, and even though he was wearing garments and armor (see 1 Nephi 4:19), he was still left unprotected because he was not obedient. Is there a message in all of this? As far as Laman and Lemuel are concerned, the message is still that half measures avail us nothing. Nephi was able to accomplish the commandments of the Lord because he was persistent, and he trusted God.

Example #2. In 1 Nephi 15, Laman and Lemuel are perplexed about what their father has told them regarding the natural branches of the olive tree and the Gentiles. Nephi poses this brilliant question to them: "Have ye inquired of the Lord?" To which they respond: "We have not; for the Lord maketh no such thing known unto us" (see 1 Nephi 15:8–9). They hadn't even asked. How would they know?

Laman and Lemuel must have had at least a mild interest in studying the gospel. They do pose a few questions, suggesting that they may have even done some reading on their own. But even if they had read, studied, and pondered, they were still only doing a half measure, because they did not pray about it. There is also an opposite kind of half measure. It is also a half measure to only pray about something without studying it out in our minds first. No one can expect to receive God's grace until he or she has done everything in his or her own power first. Oliver Cowdery learned this when the Lord said the following to him in a revelation: "Behold, you have not understood; you have supposed that I would give it unto you, when you took no thought save it was to ask me" (D&C 9:7).

Example #3. When Nephi broke his bow of fine steel, Laman and Lemuel were angry with him because they could not obtain any food (see 1 Nephi 16:18). It was always okay with Laman and Lemuel for Nephi to be the leader and the provider of physical blessings and the necessities of life. It was acceptable for Nephi to put food on the table, but when it came to spiritual nourishment, they always became angry, saying things like, "We will not that our younger brother shall be a ruler over us" (1 Nephi 18:10).

It can be easy for any addict to fall into the same trap. Addicts have a tendency to welcome the material blessings that come with sobriety—things like a nice house, a good job, two cars in the garage, and money to put food on the table. Spiritual blessings, however, come with a price. Elder Neal A. Maxwell once said, "As you and I observe the valiant cope successfully with severe and relentless trials, we applaud and celebrate their emerging strength and goodness. Yet the rest of us tremble at the tuition required for the shaping of such sterling character, while hoping we would not falter should similar circumstances come to us!" (Neal A. Maxwell, "Plow in Hope," *Ensign* [May 2001]: 59).

A verse in the Doctrine and Covenants applies here. "And he who receiveth *all things* with thankfulness shall be made glorious; and the things of this earth shall be added unto him, even an hundred fold, yea, more" (D&C 78:19). This is a concept that is easy to talk about, but hard to do. Do we recognize a blessing from God when it comes in the form of chastisement? Do we appreciate a blessing that grows out of a trial? It is usually hard to recognize the heat of the refiner's fire as a blessing or an opportunity for spiritual growth, yet if we only appreciate the blessings that come to us in the forms we envision, or the ones that come couched in good things, then we are allowing ourselves only a "half measure" of God's will for us.

It takes a full program to heal and to recover. The basics include daily prayer, daily scripture study, reading from the *Big Book* and other uplifting books, attending meetings (both Twelve Step and Church meetings), and working the Twelve Steps. If any of these basics are left out, then it becomes a "half measure," and that "avail[s] us nothing."

There is one other aspect of a half measure. Each of the Steps has a part that we must do, and a part that we need to turn over to God. Each Step starts out with an action verb: *admitted*, came to *believe*, *made* a decision, *made* an inventory, *admitted*, *were* entirely ready, humbly *asked*, *made* a list, *made* direct amends, *continued to take* personal inventory, *sought*, *having had*, *tried to carry*, and *practice*. Then there is a part of each Step that God will do for us, if we let Him. He will *restore* us to sanity (Step Two), *care* for us (Step Three), *remove* all these defects of character (Step Six), *remove* our shortcomings (Step Seven), and reveal His will for us and give us power to carry out His will (Step Eleven). In each

Step there is a covenant relationship implied. If we do our part, God will certainly do His part.

There are those in recovery who work only the first part of each Step. They admit they are addicts, take a moral inventory, make lists, make amends, share with other alcoholics, and read the *Big Book* and the scriptures. They are good at the mechanics, but some of them lack the faith needed to trust God. Some of them are not willing to let God refine them and cleanse them of impurities. Then there are those who work only the second part of each Step. They are not willing to put forth the effort to study and work, and yet they still expect God to work a miracle in their behalf. They expect God to do everything for them, while they expend little or no effort. In your own personal recovery, make sure you are working a full program, and not just half of a program! Remember, "that it is by grace that we are saved, after all we can do" (2 Nephi 25:23).

Example #4. After Lehi and his family have traveled in the wilderness for eight years, they come to the land of Bountiful. At last, they are in a desirable place with "much fruit and also wild honey" (see 1 Nephi 17:4–5). But as nice as it is, it is not to be their final destination. After many days in Bountiful, the voice of the Lord comes to Nephi, telling him to get up "into the mountain," where he will be instructed to build a ship (see 1 Nephi 17:7–8).

You can tell that it is Nephi on the mountain because of his immediate response: "Lord, whither shall I go that I may find ore to molten, that I may make tools to construct the ship after the manner which thou hast shown unto me?" (1 Nephi 17:9). This is just how specific prayers need to be in recovery. Addicts can't afford to offer vague prayers like, "Lord, keep me sober today." That's okay from someone who just got out of bed in the morning if it is your first waking thought, but it needs to be followed up by something like, "Father, please keep me on the road as I am driving past the liquor store right now" or "Father, please show me what I need to do to overcome this overpowering compulsion I am feeling right this very second." Now, if I had been on the mountain instead of Nephi, the response would have been something like, "Are you kidding? Me? Build a ship? With what? Didn't you see those wall shelves

I tried to make in eighth grade shop class? And now you expect me to build a ship?"

Laman and Lemuel must have had similar thoughts because when they saw Nephi starting to build the ship, they exclaimed, "Our brother is a fool, for he thinketh that he can build a ship; yea, and he also thinketh that he can cross these great waters" (1 Nephi 17:17).

Apparently the land Bountiful was good enough for Laman and Lemuel. After an eight-year sojourn in the wilderness, they had decided that the beach life was good enough for them. Did they really think the Lord would have them wander in the wilderness for all this time just to end up there? When they saw turbulent waters ahead, they must have said, "Whoa, this is far enough!" But to make only the land journey and not navigate the waters would only be a half measure.

The Lord has something much greater in mind for recovering addicts than just staying sober. To simply not drink or not use is only a half measure in both the Lord's eternal plan and the Lord's vision of our mortal probation.

Addicts must not be surprised if they find Satan trying to convince them to do half measures. He knows the Twelve Steps too. He knows that the *Big Book* is exactly right. He knows that if he can get anyone to do a half measure, it will avail him or her nothing, and that is exactly what he wants everyone to have in the end—nothing!

"Complete abandon"

The *Big Book* says, "We asked His protection and care with complete abandon." This is a combination of Steps Three and Eleven. We pray for God to protect us, care for us, and reveal His will for us. Then we submit and surrender to God's will and trust Him completely with the outcome. Complete abandon requires God's grace. It is not something a stubborn addict can do alone. It requires a mighty change of heart (see Alma 5:14).

Lehi was commanded "that he should take his family and depart into the wilderness." Lehi was obedient, and "he left his *house*, and the *land of his inheritance*, and his *gold*, and his *silver*, and his *precious things*, and took nothing with him, save it were his family, and provisions, and tents, and departed into the wilderness" (1 Nephi 2:2-4, emphasis added). There cannot be a greater example of complete abandon. He left all of his material things and precious belongings behind, with the exception of the most important thing—his family. We know that the property left behind was very substantial because when his sons went back to get the property to take it to Laban, Laban saw that it was "exceedingly great," and he "lust[ed] after it" (1 Nephi 3:25).

Addicts may not be required to leave behind their material property in order to obtain sobriety, but there are things that must be abandoned. We need to abandon our "stinking thinking." We need to be willing to abandon our will. Just as Lehi could never go home to Jerusalem again, there are places addicts should not revisit. Sometimes they are required to leave old friends behind. It doesn't mean they are not their friends anymore, but they cannot afford to associate with them in a dangerous environment. They cannot afford to allow themselves to be tempted. They need to abandon slippery places—bars and other locations where alcohol, drugs, or pornography are readily available. I remember someone sharing in a meeting that his sponsor told him he only needed to change one thing about himself—everything. There are certain to be old habits and old ideas that we must let go of as we begin our journey of recovery.

One of my favorite passages of scripture is found in Romans 6. Paul likens baptism to burial:

> Therefore we are buried with him by baptism into death: that like as Christ was raised up from the dead by the glory of the Father, even so we also should walk in *newness of life*.
> For if we have been planted together in the likeness of his death, we shall be also in the likeness of his resurrection:
> Knowing this, that *our old man is crucified with him*, that the body of sin might be destroyed, that henceforth we should not serve sin. (Romans 6:4–6, emphasis added)

In recovery, we also abandon the "old man"—the addicted man, the carnal man, the selfish man, or the natural man.

The lengths they are required to go will vary from one addict to another. One person's journey may be a little different from another's, but their paths are certain to cross. Both must have a willingness to go to any length—to lay it all on the line if asked. Everyone who travels this journey successfully must be willing to offer the right kind of sacrifice— that of a broken heart and a contrite spirit (see D&C 59:8; 3 Nephi 9:20).

the price of addiction versus the cost of discipleship

Every spiritual principle found in Alcoholics Anonymous is also contained in the restored gospel of Jesus Christ. Does that mean we should just ignore AA and concentrate solely on Church activity? Absolutely not! To not take advantage of the AA program and its Twelve Steps just because one has a knowledge and testimony of the gospel is as foolish as throwing out the Bible because one has the Book of Mormon. If you believe the thirteenth Article of Faith—which states, "If there is anything virtuous, lovely, or of good report or praiseworthy, we seek after these things"—then you will believe in Alcoholics Anonymous and the Twelve Steps. It certainly meets the criteria mentioned in this Article of Faith. In fact, the general editor of the Book of Mormon makes the following observation: "Wherefore, I beseech of you, brethren, that ye should search diligently in the light of Christ that ye may know good from evil; and if ye will *lay hold upon every good thing*, and condemn it not, ye certainly will be a child of Christ" (Moroni 7:19, emphasis added). It is an incredible promise, but it can only come to fruition if one is willing to lay hold upon every good thing, regardless of its origin.

DON'T LET SATAN TAKE AWAY YOUR RECOVERY WITH YOUR CHURCH MEMBERSHIP

Don't mistake or misquote me. The greatest blessings in my life today and the things that bring me the greatest joy, all come from my membership in the Church of Jesus Christ of Latter-day Saints and from activity in the gospel. But I know as surely as I know anything, that my Church membership and the gospel itself are only meaningful to me today because I am clean and sober. Without my sobriety, I would never have these great blessings.

I want to focus on a specific kind of danger. I have seen some tendencies that seem more pronounced for Church members. Some confuse a structured repentance program with a recovery program. Repentance *does* need to be an ongoing part of recovery, but recovery is more. Some people are referred to the LDS recovery program by their respective bishops or other priesthood leaders. The bishop may have given this person a program to follow to come back into full fellowship or to complete the process of repentance for serious transgressions. There may be a probationary period where specific privileges are suspended. These privileges may involve certain, sacred ordinances like partaking of the sacrament or attending the temple. Sometimes, a bishop will ask a Church member to attend the Twelve-Step meetings. The member is asked to meet with his or her bishop on a regular basis. Some of the things a bishop asks the member to do pertain only to the probationary period.

Here is the danger! I have seen many addicts come to the Twelve-Step meetings because they were referred by their bishops. I have seen some faithfully attend meetings and work a program during the time when they are meeting on a regular basis with their bishops, but once they quit meeting with the bishop, after he has deemed that they are back in good standing and full fellowship with the Church, they quit coming to meetings. Some work a program and attend meetings until they receive their temple recommends. Then they suddenly act as if they are no longer addicts, and they neglect their programs and quit going to meetings.

Some seem to have fallen off the face of the earth. We wonder where they are and how they are doing. Then, without any warning, some of them start coming back. We are always excited to see them because we love them and have missed them for so long! They start to tell their stories. We see a tear in their eyes and hear a quaking voice. We often hear the sad tale of relapse—of how well they were doing and how they thought everything was okay. There are many triggers that come up. Sometimes they just got too busy. Sometimes it was work-related. Sometimes there was a problem in the family. Sometimes sickness or surgery was involved—especially when medications are prescribed. Sometimes they just forget. They let HALT take over—they were too hungry, angry, lonely, and tired. Sometimes they became complacent and thought they had it made. Sobriety lost its urgency, and they were no longer "anxiously engaged" (D&C 58:27) in recovery.

I have seen Church members who will not go to regular AA meetings because they think they will not fit in. Some refuse to go to AA meetings because they heard someone use profanity there. Many with such attitudes relapse. I have to wonder whether they hear good, clean language out there among their old buddies who are still drinking and using.

Church activity will certainly enhance your spiritual growth, and it will definitely help you stay sober. But Church activity is not enough to ensure success in an addiction recovery program.

THE PARABLE OF THE BICYCLE (IN REVERSE)

The parable of the bicycle likens a girl's dream of having a new bicycle with our quest for the kingdom of God. Addicts can relate their dream of sobriety with the parable as well. All of these things are unachievable by virtue of our own merits.

I watched the video version of this parable one morning before getting ready to go to work. The girl in the story went to her dad and asked for a bicycle. It would not have been financially easy for her parents to buy a bike at that time, so her father said, "I'll tell you what . . . you save all your pennies, and pretty soon you'll have enough for a bike." I watched this girl in the video trying desperately to earn enough money to buy the bicycle of her dreams. She was giving the dog a bath, doing extra chores, and selling lemonade—anything to earn a little cash. The anticipated day arrived when she went to the bicycle shop with her dad.

> "She ran and jumped up on the bike and said, 'Dad, this is it. This is just the one I want.' She was thrilled.
> Then she noticed the price tag hanging down between the handlebars, and with a smile, she reached down and turned it over. At first she just stared at it; then the smile disappeared. Her face clouded up, and she started to cry. 'Oh Daddy,' she said in despair, 'I'll never have enough for a bicycle.'"

Then her father made an offer—an intercession. He said to his daughter, "'Then I'll tell you what, dear. Let's try a different arrangement. You give me everything you've got . . . and a hug and a kiss, and this bike is yours'" (as recorded in Stephen E. Robinson, *Believing Christ* [Salt Lake City: Deseret Book: 1992]: 30–32).

Then, as I gratefully and tearfully watched the video version of this great parable, I saw this young girl reach out her hand and empty everything she had into her father's hand. I saw a few coins and maybe a crumpled up dollar bill, as she literally gave everything she had. There was a look of immense love, gratitude, and trust in her eyes. She joyfully rode her new bicycle home, with her father following behind her in his vehicle.

This is a beautiful illustration of the Atonement. Our little offering, even though it is all we can give, is minuscule when compared with the requirements for our salvation and the ultimate sacrifice that satisfied the demands of justice. Again, it is the wonderful principle that "it is by grace that we are saved, after *all* we can do" (2 Nephi 25:23). We gain our sobriety and ultimately our eternal salvation through the grace of God.

As I got ready for work, I pondered these great principles with a profound feeling of gratitude in my heart for a loving, merciful Savior.

Little did I realize that the second part of this great lesson from the Spirit would be manifest within the hour.

I got on the bus and started off to work. I had to transfer buses, and while I was waiting, I went into a convenience store to buy a snack and a soda pop. My next bus was coming soon, so I was somewhat in a hurry. I saw a man in front of me and noticed he was buying a pack of cigarettes. I became more impatient—that is one of my character defects. But then I had a feeling that I needed to quit stressing out and observe what was going on in front of me. I started to watch what was happening.

I saw the man reach deeply into his pocket to pull out a crumpled up dollar bill and a handful of loose change. It looked just like the money exchanged in the video I had seen about an hour earlier. The man pulled his pockets inside out to make sure he had given every penny. I saw a trembling hand reach out to surrender his last penny. I saw a familiar look on his face. I saw fear and worry. He said something like, "I hope I have enough." My mind went back and forth between the man in front of me and the little girl in the video. I remembered the sad face on the girl and the tears in her eyes when she looked at the price tag on the bike.

I had empathy for the man; I had been there. He checked every pocket again. The cashier started counting the change, which took up the whole counter. What if he didn't have enough? Who would come to his aid? My mind raced back in time to desperate moments. I remembered racing in my car one Saturday night after discovering that my stash of liquor bottles was running low and dry. I had ten minutes to get to the liquor store before it closed for the rest of the weekend. I ran a red light because I only had about two minutes left and was still six blocks away. What if I had to go through Saturday night, all of Sunday, and Sunday night dry? I risked my own life and the lives of others just to make it there in time. I was sweating profusely as I turned the corner into the parking lot. I jumped out of my car and ran to the door only to see the store clerk on the other side of the door with the key already in the keyhole. Fortunately, he knew me well. I was probably their best customer. He smiled, unlocked the door, and said, "You're cutting it a little close tonight!" I would survive another day!

What about that guy in front of me? The little girl had an advocate—

a mediator. I remembered what it was like to not have a mediator in my life. I had pushed Him away long ago. At last the suspense was over. The store clerk looked up and said, "Close enough." The man turned around with his treasure, wiped the sweat off his brow, and apologized for making me wait. I said, "No, really it's okay!" I watched him walk out of the store with empty pockets.

SIX-DIMENSIONAL EXPERIENCES

The events of that morning constituted what I like to call a six-dimensional experience. A six-dimensional experience combines the operation of the five senses with the sixth sense—the witness of the Holy Ghost. The physical realities were evident. I could *see* the money and the expressions on the faces. I could *hear* the man and the girl talking. But there was also a spiritual reality borne of the Spirit and witnessing of the truths and the principles relating to these two actual events.

I continued to have thoughts and feelings about this experience. At first the similarities were obvious. I could see the parallel between the cost of discipleship and the price of addiction. They both require everything we have. I thought of my own addictions and how I was always willing to give up everything just to have my next drink. I thought of recovery, and I took a good, hard look at my willingness. Was I willing to lay down all of my sins, character defects, and unrighteous desires in order to have an intimate relationship with my God? Was I willing to give up everything else for the cause of discipleship? These were soul-searching inventory questions because I knew how willing I had been to lose everything else in order to drink and practice my addictions. I knew I had been "willing to go to any length" to drink and live in denial. There was a definite parallel. Addictions require us to give up everything. We eventually lay it all down on the table. I somehow knew that the man in the convenience store would have given up food for the day in order to buy that pack of cigarettes. I knew there was a time when I would have starved myself or done anything else just to drink. Like the last remaining Jaredites, I "ate and slept" my addictive lifestyle "and prepared for death on the morrow" (Ether 15:26).

I also know that true discipleship requires our all. We must have complete abandon and total surrender. We must be willing to place everything else on the altar and put God first. Spiritual tutoring comes at an enormous cost. I had to ask myself, "Am I willing to deny myself of all ungodliness? Do I love the Lord with all my might, mind and strength?" (see Moroni 10:32). Am I willing to empty my pockets for the cause of discipleship?

On that morning as I walked out of that store, the world of addictions seemed like the perfect counterfeit. The father of lies and the author of all sin (see 2 Nephi 2:18 and Helaman 6:30) had devised another counterfeit scheme to divert the affections of the heart away from God. Addiction seemed like a copycat of two of God's highest laws—the law of sacrifice and the law of consecration.

Then all of the differences started to come to the surface. Really, the only similarities I could think of were the money exchanged and the empty pockets at the end of the transactions. Both the little girl in the video and the man at the counter gave their all as I stood there and watched. Even the money looked the same in both events. The monetary offering was probably even similar in dollars and cents; neither was large in monetary terms. But that is where the parallel ends.

You cannot compare the value of the bicycle with the value (or lack thereof) of the cigarettes. Both individuals were very motivated. The girl was obviously filled with desire and joy. The man was compelled by urgent need. The girl looked forward with anticipation for her new bicycle. The man seemed fearful and nervous. What if he didn't have enough?

I saw two completely different faces. On the face of the man I saw fear, worry, and frustration followed by a look of relief. On the face of the young girl I saw trust, gratitude, joy, and, most importantly, love. She was following her dream, she was being led, and she was pursuing a goal, even though it was unattainable on her own. The man on the other hand seemed to be driven by a need for instant gratification. I viewed it through my own addictive eyes. I could almost feel him being kicked right into that store and pushed from behind. He was being driven! I remembered times when I didn't even want to drink anymore, but I was compelled to. I drank for years after I had stopped enjoying it. It may have been the same for that man.

Noticeably absent from the event at the convenience store was the role of an advocate or mediator. The man had no one who would step in to cover the cost and meet the demands of justice. He would have suffered physically and emotionally for a time if he had not been able to pay the full price. This is one of the reasons addicts live in fear and impending doom while they are practicing their addictions. I had a great fear of losing my job back then. Today I believe that if I were to lose my job, it would be extremely difficult, but I don't think my family and I would starve to death. When I was drinking every single day, the idea of losing my job or getting sick and going to the hospital filled me with terror. Where would I get my booze?

Without the Atonement and without recovery, addicts are "exposed to the whole law of the demands of justice" (Alma 34:16). Likewise, they are exposed to the concrete wall of reality with all of its rough edges. They are exposed to the whole law of natural consequences—things like hangovers, hurt relationships, broken homes, lost jobs, jail sentences, and a feeling of impending doom. They eventually are left alone in the wilderness with their addictions. Satan may have been there in the beginning to entice them. The first time they ever drank or used, he may have whispered. "Just one beer won't hurt anything" or maybe "Just one little peek at some pornographic pictures won't hurt," but as they near their respective bottoms, Satan abandons them, leaving them alone in their misery.

One of the deepest and richest blessings of sobriety is for addicts to know that they are never alone. They can come to a sure peace and knowledge that our glorious Savior paid the full price for every single addiction and every single sin. They can know that if they give Him all that they have, regardless of how small it is when compared with the total price, "then is his grace sufficient" (Moroni 10:32, see also Ether 12:27 and 2 Corinthians 12:9).

I am grateful to the man in the store, who apologized for taking my time. I am even more grateful for a loving Heavenly Father, a loving, merciful Savior, and for the Holy Ghost, who bears witness of the Father and Son. The man at the counter gave me something to pray about. Every day I pray that I might be able and willing to empty my pockets—

that I might come to know my Father and His Son a little better and to draw closer to Them.

LED VERSUS DRIVEN

There is a stark contrast between addiction and consecration. Both may cause us to empty our pockets. However, the motivating forces are completely different.

Consider the descendants of King Noah's priests:

> And he (Abinadi) said unto the priests of Noah that their seed should cause many to be put to death, in the like manner as he was, and that they should be scattered abroad and slain, even as a sheep having no shepherd is *driven* and slain by wild beasts; and now behold, these words were verified, for they were *driven* by the Lamanites, and they were hunted, and they were smitten." (Alma 25:12, emphasis added)

We can be driven and slain by beasts like alcohol, drugs, and immorality.

Now let's consider the other option—being led by the Lord. Compare the scripture above with the following scripture: "And I will also be your light in the wilderness; and I will prepare the way before you, if it so be that ye shall keep my commandments; wherefore, inasmuch as ye shall keep my commandments ye shall be *led* towards the promised land; and ye shall know that it is by me that ye are *led*" (1 Nephi 17:13, emphasis added).

Life is far sweeter being led by the Good Shepherd than it is being driven by wild beasts in the wilderness. "The good shepherd giveth his life for the sheep" (John 10:11).

No one has to be driven by addiction. All can be led by the Lord— following His Spirit in all things. The path was clear for the children of Israel: "And the Lord went before them by day in a pillar of a cloud, to *lead* them the way; and by night in a pillar of fire, to give them light to go by day and night" (Exodus 13:21).

As we allow the Lord to lead us in the wilderness of recovery, we will end up in the promised land—ultimately in celestial glory and exaltation!

pharmakeia: the babylonian drugstore of the seventh seal
(and other prophecies of addiction)

Alcohol and drugs are not new to society. Neither is addiction. We can find signs of drunkenness in pretty much all dispensations in the scriptures and other historical records. One interesting aspect of addiction is the warning label attached to stories in holy writ. Some of the warnings and prophecies are short-term and some are long-term, but warning labels attached to the last days are very interesting.

PHARMAKEIA—A SIGN OF THE TIMES

There is a word in the scriptures that is used only seven times. It appears in Mormon's own record shortly before the final destruction of the Nephites (Mormon 1:19). It appears twice in Revelation as John describes the seventh seal and then the fall of Babylon (see Revelation 9:21; 18:23). The reality that this one word comes right before three major destructions (two in the past and one in the future) should get our attention! The word is *sorceries.*

Sorceries and the occult are signs of the times, and we would expect to see sorcery as one of Satan's counterfeit schemes. We should not be surprised to find it in the scriptures. It appears only three times in the New Testament—twice in Revelation. In Acts a man named Simon (not Simon Peter who was the Apostle of Jesus) used sorceries to bewitch the people of Samaria (see Acts 8:9–11). In this instance the Greek word for *sorceries* is *mageia* (see *Strong's Exhaustive Concordance of the Bible* #3095). You will recognize its English counterpart as *magic*. Mormon even calls it "magics" (Mormon 1:19). It is what you would expect the definition of *sorceries* to be.

When the word *sorceries* appears in Revelation, however, it is translated from a different Greek word: *pharmakeia*. Its English counterpart is *pharmacy*. This is probably not the pharmacy that a doctor refers you to. It's the Babylonian drugstore of the seventh seal.

I am not downplaying the evils of witchcraft and the occult. Unfortunately we have that to deal with as well, but let's look at the definition of *pharmakeia*. The word has four definitions: (1) the use or the administering of drugs, (2) poisoning, (3) sorcery and magic arts, often found in connection with and fostered by idolatry, and (4) a metaphor for the deceptions and seductions of idolatry (see *Strong's* #5331). It is clear from these definitions that this is not the medicinal use of drugs. The definition includes poisoning, witchcraft, and idolatry. The word *pharmakeia* deals with the abuse of drugs and its poisoning effects.

Here is the first case where *pharmakeia* appears as *sorceries*: "Neither repented they of their murders, nor of their *sorceries*, nor of their fornication, nor of their thefts" (Revelation 9:21, emphasis added).

I like to call this "the addiction sandwich." One slice of bread is murder, the other is theft, and in the middle you have two addictions—drugs (including alcohol) and fornication (including all forms of sexual addiction). How telling this prophecy is considering the fact that crimes like murder and theft are often driven by drug addictions, alcoholism, and sexual immorality. The chapter heading of Revelation 9 says, "John also sees the wars and *plagues* poured out during the seventh seal and before the Lord comes" (emphasis added). Addiction certainly is a plague that is sweeping the world.

President Hinckley had something to say about another horrible plague of our day. He is speaking of pornography, and his words apply to other addictions as well:

> Leave it alone! Get away from it! Avoid it! It is sleazy filth! It is rot that will do no good! You cannot afford to watch videotapes of this kind of stuff. You cannot afford to read magazines that are designed to destroy you. You can't do it, nor even watch it on television. . . . Stay away from it! Avoid it like the *plague* because it is just as deadly, more so. The *plague* will destroy the body. Pornography will destroy the body and the soul. Stay away from it! It is as a great disease that is sweeping over the country and over the entire world. Avoid it! I repeat, avoid it! (Jordan Utah South Regional Conference, Priesthood Session, March 1, 1997)

Could the prophet be any more direct?

The first verse in Revelation 9 begins as follows: "And the fifth angel sounded, and I saw a star fall from heaven unto the earth: and to him was given the key of the bottomless pit." As we approach the Second Coming of the Lord, the wickedness of men will descend lower and lower. It will be similar with addictions. The point at which we hit bottom will also descend lower and lower.

"AND THE LIGHT OF A CANDLE SHALL SHINE NO MORE AT ALL IN THEE"

The next prophecy deals with the spiritual fall of Babylon on a macro scale. On the micro scale, it warns about the consequences of not fleeing spiritual Babylon, and on an even smaller scale it warns about the effects of drugs (pharmakeia) on the individual. Remember that the term *drugs*, for our purposes, includes all forms of addiction, including pornography and sexual addiction.

Here is *pharmakeia* (or sorceries) in case two:

> And the voice of harpers, and musicians, and of pipers, and trumpeters, shall be heard no more at all in thee; and no craftsman, of whatsoever craft he be, shall be found any more

in thee; and the sound of a millstone shall be heard no more
at all in thee;

And the light of a candle shall shine no more at all in
thee; and the voice of the bridegroom and of the bride shall
be heard no more at all in thee: for thy merchants were the
great men of the earth; for by thy *sorceries* were all nations
deceived.

And in her was found the blood of prophets, and of
saints, and of all that were slain upon the earth. (Revelation
18:22–24, emphasis added)

Have you ever seen the lights go out in the eyes of an addict? If you
are a codependent, have you ever gazed into the face of a loved one and
wondered who was in there? These verses are beautifully written, yet
they tell a sad story. It isn't just hyperbole; it is real life.

Let's look at each symbol or element in these verses.

Music and musical instruments are usually placed in the scriptures
to emphasize true joy and cause for celebration, as opposed to partying
and reveling, which addicts may be used to. Music in this context is
probably not the most uplifting kind since it originates in Babylon. The
scripture makes a good point. If we pursue our addictions long enough
and hard enough, the party will eventually end. Only the compulsion
will remain.

Craftsmen and crafts represent those who are proficient in a skill or
trade. A craft could be a talent or ability. Millstones were used to grind
grain into flour (see Bible Dictionary, "Millstone"). A millstone could be
likened to a modern-day factory or production line.

When Jesus gave the Sermon on the Mount, He said, "Neither do
men light a candle, and put it under a bushel, but on a candlestick; and it
giveth light unto all that are in the house. Let your light so shine before
men, that they may see your good works, and glorify your Father which
is in heaven" (Matthew 5:15–16). Besides setting a good example for
others with the motive of glorifying God, there lies a deeper meaning.
Notice that the Lord says the candle belongs on the candlestick; and
the candlestick was made to be placed in the tabernacle and later in the
temple (see Bible Dictionary, "Candlestick"). We have the opportunity

to be "a light unto the world, and to be the saviors of men" (D&C 103:9) as we participate in family history and temple work for ourselves and others.

The bridegroom represents the Savior. In the parable of the ten virgins, the virgins "went forth to meet the bridegroom" (Matthew 25:1). In several passages of scripture we are admonished to "be ready at the coming of the Bridegroom" (D&C 33:17; see also D&C 65:3 and 133:10). The bride represents the Church. The following scripture is an example:

> That thy *church* may come forth out of the wilderness of darkness, and shine forth fair as the moon, clear as the sun, and terrible as an army with banners;
> And be adorned as a *bride* for that day when thou shalt unveil the heavens, and cause the mountains to flow down at thy presence, and the valleys to be exalted, the rough places made smooth; that thy glory may fill the earth. (D&C 109:73–74, emphasis added).

Taken together, references to brides and bridegrooms can also suggest a family or marital relationship.

The word *merchants* in verse 23, suggests that the forces driving addiction are well-organized. Drug trafficking is big business. Millions of dollars are spent to advertise alcoholic beverages. President Gordon B. Hinckley said that pornography is a $57 billion industry worldwide (Gordon B. Hinckley, "A Tragic Evil Among Us," *Ensign* [November 2004]: 59).

Using the foregoing symbols, a possible interpretation of this prophecy (Revelation 18:22–24) would be as follows: For addicts, the joy and celebration are gone from life. Job performance has slackened and work ethic has faded away. The light in their eyes is dim. Temple blessings are absent from life. The Savior is calling them back, but they won't listen. Their spouses and children weep each day, but all of their money goes to their drug of choice, and someone else is getting rich. They have been deceived in a deadly game.

"I WILL FEED THEM . . . WITH THEIR OWN FLESH; AND THEY SHALL BE DRUNKEN . . . AS WITH SWEET WINE"

Isaiah's version of this quote as found in the King James version of the Bible is: "And I will feed them that oppress thee with their own flesh; and they shall be drunken with their own blood, as with sweet wine: and all flesh shall know that I the Lord am thy Saviour and thy Redeemer, the mighty One of Jacob" (Isaiah 49:26).

Clearly this prophecy pertains to the enemies of the house of Israel as they "war among themselves." Their own sword will fall upon their own heads, and they shall be "drunken with their own blood" (see 1 Nephi 22:13–14). But could there be another spiritual message? What about being fed with their own flesh? And what about being "drunken" with the things of the flesh?

Nephi clearly connects this prophecy with those who are "in the flesh," those who seek to "get power over the flesh," and those who "seek the lusts of the flesh" (see 1 Nephi 22:22–23). That gives this verse a whole new spin.

Our minds and souls feed on those things we put into them. Indeed unsavory and unwholesome thoughts and images are not readily digested. They poison the mind for a long time. When we feed on flesh, it creates an appetite for itself, and we chase after the grosser and harder forms.

Don't be confused by the beginning of this Isaiah verse, which says, "And *I* will feed them . . . with their own flesh." The Lord does not feed us this kind of trash any more than he causes the enemies of the house of Israel to turn on each other. Isaiah uses figurative and poetic imagery. A more literal wording might be, "I allow men their agency, even if that means they turn against each other or choose to chase after the things of the flesh and use their agency in an unrighteous manner."

This imagery of Isaiah brings out an important point with the phrase, "drunken . . . as with sweet wine." Anyone can become drunken and out of control with any addiction! The Jaredites, near the end of their civilization, were "drunken with anger" (see Ether 15:22). They slept on their swords. I have heard some with eating disorders say they were drunken with binge eating, even though they had never drank a drop of alcohol. People also become drunken (or out of control) with pornography and sexual addictions.

Many who have overcome alcohol or drug addiction have also struggled with these addictions of the flesh. There is not a stronger addiction than pornography or sexual immorality. Personally, I believe these are the very toughest to overcome. Those of us who are active in Twelve-Step recovery and have held service positions in the program, especially in the LDS Church program, will agree that the most spiritually threatening addiction out there is pornography, along with its spin-off—sexual immorality. I think we are only seeing the tip of the iceberg. I will go on record saying that this problem is the biggest threat and hindrance to the functioning power of the priesthood of God. It is that serious. There are also countless numbers who live in secret shame. They will not come to meetings nor seek help because of the stigma associated with doing so. I see this problem as the biggest addiction problem in the Church. Period. No wonder the brethren are devoting so much attention to this issue in general conference and other Church meetings.

As severe as this problem is, however, there is still hope. The Son of Man suffered "temptations of *every* kind; and this that the word might be fulfilled which saith he will take upon him the pains and the *sicknesses* of his people" (Alma 7:11, emphasis added). Every addiction is also a spiritual disease, and pornography and sexual immorality are of the sickest. The good news of the gospel is that the Savior descended below all these things, so He could overcome all things of the world—even the things of the flesh (see John 16:33). Therefore, we all can "be of good cheer" even if we suffer from such temptation, and even if we have fallen prey to addictions of this kind. Jesus, "who wrought out this perfect atonement through the shedding of his own blood" (D&C 76:69), now stands anxiously ready, willing, and able to act as a personal mediator and advocate. With "His own blood" he now can and will guide, empower, and rescue those who are "drunken with their own blood" (Isaiah 49:26).

His plea to the Father is:

> Father, behold the sufferings and death of him who did no sin, in whom thou wast well pleased; behold the blood of thy Son which was shed, the blood of him whom thou gavest that thyself might be glorified;
> Wherefore, Father, spare these my brethren that believe on my name, that they may come unto me and have everlasting life. (D&C 45:4–5)

The translation for the Greek word *pharmakeia* into the English word *sorceries* seems quite fitting. Sorcery is an evil, false, and counterfeit form of worship where Satan is attempting to imitate the power of God. I never considered myself a "sorcerer" when I drank alcohol every day, but I really was. I was bowing down to the god of alcohol just as others bow to gods with names like meth, cocaine, marijuana, pornography, etc.

In summary, we live in a world filled with addictions of every kind. It is one of the hallmarks of our day.

building your ship—
your program

I will now continue with the story of Nephi and his family from the Book of Mormon. After eight years of sojourning in the wilderness, Nephi and his family arrived in the land of Bountiful, a place on the seashore noted for its "much fruit and also wild honey" (1 Nephi 17:5). Then Nephi records:

> And it came to pass that after I, Nephi, had been in the land of Bountiful for the space of many days, the voice of the Lord came unto me, saying: Arise, and get thee into the mountain. And it came to pass that I arose and went up into the mountain, and cried unto the Lord.
>
> And it came to pass that the Lord spake unto me, saying: Thou shalt construct a ship, after the manner which I shall show thee, that I may carry thy people across these waters." (1 Nephi 17:7–8)

Fortunately, Nephi had more faith than I would have had under such circumstances. He simply said, "Lord, whither shall I go that I may find ore to molten, that I may make tools to construct the ship after the manner which thou hast shown unto me?" (1 Nephi 17:9) Nephi gets an answer to his prayer, and then he goes to work.

Nephi is trying to cross some turbulent waters, just as many addicts are. They can glean many principles of recovery from Nephi. After all, both of them are all trying to get to the same place—the promised land, or, in other words, exaltation and eternal life. It is their ship, or, in other words, their program, that will carry them across the turbulent waters of trial and temptation and deliver them safely at the shores of recovery. Remember, the Lord has promised every addict full recovery in spite of their imperfections, if they are faithful and will work some difficult but simple steps.

Nephi was not building this ship after a design he learned in his shop class or from something he read in a book. He said, "And the Lord did show me from time to time after what manner I should work the timbers of the ship. Now I, Nephi, did not work the timbers after the manner which was learned by men, neither did I build the ship after the manner of men; but I did build it after the manner which the Lord had shown unto me; wherefore, it was not after the manner of men" (1 Nephi 18:1–2). Nephi emphasized three times the idea that he did not build the ship after the manner of men.

There are two good reasons for building a program of recovery after the manner of the Lord and not after the manner of men. Addicts can go to many programs, self-help books, therapy groups, and rehab centers, and come away with some good ideas. Certainly treatment centers and hospitals have their place in recovery, but the learning of men will focus on many of the physical symptoms and not address the spiritual aspects of recovery. Addicts have a spiritual disease, and it requires a spiritual cure. They may be able to successfully dry you out for thirty days; but you will still need to learn how to live "life . . . on life's terms" (*Big Book of Alcoholics Anonymous*, p. 417) if you expect any form of quality sobriety, length of sobriety, and happiness in your life.

We are trying to combat the disease of alcoholism—not just fight alcohol. The real disease of alcoho*lism* is the *ism* at the end. It stands for "I," "Self," and "Me." Alcoholism is the disease of bondage of self. It is so much more than just not drinking. It is not politically correct in today's world for institutions other than churches to address spiritual issues. Let me make one thing clear. Alcoholics Anonymous and the Twelve Steps are not remedies after the manner of men. They are directly inspired of God

There is a second reason for building your program after the manner of the Lord. The reason is this: No one can tell anyone else exactly how to build his or her program. I, for example, can tell someone what constitutes a successful program for me, because the Lord has prompted me through His Spirit to help me know what works for me. Someone may have some of the same addictions that I have, but we don't have the same set of temptations, triggers, and trials. We may be motivated differently. Something that works for someone else may not work as well for me. Thus, the Lord, who knows each of us intimately, can create for each of us, a tailored battle plan of recovery and healing. He will give addicts specific insights into their own personal life, if they seek Him.

There are a couple of things we can observe from Nephi that are essential for building a successful ship—or, in our case, a successful program. Immediately after Nephi gets his assignment, he prays to the Lord and asks Him specifically where he should go to get ore to make tools. He prays for assistance since he is not capable of building a ship by himself. As a matter of fact, his brothers Laman and Lemuel ridicule him for even thinking he can build a ship. The idea is outrageous in their minds. But Nephi has faith and trust in the Lord.

Recovering addicts may have friends, relatives, and others scoff at their desire to become clean and sober. Others may question their abilities and motives, and they will probably have many doubts and reservations themselves, but the good news is that they do not have to build this ship alone. They get to partner up with the "One who has all power." The Savior invites all of us to enter into a partnership with Him when he says, "Take my yoke upon you, and learn of me; for I am meek and lowly in heart: and ye shall find rest unto your souls. For my yoke is easy, and my burden is light" (Matthew 11:29–30).

The dictionary defines a yoke as "a wooden bar or frame by which two draft animals" such as oxen, "are coupled at the heads or necks for *working together.*" The imagery of this symbolism sometimes brings me to tears of gratitude! I imagine the Savior addressing me by name and saying, "Come, get in the blocks with me—side by side—and we will work together. When you are too weak and cannot carry the load anymore out of sheer exhaustion, I will pull the load for you. I will strengthen you and help you. I will steer the course and guide the way, 'that where I am, there ye may be also'" (John 14:3). The Savior invites us to work side by side *with* Him; He doesn't drag us. It brings me immense gratitude and comfort to know that as long as I stay yoked to Him, I will end up in the same place with Him.

Recovering addicts may have a greater appreciation for the principle of grace and a better understanding of the balance between grace and works than many of their brothers and sisters in the Church. However, you don't have to commit sin and you don't have to be an addict to understand grace. In fact, I firmly believe that those who are continually striving to be righteous have the greatest appreciation and understanding of the concept of grace. Abraham, who was always a "follower of righteousness" and who desired to be a "greater follower of righteousness" (see Abraham 1:2), had superb appreciation and understanding of grace, when he was "fully persuaded that, what [God] had promised, he was able also to perform" (Romans 4:21). Thus, Abraham was enabled to perform extraordinary works.

Recovering addicts will have a beautiful view of grace if they stay clean and sober, because they will realize they are only able to gain and keep sobriety by the grace of God. They will not see grace as a "freebie" or a free pass, but rather as "an enabling power that allows men and women to lay hold on eternal life and exaltation after they have expended their own best efforts" (Bible Dictionary, "Grace").

The ship needs to be balanced to sail properly. If there is too much weight on the side of grace, the ship will capsize. The same will happen if there is too much weight on the side of works.

Nephi is a prime example of how to work a program. Notice the balance between grace and works as the Lord commands Nephi, "Thou shalt construct a ship, after the manner which I shall show thee, that I may carry thy people across these waters" (1 Nephi 17:8). Nephi is going to be doing a lot of work as he builds the ship. Grace is also apparent as the Lord shows Nephi how to build the ship and as the Lord is going to "carry" them across the waters. The Lord does not say He will magically transport or transfer them to the promised land, which is symbolic of exaltation. Nor does He expect Nephi to navigate the waters successfully by himself. Nephi understands his role of working closely with the Lord, nevertheless he is still working when he asks "Lord, whither shall I go that I may find ore to molten, that I may make tools to construct the ship after the manner which thou hast shown unto me?" (1 Nephi 17:9). This is an important concept because it affects how an addict will work every aspect of his or her program. Nephi received his assignment and then went right to work. So let's do the same thing.

A good personal recovery program will include the following components.

MIGHTY PRAYER

First Nephi Chapter 1 is a good place to start studying the Book of Mormon, and it is a good place to start your program. Here is a synopsis of the narrative.

> Verse 1: Nephi introduces himself, speaks of the goodness of God, and states his intent to write a record.
> Verse 2: He reveals the language of the record, which consists of reformed Egyptian and the learning of the Jews.
> Verse 3: Nephi bears testimony of his own record.
> Verse 4: He gives us the starting date of his record and the setting of Jerusalem to let us know where the events are taking place.
> Verse 5: Now that Nephi has given the background for his record, he begins the actual narrative by saying, "Wherefore it came to pass that my father, Lehi, as he went forth *prayed* unto the Lord, yea, even with *all his heart*" (emphasis added).

You can't even turn the first page of the Book of Mormon without finding a prayer. The first four verses are background verses, so the first actual event pertaining to Nephi and his family is a prayer given by his father, Lehi. Notice also that this is a prayer of the heart. Lehi does not hold in any of his feelings.

As a result of Lehi's prayer and accompanying faith, he sees the heavens open, God sitting on His throne, concourses of angels, the Savior Himself, and twelve others following Him. He learns that Jerusalem will be destroyed. He praises God for His mercy, power, and goodness—all attributes of God that He willingly shares with us and that are necessary for healing the wounded soul. Lehi praises God for His goodness and because Lehi and his family will be saved from a terrible, impending destruction.

Often for the addict such a heart-felt prayer is the beginning. It is the wake-up call with the realization that one can be saved from a terrible destruction, both physically and spiritually. I vividly remember my own first prayer of recovery on July 31, 1989—my sobriety date. I remember that hour-long battle with the enemy before I could humble myself enough to fall down on my knees. I remember his rhetoric: "You can't pray to God now after all the terrible sins you have committed and after all the lives you have ruined. It is too late for you. Why should God help you now? You've gone too far; no one can help you now!" About two years later I was reading the scriptures one day, and I came to understand that Satan tells this pack of lies to everyone with a sinful past who is now ready to turn to the Lord. "For the evil spirit teacheth not a man to pray, but teacheth him that he must not pray" (2 Nephi 32:8). An addict beginning recovery can expect this to happen.

I finally got on my knees, and the words started coming out awkwardly. The tears began to flow like a well. I am kind of embarrassed to admit it, but it may have been the first prayer of my life having "real intent" (see Moroni 10:4). I can't live long enough to forget the feeling of incredible peace that overwhelmed me. It surprised me terribly! I knew I didn't deserve any peaceful feelings, and they certainly weren't expected. But a loving Father enveloped me in His love nonetheless. I didn't hear a voice. I didn't need to; I felt Him whisper calmly to my soul, "It's going to be alright. I can heal you." I dared to hope that I could be rescued from a terrible destruction. God is real and stands willing with great desire to rescue us all.

Nephi continues the narrative. The first testimony of the coming of the Messiah comes only nineteen verses into this marvelous book. Then comes Nephi's remarkable testimony, which has a profound application to the addict: "But behold, I, Nephi, will show unto you that the tender mercies of the Lord are over all those whom he hath chosen, because of their faith, to make them mighty even unto the power of deliverance" (1 Nephi 1:20). Prayer is a catalyst to activating the power of deliverance.

In chapter 2, Lehi is commanded to take his family and depart into the wilderness. He abandons everything—his neighborhood, his house, his gold, his silver, and his "precious things" (see 1 Nephi 2:4). Recovering addicts must also abandon everything that is tied to addiction. They may even have to leave their old drinking and using buddies behind. That doesn't mean they don't love them anymore; they just cannot afford to have those friends drag them down to their old ways.

You will notice that, so far, Nephi has only been writing about the experiences of his father. He continues the story by recounting a talk Lehi had with his sons Laman and Lemuel. This talk ends in verse 14 when Laman and Lemuel are confounded by the words of their father. Verse 15 ends the narration of Lehi's story for a while, with the comment, "And my father dwelt in a tent."

In verse 16 the focus shifts to Nephi. Nephi tells us a little bit about himself. He says he is large in stature, young, and desires greatly "to know of the mysteries of God." So, what is the first actual event that Nephi records about his own life? He says, "Wherefore, I did cry unto the Lord; and behold he did visit me, and did soften my heart that I did believe all the words which had been spoken by my father." Nephi's first recorded event, like Lehi's, is a prayer of the heart.

A great source of Nephi's power is this: he always gives the Lord credit for his blessings. It was the Lord who softened his heart. Can you imagine Nephi with even an ounce of rebellion or any lingering doubts? It is hard to imagine because we see Nephi and his character only *after* the Lord has already changed his heart. Addicts will be more successful in their recovery, if they always remember the Lord and give Him due credit. Yes, they must work the Twelve Steps and perform the basic requirements, but they know they cannot stay clean and sober without the grace of God.

Lest anyone should think of Lehi and Nephi's experience with prayer as an aberration, here is another example of a record beginning with great prayer. The Nephites and the Lamanites were not the only civilizations that existed in Book of Mormon times. There was also the Jaredite civilization. Here is a synopsis of some of the verses at the beginning of this record in the first chapter of Ether.

Verse 1: Moroni tells us he is giving an account of the Jaredites, who were destroyed.

Verse 2: He tells of the source of his account—the twenty-four plates found by the people of Limhi (a group that the Lord delivered from bondage).

Verses 3–4: He omits the part of the record that discusses everything from the creation of the world to the Tower of Babel, or, in other words, the first ten chapters of Genesis, supposing that this account is also had among the Jews, and, therefore, it will be in our Bibles.

Verse 5: Moroni says he is not giving the full account contained in the record. He says his account begins with the Tower of Babel and ends with the destruction of the Jaredites.

Verse 6: He introduces the writer of the record, Ether.

Verses 6–32: The ancestry of Ether is given, going all the way back to Jared.

Verse 33: Moroni takes us back to the days of Jared, who came to the promised land with his brother, their families, and many others at the time of the Tower of Babel, during which time the language of the people was confounded, and the people were scattered.

Verse 34: The brother of Jared is introduced as "a large and mighty man" (like Nephi). Jared asks his brother to cry unto the Lord and ask that their language not be confounded.

Verse 35: The brother of Jared cries unto the Lord, and the Lord has compassion upon him. Their language is not confounded.

Verses 36–37: Jared asks his brother to pray again that the language of their friends not be confounded. The brother of Jared complies with his request.

Verse 38: Jared asks his brother to inquire of the Lord whether they shall be driven out of the land and, if so, where they shall go. Jared speaks of a choice land for their inheritance and asks his brother to inquire of the Lord concerning these matters.

Verse 39: The brother of Jared prays again.

Verses 40–43: The Lord promises to lead them to a promised land, where He will bless them and make them a great nation.

Once again, just like in First Nephi, the first actual event of the Jaredite record is a series of prayers offered by the brother of Jared. Everything prior to this is simply background information.

There are some very interesting characteristics of these prayers. Notice that the brother of Jared prays for himself and his brother the first time. That simple prayer is answered. The scripture says, "And Jared and his brother were not confounded" (Ether 1:35). Then, like Nephi, Enos, King Benjamin, Alma, Mormon, and many others, he begins to pray for others. In the spirit of Step Twelve ("Having had a spiritual awakening as the result of these steps, we tried to carry this message to alcoholics, and to practice these principles in all our affairs"), it becomes as natural as breathing to share blessings and spiritual principles with others. The brother of Jared then prays for his and his brother's friends and their families.

The Lord makes a promise to the brother of Jared and those who will go with him. If you compare verse 43 with the Abrahamic covenant found in Abraham 2:8–11 and Genesis 12:2–3, you will find several of the promises being repeated. There is the promise that the Lord will make them into "a great nation." They will be blessed beyond measure. The blessings are perpetuated through their seed with each successive generation. Part of the Abrahamic covenant is the promise of "certain lands as an eternal inheritance" (see Bible Dictionary, "Abraham, Covenant of"). Nephi and the brother of Jared were both promised that they would be led to a choice land. Likewise, addicts are promised that if they will follow certain basic principles, they can land safely in the promised land of sobriety, where they will experience joy, happiness, and healing.

The brother of Jared is promised all of these great blessings of the Abrahamic covenant. The Lord said, "And thus I will do unto thee because this *long time* ye have cried unto me" (Ether 1:43, emphasis added). Persistence in prayer pays off.

In summary, the blessings of both the Nephite and the Jaredite civilizations begin with prayer. Real recovery also begins with sincere prayer.

Next we will look at the components of effective prayer.

1. Mighty prayer is a function of the Spirit and involves real desire.
2. We pour out our hearts in mighty prayer.
3. Mighty prayer recognizes both grace and works.
4. Mighty prayer embraces principles of serenity.
5. Mighty prayer is specific in nature.
6. We can be "bold in mighty prayer" before God (2 Nephi 4:24).

Mighty Prayer Is a Function of the Spirit and Involves Real Desire

Step Eleven states, "Sought through prayer and meditation to improve our conscious contact with God as we understood Him, praying only for knowledge of His will for us and the power to carry that out." Conscious contact implies a two-way communication process. When we, and this is true for addicts and non-addicts, learn to pray (or re-learn for some of us), we learn to listen and not just talk. We begin to feel promptings of the Spirit. I find that some of my most effective personal prayers have pauses in the middle. I sometimes stop to listen and feel.

When the Savior visited the American continent, His disciples prayed unto Him. The scripture records, "They did still continue, without ceasing, to pray unto him; and they did not multiply many words, for it was given unto them what they should pray, and they were filled with desire" (3 Nephi 19:24). Desire and energy of heart are more important than wordiness and lip service when praying. Often, as in this case, the best prayers are those that come from the promptings of the Spirit. When an addict kneels down and prays for sobriety, the Lord knows how bad he or she wants it.

One of my favorite prayers recorded is the prayer offered at the dedication of the Kirtland Temple. It is section 109 of the Doctrine and Covenants. The section heading tells us that this prayer was given to the Prophet Joseph Smith by revelation. Prayers will be richer, more meaningful, and more powerful when they are guided by the Spirit.

We Pour Out Our Hearts During Mighty Prayer

In the Book of Mormon, the people of Alma the Elder serve as an excellent model of mighty prayer. They were in bondage to the Lamanites, and they were delivered by God. They'd had taskmasters placed over them. Amulon had commanded them that they should not pray. Guards were placed over them, and anyone caught praying was put to death.

The people of Alma did not pray out loud to the Lord, but they "did pour out their hearts to him; and he did know the thoughts of their hearts" (Mosiah 24:12). The imagery of the word *pour* is very interesting. If you pour out a glass of water, everything comes out of the glass. If there is mud in the water, it comes out too. Nothing is held back. By pouring out our hearts, we become rigorously honest with God. The people of Alma had some pretty good reasons for resentment and frustration. They were treated unfairly and cruelly afflicted. Amulon falsely blamed Alma for Amulon's being subject to the king of the Lamanites. There must have been some hard, bitter feelings in their hearts, but in the spirit of Step Three, they turned everything over to the Lord—the good and the bad.

No one needs to sugarcoat his or her feelings with the Lord. Be honest and pour everything out of your heart when you pray. Acknowledge the feelings in your heart, even if you are not proud of all of them. Like this scripture illustrates, the Lord knows your feelings and thoughts anyway. If you pour out your heart to God and keep His commandments, He will "pour you out a blessing, that there shall not be room enough to receive it" (Malachi 3:10).

Mighty Prayer Recognizes Both Grace and Works

When Laman and Lemuel tied up Nephi with cords (for the first time) with the intention of leaving him in the wilderness to be devoured by wild beasts, Nephi uttered a mighty prayer. He prayed, "O Lord, according to my faith which is in thee, wilt thou deliver me from the hands of my brethren; yea, even *give me strength* that I may *burst these bands* with which I am bound" (1 Nephi 7:17, emphasis added). The bands were then loosed from his hands and feet. Notice the spiritual maturity reflected in the prayers of the prophets. This prayer is vastly different from a prayer like, "Lord, come down and untie me" or a vague plea like, "Get me out of this mess!" Nephi could have asked the Lord to break the bands for him.

Likewise, addicts will find their prayers to be more effective when they pray for strength to overcome—when they pray for strength to break the bands of addiction. Alma offered a similar prayer: "O Lord, give us strength according to our faith which is in Christ, even unto deliverance" (Alma 14:26). Alma and Amulek were in prison and bound with cords. The result of Alma's prayer is in that same verse: "They broke the cords with which they were bound." Again, the Lord gave them strength rather than appearing on the scene with a knife to cut the cords.

After Alma the Elder and his people poured out their hearts to God, they received an answer to their silent prayers. The Lord said, "I will also ease the burdens which are put upon your shoulders, that even you cannot feel them upon your backs" (Mosiah 24:14). Indeed, there are two ways the Lord could accomplish this. He could reduce the actual weight of the load or He could strengthen their backs. The next verse (Mosiah 24:15) tells us that He chose the latter method. As a result, the people were able to "submit cheerfully and with patience to all the will of the Lord." Thus, they were able to work an excellent Step Three ("Made a decision to turn our will and our lives over to the care of God as we understood Him").

Remember to pray for strength, not for the "easier, softer way."

Mighty Prayer Embraces Principles of Serenity

Many recovering addicts carry around anniversary or birthday medallions representing the number of years they have been sober. Many of them, including mine, have the Serenity Prayer on the back. This is a prayer originally written by Reinhold Niebuhr and adopted by Alcoholics Anonymous. AA's slightly edited version reads, "God grant me the serenity to accept the things I cannot change; courage to change the things I can; and the wisdom to know the difference."

Too often in my prayers, I confuse the things I cannot change—such as other people, places, and things—with the one thing I can change—me. We often see spouses and parents come to a Twelve-Step meeting with the idea that they are there to support an addicted spouse or child. One day they begin to surrender their old ideas. Eventually they understand that they really cannot fix that wayward spouse or child, and they start to work a personal program for themselves to get well.

Another spiritually mature prayer is given by Alma while he is on a mission to the Zoramites: "O Lord, wilt thou give me strength, that I may bear with mine infirmities. For I am infirm, and such wickedness among *this people* doth pain my soul. O Lord, my heart is exceedingly sorrowful; wilt thou comfort my soul in Christ. O Lord, wilt thou grant unto me that I may have strength, that I may suffer with patience these afflictions which shall come upon me, because of the iniquity *of this people*" (Alma 31:30–31, emphasis added). Then he prays a similar prayer on behalf of his missionary companions, asking that they will be able to endure patiently the afflictions caused by the Zoramites.

I am afraid I might have uttered a prayer like this: "Please help these people. They are so messed up. Don't let us suffer because of them. They are the ones who are unrighteous. Please fix them, and fix them now!"

Notice that Alma acknowledges the fact that he is inevitably going to suffer afflictions. Nevertheless, he still prays that the Zoramites might be brought back to Christ. After he does all he can for them, and after he prays for them with all of his heart, he turns the rest over to the Lord and calmly accepts the outcome.

Step Eleven teaches us all much about the proper method of prayer. Prayers need to be focused on the things the Lord can help us change.

This step teaches people to pray "only for knowledge of His will for us and the power to carry that out." Otherwise, prayers can be taken over by self-will. In harmony with the other steps, we seek God's will for us and not our own selfish interests. Praying in this manner helps us learn to trust God. We can have peace and serenity by knowing that if we seek to do His will, then "all things shall work together for [our] good" (D&C 90:24). Our prayers will be more effective if we aren't asking the Lord to fix everyone and everything around us.

Mighty Prayer Is Specific in Nature

Prayers in recovery need to be specific and realistic, rather than vague and hypothetical. The scriptures can teach us much about prayer. When Nephi builds his ship, he offers specific prayers. He prays, "Lord, whither shall I go that I may find ore to molten, that I may make tools to construct the ship after the manner which thou hast shown unto me?" (1 Nephi 17:9) This is a much better prayer than "Lord, help me get to the promised land in safety."

The brother of Jared turns to the Lord after he has built the barges to cross the sea and expresses his concern regarding two major problems. The barges have neither light nor ventilation. The Lord solves the problem concerning the air in the vessels, but in reference to the lack of light, He says in effect, "What would you have me do about it?" I am sure that was not the answer the brother of Jared was looking for. (See Ether 2:19–25.)

Then the brother of Jared becomes a little more specific in his request. He moltens out of a rock sixteen small stones and carries them in his hands to the top of the mount. Then he cries to the Lord and proposes that the Lord touch each of the stones with His finger so that they may give light. That is a far cry from, "Help us have light in our vessels." (See Ether 3.)

Admittedly, a prayer saying, "Help me stay sober" is better than no prayer at all. But many will find their prayers becoming more powerful when they ask God for specific things, like, "Give me strength to overcome the terrible compulsion I am feeling at this very moment." Indeed, there are times when addicts must ask the Lord to remove an immediate compulsion to drink or use. The *Big Book* accurately states, "The alcoholic at certain times has no effective mental defense against the first drink. Except in a few rare cases, neither he nor any other human being can provide such a defense. His defense must come from a Higher Power" (p. 43).

Remember, specific prayers bring specific results.

We Can Be "Bold in Mighty Prayer" before God (2 Nephi 4:24)

Perhaps another reason why the Lord did not immediately answer the brother of Jared's prayer concerning light in the vessels was because the Lord wanted to let him have a faith-stretching and faith-promoting experience. Perhaps the Lord wanted to force his hand to come back and ask for a specific miracle. Either way, the brother of Jared is now required to be bold enough to ask the Lord to touch each stone. The result is that he sees with his eyes what before he had only viewed in his mind with "an eye of faith" (Ether 12:19)—the finger of the Lord coming down to touch each stone. Is there not a type here? Isaiah counsels, "Look unto the rock whence ye are hewn" (Isaiah 51:1). In other words, he might say, "You come from some pretty good stock! You are a descendent of Abraham and Sarah (see Isaiah 51:2). Like Moses, you are a child of God, 'in the similitude of his Only Begotten' (Moses 1:13). You have infinite potential!" It brings up two questions. Do we really view ourselves this way? And do we really dare to ask God to touch our personal lives, as He did the sixteen stones, so that we "may shine forth in darkness" (Ether 3:4)?

The good news is that it is not only permissible, but also encouraged by God that we ask for the big miracle. Addicts in recovery will find that when God pours out blessings, He will give them way more than they ever thought possible or more than they ever felt they deserved. I have said this before, but it is true. If I had dared to write down my wildest dreams going into recovery, I would have cheated myself big time compared to what God has restored and added to my life. Nephi said, "And mine eyes have beheld great things, yea, even too great for man." And all this happened because he first "waxed bold in mighty prayer before [God]" (see 2 Nephi 4:24–25).

I remember the day my bishop called me in for an interview. I had been sober for several months, but I had not yet dared to work Step Five with him. Step Five is "Admitted to God, to ourselves, and to another human being the exact nature of our wrongs." I had worked this step some with my sponsor, but it was my bishop who approached me. I hasten to add that it should have been the other way around. If you are an addict, go to your bishop. You will feel better.

I had scarcely sat down in his office when he proceeded to tell me that he wanted me to return to the temple. I must have looked shocked as I sat there and stared at him in silence for about ten seconds. Then I said, "Well, bishop, I don't see how that is possible, since I'm an alcoholic." Then he asked me a few questions, including what the length of my sobriety was, and he proceeded to give me a plan whereby I could get my temple recommend back. I was still in shock. For several months the only thing on my mind had been to stay sober. I had tunnel vision. The dream of ever going back to the temple had become a fantasy for me years before. I had written that one off a long time ago. But, over time, it finally happened.

As Paul puts it, "For we have not an high priest which cannot be touched with the feeling of our infirmities; but was *in all points* tempted like as we are, yet without sin. Let us therefore come *boldly* unto the throne of grace, that we may obtain mercy, and find grace to help in time of need" (Hebrews 4:15–16, emphasis added). It cannot be stated more beautifully. Because our Savior descended below all things, he experienced firsthand every sorrow, every broken heart, every pain, every sickness, every effect of every sin, and every effect of every addiction. Indeed, He experienced the gamut of human emotion, and His only motivation was His infinite love. We don't need to be timid in approaching the Lord, wondering whether He will really understand our suffering and whether He can really "help in time of need."

There is a silver lining in the cloud of powerlessness. One of the greatest potential blessings for recovering addicts comes from being powerless in their addiction. If they are to overcome successfully, they will have experienced the grace of God. They will also experience mighty prayer. They will be put in a position where they must plead with the Father with "all the energy of heart" (Moroni 7:48) that He will deliver them from the clutches of addiction, because they will understand fully in their most honest moments that they simply cannot do it themselves.

I say this to the recovering addict: When it is crunch time, you learn how to talk with God. You will learn more than just the format of prayer. I promise you that if you will work the Twelve Steps to the best of your ability, and then go to the Lord in mighty prayer, He will bridge the gap between your own abilities and the righteous desires of your heart. You will feel His power, and you will know you are receiving help beyond your own abilities. Jesus Himself made this promise: "And whatsoever ye shall ask the Father in my name, *which is right*, believing that ye shall receive, behold it shall be given unto you" (3 Nephi 18:20, emphasis added). It is the right thing to do to get clean and sober and stay clean and sober. I know of the validity and truthfulness of this promise.

You will find the "One who has all power," as you are prayerful and obedient to His commandments.

"May you find Him now!"

"try the virtue
of the word"

The next three chapters are a continuation of the previous chapter. Addicts are still building the ship and fortifying themselves against the turbulent waters and "fiery darts," (1 Nephi 15:24) which are bound to occur. The adversary is not going to let them out of his plan of bondage without a hard fight! In the last chapter we looked at the necessity of mighty prayer, as the beginning of a recovery program. This chapter will examine another critical part of the framework of our ship—namely, it is to "feast upon the words of Christ." After all, "the words of Christ will tell [us] all things what [we] should do" (2 Nephi 32:3).

Returning to the story of Lehi and his family, after Lehi prayed, and was warned of the impending destruction of Jerusalem, and was commanded to take his family and depart into the wilderness, and after Nephi prayed and the Lord softened his heart, and after the entire family was safely in the wilderness, Lehi was commanded to send his sons back to Jerusalem to obtain the record on the brass plates.

Recovering addicts are navigating their way through a new, unknown wilderness, as they start out in their newfound sobriety. They must re-learn how to cope with their feelings and emotions and how to live life on life's terms. They have numbed everything for years and must now start over. As they start out, possibly somewhat disoriented, the scriptures can be a guide for them. The "word is a lamp unto [their] feet, and a light unto [their] path" (Psalms 119:105).

A few chapters later, Lehi awakens to find a "ball of curious workmanship" outside his tent door. The ball has two spindles. Nephi records, "And the one pointed the way whither we should go into the wilderness" (1 Nephi 16:10). The scriptures can and will guide recovering addicts in making important decisions concerning their sobriety. Alma draws the following parallel:

> For behold, it is as easy to give heed to the word of Christ, which will point to you a straight course to eternal bliss, as it was for our fathers to give heed to this compass, which would point unto them a straight course to the promised land. And now I say, is there not a type in this thing? For just as surely as this director did bring our fathers, by following its course, to the promised land, shall the words of Christ, if we follow their course, carry us beyond this vale of sorrow into a far better land of promise. (Alma 37:44–45)

The word of Christ, if they follow its precepts, will carry addicts into the promised land of recovery where they will be free from bondage.

The second lesson in the story of Lehi and his family is that addicts actually cannot work the Twelve Steps without the word of God. Later on in the Book of Mormon, some of the Nephites encounter the people of Zarahemla—the Mulekites. They descended from Mulek, the only surviving son of Zedekiah, who was the king of Judah at the time Jerusalem was besieged by Babylon. Nebuchadnezzar, the Babylonian king, slew the sons of Zedekiah before Zedekiah's eyes—all except Mulek (see 2 Kings 24:11,17–18; Jeremiah 52:10; 1 Nephi 1:4; and Helaman 6:10; 8:21). Mulek and Nephi were contemporaries.

A group of Nephites meets up with a group of Mulekites in the Americas sometime between 300 and 500 years after their departure from Jerusalem. The Mulekites are described as having had many "wars and serious contentions." Unlike the Nephites, the Mulekites had not brought records with them. Their language had become corrupted, and the Nephites could not understand them, even though both groups migrated from Jerusalem. The most significant difference of all was that the Mulekites "denied the being of their Creator" (see Omni 1:17).

The first thing we learn about the character of Laman and Lemuel is that "they knew not the dealings of that God who had created them" (1 Nephi 2:12). That was the underlying problem affecting their behavior and attitude. Through prayerful and diligent study of the scriptures, we will come to understand the dealings of God. This is critical for addicts in early recovery, because their faith, hope, and trust levels are not very high when they first start out. When active in their addictions, addicts tend to project their motives and character traits on others. This affects their relationship with others, as well as God. They once trusted only their drug of choice. When that also goes south, they may start to feel like they can't trust anything. Many enter recovery either mad at God or afraid of Him.

Addicts have a lot of wreckage to overcome in their relationship with God, therefore it behooves them to come to an understanding of the true nature of God. It will automatically improve their relationship with others as well. One of the best ways I know of to gain an understanding of God and to have a relationship with Him is to immerse one's self in the scriptures. The *Big Book of Alcoholics Anonymous* will have a similar effect. These great books illustrate how God's influence and power have affected the lives of others. By reading them, addicts will begin to have some hope for themselves.

By feasting on the words of Christ every day, one can begin to understand and appreciate the true nature and characteristics of God— His mercy, patience, long-suffering, infinite power, love, wisdom, and grace. In 2 Nephi 9, for example, Jacob lists many of the attributes of God, and then expounds on them to fully explain how each attribute is a blessing in our lives.

The basics of the Twelve Steps are simple. I have to work the first three steps every day. Step One: I am powerless by myself. Step Two: I believe God can restore me. Step Three: I trust Him enough to turn it over to Him. In other words, I can't; God can; I will let Him. How can we trust someone we do not know? How can we trust the Lord, if we don't know how He operates? No wonder the Lord said, "Take my yoke upon you, and *learn of me*; for I am meek and lowly in heart: and ye shall find rest unto your souls. For my yoke is easy, and my burden is light" (Matthew 11:29–30, emphasis added). Most of us need to learn something about Him before we will get in the yoke with Him.

When Lehi found the Liahona outside his tent, and his family began to use it, they discovered a few interesting things about it. It worked "according to the faith and diligence and heed" (1 Nephi 16:28) that they gave to it. The scriptures work the same for us. If we are obedient and diligent in following the counsel given therein, we will discover the value and the power of the scriptures. They will begin to change our lives as we receive enrichment from them.

Nephi also observed that the pointers on the Liahona contained a "new writing" that gave them "understanding concerning the ways of the Lord" (1 Nephi 16:29). Likewise, the scriptures can teach us much about the Lord and His ways. We can all gain the ability to trust in the Lord as we learn about His dealings with others and as we liken these principles to ourselves.

Nephi also observed that the writing "changed from time to time" (1 Nephi 16:29). When I got sober and began reading the scriptures again, I noticed that certain verses would have a different meaning for me than they had had in the past. This is one of the greatest things about the words of Christ. I testify to those in recovery that as you read by the light of the Spirit, you will find that the same scripture will have different meanings as you read it over and over. You will gain insight regarding specific things you need to do to enhance your recovery or to keep your sobriety. If you will prayerfully search the scriptures, you will find the strength and insight you seek.

I have heard participants in Twelve-Step meetings share similar experiences. Once I heard someone share how he would read in the *Big Book* on a regular basis. He said he thought his *Big Book* was magical. He would read a page, close the book, set it down, and come back to it later. He would read the same page again—but this time it would have a different meaning. He said he could have sworn that the writing was being changed in his book! He would find new spiritual messages each time he read. The same principle applies to the scriptures, except on a much larger basis. With most books I read, I learn less new material with each successive reading, but with the scriptures it is just the opposite. The more times I read the scriptures (especially the Book of Mormon) the more new insights I am able to gain.

"THE WORD OF GOD . . .
IS QUICK AND POWERFUL"

There is another great reason to prayerfully study the word of God. Step Eleven teaches that addicts (though this applies to everyone) should seek to obtain two things from God—knowledge and power. It is quite evident that they will improve their knowledge of God and His ways as they search the scriptures. However, it is not as apparent that they will also gain power and grace as they study the word of God.

When all else fails, rely on the power of the word of God. When Alma saw the people around him falling into a state of apostasy, he called upon the power of the word to rescue them. The scripture records: "And now, as the preaching of the word had a great tendency to lead the people to do that which was just—yea, it had had more *powerful* effect upon the minds of the people than the sword, or anything else, which had happened unto them—therefore Alma thought it was expedient that they should try the virtue of the word of God" (Alma 31:5, emphasis added).

Our modern apostles and prophets have taught similar concepts. One of my favorite quotes was given by Elder Boyd K. Packer. He said the following: "True doctrine, understood, changes attitudes and behavior. The study of the doctrines of the gospel will improve behavior quicker than a study of behavior will improve behavior" (Boyd K. Packer, "Little Children," *Ensign* [November 1986]: 6). There is great truth and power in this statement. The wisdom of the world would have addicts focus on their addictive behaviors in an attempt to eliminate them. A more spiritual approach would foster daily scripture study, which in time will lead to a correct understanding of true doctrine. True doctrine then has the power to change addicts from the inside out; their very natures are changed.

Addicts in recovery are definitely seeking to change their behavior. When I entered the rooms of Alcoholics Anonymous, I believed if I could only stop drinking, then virtually every problem in life would be eliminated. I had hopes of changing only one little behavior, which by that time was not so little anymore. Indeed, it had grown into a monster. Today, with 20/20 hindsight, I can see that my life would still be quite empty if it were only about not drinking. The Twelve Steps are all about having a spiritual awakening, and it is that very spiritual awakening that will give us the power to stay clean and sober. A wise friend of mine who is in the program and who I look up to as a spiritual giant used to always say that his sponsor told him he needed to work the steps to stay sober, and he needed to stay sober to work the steps. At first, this sounded like one of those dumb AA sayings, but time has shown me just how profound this statement is.

Helaman 3:29 is a great summary verse in the Book of Mormon that discusses the power of the word of God. "Yea, we see that whosoever will may lay hold upon the word of God, which is quick and powerful, which shall divide asunder all the cunning and the snares and the wiles of the devil, and lead the man of Christ in a strait and narrow course across that everlasting gulf of misery which is prepared to engulf the wicked."

The word *quick* in the scriptures does not necessarily relate to speed or length of time as we would use the word today. The word *quick* means to enliven or make alive. In Greek it means to enjoy real life (in AA we would say enjoy "living life on life's terms"), to be in full vigor, or living water having vital power in itself and exerting the same upon the soul (see *Strong's* #2198). The term *living water* also draws the power of the Savior into the picture (see John 4:10–14).

I feel impressed to stop here and share an experience, which happened within an hour of writing the paragraph above. After returning home from an errand, I noticed an AA publication entitled *Twenty-Four Hours a Day* in the corner of the room. The book was written for daily meditation, but I must confess, I rarely read it. I felt a distinct feeling that I should read the thought for the day. I flipped it open near the beginning to find January 15, but I missed and accidentally turned to January 20. The words at the top of the page caught my eye, and interestingly enough the *Big Book* says "Nothing, absolutely nothing, happens in God's world by mistake" (p. 417). Compare this thought with the previous paragraph concerning the verse in Helaman.

> In A.A., we're all through with lying, hangovers, remorse, and wasting money. When we were drinking, we were only *half alive*. Now that we're trying to live decent, honest, unselfish lives, we're *really alive*. Life has a new meaning for us, so that we can really enjoy it. We feel that we're some use in the world. We're on the right side of the fence, instead of on the wrong side. We can look the world in the face instead of hiding in alleys. We come into A.A. to get sober and if we stay long enough, we learn a new way of living.

The word of God really is "quick and powerful." It really does make us "alive in Christ." (See Moroni 8:22; 2 Nephi 25:25.)

Returning to Helaman 3:29, the word of God has power to cut through any snare or trap laid by the adversary. Paul uses similar language: "For the word of God is quick, and powerful, and sharper than any two-edged sword" (Hebrews 4:12). When John sees the Lord, he declares that, "out of his mouth went a sharp twoedged sword" (Revelation 1:16). Thus, the word of God becomes a two-edged sword that divides the "gulf of misery" from eternal joy in the "kingdom of heaven" (Helaman 3:30), but we don't have to wait for heaven to experience the difference. The word of God is powerful enough to transport us across that "gulf of misery" into a better place where we can be "happy, joyous, and free." Those of us who have suffered through addictions know all too well about that "everlasting gulf of misery," but the flip side of life with God's promised blessings is every bit as real.

The imagery in Helaman 3:29 is beautiful and powerful. The dictionary defines *wile* as "a trick or stratagem intended to ensnare or deceive." When addicts see words like *wile* or *snare* in the scriptures, especially when these words are used in conjunction with language from the *Big Book* such as "cunning, baffling, powerful," then they, myself included, know it is high time to perk up and pay attention! The scriptures give us an antidote for Satan's snares.

The healing, cleansing power of the Savior is evident throughout the scriptures. One example is evident in the story of the woman who had an issue of blood. Her condition had plagued her life for twelve years. She had "spent all her living upon physicians" (Luke 8:43), and nothing could heal her. Many addicts can sympathize. I drank for seventeen years, and for the last ten, it was a daily occurrence. I spent all my living on my booze—more than just money. Alcohol consumed every facet of my life. It reduced living to a mundane existence. Every thought and decision was based on my drinking. It became the most important piece of my life. I only hope that someday I can expend as much in time, energy, and resources for the cause of discipleship as I did for the cause of alcoholism. When I had finally had enough and was sick and tired of being sick and tired, it seemed like nothing worked. I couldn't stop, and there seemed to be no cure in sight. My own efforts could take me nowhere.

If we read Leviticus 15, it is plain to see that this poor woman with an issue of blood suffered more than physical torment. She was isolated. She became an outcast. Everything and everyone that she touched became unclean. Under the law of Moses, if she touched someone, even accidentally, then that person would need to "wash his clothes, and bathe himself in water" (Leviticus 15:27). When she touched the Savior, something happened outside the norm. Instead of Jesus becoming contaminated by the woman, she is actually cleansed and healed. The Savior has power over every form of uncleanness.

In twelve-step programs, addicts often refer to their length of sobriety as "clean time." Whether the addiction happens to be alcohol, drugs, the uncleanness that comes from pornography and sexual immorality, or any other addiction, if they will draw close to the Savior and let Him touch their lives, they will be healed and cleansed from those things that would otherwise destroy them.

The woman with the issue of blood walked behind the Savior and touched the border of his garment. She was immediately cleansed and healed. Then something very interesting happens. Jesus asks, "Who touched me?" Peter and the others who were there think this is a silly question. After all, there is a crowd of people thronging Jesus. He then responds, "Somebody hath touched me: for I perceive that *virtue* is gone out of me" (Luke 8:46, emphasis added). The Greek word for *virtue* means power (see footnote a for Luke 8:46 and *Strong's* #1411). In a very literal way, Jesus has the power to make all of us clean—every whit!

I want to compare this story to Alma 31:5, which was previously discussed in this chapter. Alma proclaims that the word of God has a more powerful effect upon the people than anything else. "Therefore Alma thought it was expedient that they should try the *virtue* of the word of God" (emphasis added). We now know that virtue means power. Thus, if the Savior's power can go from Him into the woman with the issue of blood to make her clean, even so can His power go forth from His words and into addicts to give them power to become clean, whole, and restored.

Recovering addicts will learn much more about the Twelve Steps as they study the scriptures every day. I am not sure I could read even one page without finding at least one of the steps. They will find themselves tripping across the steps as they prayerfully study the scriptures. Besides the knowledge they will gain, they will find great power. They will notice their faith increasing as they read about real people who have overcome great challenges by receiving of the Lord's grace and power.

There is another power source in the word of God. Nephi teaches us that "Angels speak by the power of the Holy Ghost; wherefore, they speak the words of Christ. Wherefore, I said unto you, feast upon the words of Christ; for behold, the words of Christ will tell you all things what ye should do" (2 Nephi 32:3). This brings up an interesting question. If a message is doctrinally correct, but is not conveyed by the Holy Ghost, is it still the word of God? We can probably answer that question by referring to D&C 50:17–20.

> Verily I say unto you, he that is ordained of me and sent forth to preach the word of truth by the Comforter, in the Spirit of truth, doth he preach it by the Spirit of truth or some other way?
>
> And if it be by some other way it is not of God.
>
> And again, he that receiveth the word of truth, doth he receive it by the Spirit of truth or some other way?
>
> If it be some other way it is not of God.

One of the qualifiers of the word of God is that it must be spoken and received by the power of the Holy Ghost. Neither the learner nor the teacher is excused from responsibility. When we receive the words of Christ as conveyed by the Holy Ghost, who is a source of power according to 2 Nephi 32:3, we are automatically receiving both knowledge and power—exactly what Step Eleven suggests we seek after.

Alma told his son Helaman that the Liahona "was prepared to show unto our fathers the course which they should travel in the wilderness" (Alma 37:39). Likewise, the Holy Ghost can show addicts the course they should travel in sobriety. He can point them in the right direction, and give them guidance and strength to make important decisions.

Nephi was able to accomplish many great things because of his diligence in following the directions of the Liahona. He states, "And it came to pass that I, Nephi, did go forth up into the top of the mountain, according to the directions which were given upon the ball. And it came to pass that I did slay wild beasts, insomuch that I did obtain food for our families" (1 Nephi 16:30–31).

Whenever I see the word *mountain* or *mount* I immediately start to think of a temple. There are some good reasons for this. For example, 2 Nephi 12:2–3, part of the Isaiah chapters, states "the mountain of the Lord's house shall be established in the top of the mountains." If you take this literally, you are stacking mountains on top of mountains, and it doesn't make much sense. Verse 3 says, "And many people shall go and say, Come ye, and let us go up to the mountain of the Lord, to the *house* of the God of Jacob; and he will teach us of his ways, and we will walk in his paths" (emphasis added). The temple is the house of God, and it is where we learn of his ways and how to "walk in his paths." Moses had a temple-like experience on Mount Sinai, where he was with the Lord for forty days (see Exodus 34). Nephi was "caught away . . . into an exceedingly high mountain" (1 Nephi 11:1), where he saw in vision the tree of life, the mission of the Savior, his descendants and their destruction, the Apostasy, the Restoration, and everything John saw in the Book of Revelation. The brother of Jared went up into the Mount Shelem, which was named for its "exceeding height," where he was brought back into the presence of the Lord (see Ether 3).

The symbol of the mountain, as meaning the "mountain of the Lord's house," does not always apply, but often it does. I think there is a connection in 1 Nephi 16—at least symbolically. Nephi *is* actually hunting in the mountains for food, but there are also symbolic meanings.

First, he followed the directions of the Liahona, which led him into the top of the mountain. If addicts (though this principle applies to everyone) follow the counsel in the scriptures and listen to the promptings of the Spirit, they will be led to the temple. Also, because Nephi hearkened to the word of the Lord, he was able to "slay wild beasts" and provide food for his family. Hearkening to the word of the Lord, diligently studying the scriptures, listening to the Spirit, and attending the temple, allows them to "slay the wild beasts" of the natural man—those irrational, animalistic urges that drive their addictions. They'll also receive spiritual nourishment in the process.

The third verse of 2 Nephi 32 teaches that the words of Christ are necessarily conveyed by the Holy Ghost. This means there are two ways to receive the words of Christ. One way to receive them is by reading and listening to the words of ancient and modern prophets and having the Holy Ghost bear witness of the truthfulness of their messages. Scripture is not confined to the Bible, Book of Mormon, Doctrine and Covenants, and Pearl of Great Price. It also includes the words of modern-day prophets, apostles, and general authorities. Therefore, the general conference issues of the *Ensign* (the May and November issues) are volumes of scripture. Messages given by the First Presidency also qualify as scripture. In fact, the words of our current prophet and apostles are the most important scriptures for our day because they apply specifically to the time we live in.

The other way we can receive the "words of Christ," according to this definition, is by revelation through the Holy Ghost. If we have been baptized and given the gift of the Holy Ghost, we are entitled to receive personal revelation, if we live worthy of receiving it. Like the Liahona, the Holy Ghost is most effective in our lives when we give diligent heed to His promptings.

There are two ways in which we can receive personal revelation. One way is by receiving revelation directly through the Holy Ghost, who "will tell you in your mind and in your heart," (D&C 8:2) specific things you need to do to enhance your spiritual progress. Revelation is also received through the inspiration of the Holy Ghost as it is given to those priesthood leaders who have stewardship over us. I highly recommend that all addicts work a program with the help of both their sponsor and their bishop. Bishops can receive revelation that will help them fine-tune their personal recovery programs.

Now that we have defined the word of God to include both the words of the prophets and also the power and influence of the Holy Ghost, it is time to look at some important principles. Notice that Alma compares the Liahona to the "word of Christ" (Alma 37:44). Thus, the Liahona can be likened to both scripture and the Holy Ghost.

Now let us return to Nephi and his ship. When the ship is completed, Nephi, his family, and the family of Ishmael board the ship. They are then "driven forth before the *wind* towards the promised land" (1 Nephi 18:8, emphasis added). There is a very important, symbolic lesson here.

The word *wind* becomes very important—it portrays a critical concept. The Savior talked about the wind during His mortal ministry. He spoke of being "born of water and of the Spirit" (John 3:5). He spoke of baptism, the Holy Ghost, and spiritual conversion. It is the "born again" concept. It relates to the "spiritual awakening" mentioned in Step Twelve. Then the Lord gives an interesting example. He said, "The *wind* bloweth where it listeth, and thou hearest the sound thereof, but canst not tell whence it cometh, and whither it goeth: so is every one that is born of the Spirit" (John 3:8, emphasis added). The original Greek word for *wind* means spirit, wind, or Holy Spirit (see *Strong's* #4151; John 3:8, footnote a). In fact, the word *wind* at the beginning of this verse, and the word *Spirit* at the end of the verse are actually the same word, *pneuma*, in Greek. Jesus compared the Spirit to the wind. We cannot see the wind nor where it is coming from, but we can certainly feel the effect of the wind. The Spirit operates in a similar fashion. We can feel the witness of the Holy Ghost within our hearts. We can know of things we cannot see.

If we substitute the word *Spirit* for the word *wind*, the above verse would read, "We did put forth into the sea and were driven forth before the *Spirit* towards the promised land." Remember, the promised land is symbolic for heaven, exaltation, or the celestial kingdom. For the purposes of this book, we will also liken the promised land to recovery. The

Holy Ghost will give us power and inspiration that will lead us along the path to our eternal home.

Every recovery program needs to be powered by the Holy Ghost! Once addicts have built their recovery ship—complete with mighty prayer, daily meaningful scripture study, attendance at Twelve-Step meetings, work with a sponsor, work with their bishops, and sobriety between meetings—they will need to receive spiritual strength and guidance from the Spirit.

Another key concept appears a few verses later. Laman, Lemuel, and others begin partying and getting carried away in "exceeding rudeness" (1 Nephi 18:9). When Nephi objects to their behavior, they become angry and tie him up again. Nephi records, "And it came to pass that after they had bound me insomuch that I could not move, the compass, which had been prepared of the Lord, did cease to work" (1 Nephi 18:12).

If the Liahona is a type for the Holy Ghost, then the spiritual message is quite apparent. The cords with which Nephi is bound become a symbol of addiction. Ropes and cords are often symbols of bondage and addiction in the scriptures. An example would be, "[Satan] leadeth them by the neck with a flaxen cord, until he bindeth them with his strong cords forever" (2 Nephi 26:22). A flaxen cord is made from very thin fibers, which are easily broken as individual strands, but, like an addiction, when the fibers are woven together into a cord, they become unbreakable. Another example would be the following Isaiah passage. "Wo unto them that draw iniquity with cords of vanity, and sin as it were with a cart rope" (2 Nephi 15:18). The cords of addiction are woven with vain imagination and insanity. It is hard for the outsider to tell whether *addicts* drag the addictions or addictions drag *them*. They are tied to their addictions like the cart and the rope. For years, no one ever saw me without my booze and other addictions trailing closely behind.

The symbolic message in the case of Nephi and the compass is this: The Spirit will cease striving with us when we are bound up with the "strong cords" of addiction.

We have looked at, analyzed, and thoroughly examined many passages of scripture. I could share what various scriptures mean to me. I could give you my take on scriptural passages as they have been revealed to me by the power of the Holy Ghost. I could only attempt to portray the feelings I have associated with specific scriptures—a sometimes poor attempt to express supernal, sublime feelings. But there is something great and marvelous that I cannot share with you. The scriptures and the Holy Ghost can become your own personal Liahona. I cannot tell you what the Spirit will reveal to you as you prayerfully and diligently search the scriptures. The Spirit will give you your own personalized version of scriptural passages. You must study it out on your own and then seek the Lord's guidance through His Spirit if you are to experience and internalize God's message for you.

Here are just a few tips to help in daily scripture study:

First, set aside a specific time period each day to study the scriptures. Reserve that time period every day for you to have a little "one on one" time with the Lord. I find that I need to pray earnestly before engaging in scripture study if I am to receive the full effect. I try to have my daily morning prayer as soon as I am awake enough to talk coherently with the Lord. I take the bus to and from work, and the morning commute is the best study time for me. I get more out of the scriptures in the morning than I do late at night. Some people are different. Do whatever works best for you, but reserve a specific time each day to study.

Second, don't try to speed-read the scriptures. The amount of time you spend reading, reflecting, and pondering the scriptures is more important than the amount you actually read. Take time to look up the footnotes and cross-references. You will gain great insights if you will do this. Read some of the cross-references and related passages. I find if I am reading a doctrinally-packed chapter like 2 Nephi 2, 2 Nephi 9, Alma 5, Ether 12, Hebrews 11, one of the Isaiah chapters, or the Sermon on the Mount, I am sometimes only able to cover a few verses in an hour by the time I look up related cross-references and other passages pertaining to the chapter I am reading. That's okay. Read the chapter headings. They were written by Elder Bruce R. McConkie and approved by the Brethren. Don't hesitate to use the Topical Guide and the Bible Dictionary.

Don't be afraid to mark up your scriptures and make notes in the margins. Mark the chapter headings and important things in the Bible Dictionary as well. I used to mark entire verses with my pink marker whenever I found something important or exciting. Once, when I was taking a Church Educational System class on the Book of Mormon, my instructor, who was also my former stake president, had me hold up my scriptures with the pages open. Everyone had a good laugh! The pages were all pink.

I finally broke down and bought a new set of scriptures. At first, I was careful to keep these scriptures clean and unmarked, but after a while, I couldn't stand it any longer. I rushed to the grocery store and bought a new marker. I was sick of pink—so I bought orange! At first, I was very frugal about marking. I would only circle the important words. Then I started drawing orange lines from the key words to the footnotes, and then to little orange notes in the margins. The next thing I knew, I started making little orange comments like "Step 3" or "bondage" or "surrender." Suddenly, I was out of control again. The little orange lines got all crisscrossed and tangled up. Circles overlapped circles—so I started highlighting the words again, so that I could see which ones were marked. Now, it is just one big orange blur!

I guess I might be a little compulsive about studying and marking the scriptures. I am an addict after all. But my compulsive scripture study has never landed me in jail. I don't get hangovers or blackouts. I can remember what I read yesterday. Best of all, I can feel my Savior nearer to me when I get caught up in the scriptures, instead of feeling like running away from Him, as I used to.

Third, follow the Spirit while "feasting on the word" (see 2 Nephi 32:3). "Let your soul delight in fatness" (2 Nephi 9:51). Develop an appetite for the things of the Spirit. Then savor and enjoy a spiritual feast, just as you would a good meal.

As you feel the promptings of the Spirit, you will discover "hidden treasures" (D&C 89:19) while studying and pondering scripture. This is a promise of the Word of Wisdom—the commandment admonishing us to stay clean and sober. Scripture study by the light of the Spirit and being clean and sober both have their rewards.

Often I will immerse myself in the scriptures and feel goose bumps all over my body and tears in my eyes. It is a feeling I would never trade for any head rush or euphoric high caused by alcohol or drugs.

There are helps and study aids that can be useful in helping us understand the scriptures, but there are really no shortcuts. We can only read them, ponder them, and pray about them. For me, that is just fine. I look forward to my daily scripture study. It is not a chore or a duty for me. It is a rich blessing. It is usually the best part of my day.

When the things in the scriptures come alive for you (see Moses 6:61), you will know you are doing it right. When the people are no longer characters in a story, but real people with real lives, then you can be sure you have the Holy Ghost as a study companion. If you stop and ponder in serious reflection, if you feel goose bumps running up and down your spine and tears welling up in your eyes, if you feel something so incredible that you just want to stop for a minute and thank your Heavenly Father for His gracious blessings, if you rejoice and mourn with the prophets of old and can't wait for the day when you can see them face to face and give them a great big hug, if you can taste of the goodness of your Savior and His love for you, if the words seem to jump off the page or the message comes so intimately that you feel someone is talking directly to *you*, and finally, if you marvel that you can carry around so much power when you carry the scriptures, *then* the scriptures are having an impact in your life. You know you have something marvelous, wonderful, and eternally sublime.

"let us be strong like unto moses"

This chapter addresses another component of a recovery ship. Addicts will probably not be content with waiting for arrival in the promised land to become "happy, joyous, and free" (*Big Book of Alcoholics Anonymous*, p. 133). They are, after all, accustomed to instant gratification. Why wait? I am sure that exaltation in the celestial kingdom is going to be far more joyous and glorious than anything experienced or imagined in mortality, but if the addict in question is like me, then life today has to offer him or her something better than the liquor store.

The word of God, as discussed in the last chapter, gives us permission to be happy right at this very moment. "Men are that they might have joy" (2 Nephi 2:25). Amulek taught: "For behold, now is the time and the day of your salvation; and therefore, if ye will repent and harden not your hearts, *immediately* shall the great plan of redemption be brought about unto you" (Alma 34:31, emphasis added). *The Big Book*, once again, agrees with the scriptures one hundred percent. It states: "We are sure God wants us to be happy, joyous, and free. We cannot subscribe to the belief that this life is a vale of tears," —Alma 37:45 calls it a "vale of sorrow"—"though it once was just that for many of us. But it is clear that we made our own misery. God didn't do it. Avoid then, the deliberate manufacture of misery, but if trouble comes, cheerfully capitalize it as an opportunity to demonstrate His omnipotence" (p. 133).

So we are determined to capitalize on recovery! We get to live in the here and now. We can enjoy today! We get to be clean and sober ONE day at a time. We are not torn apart by the guilt and anger of yesterday and the fear of tomorrow, as we once were. So we are going to enjoy the ride—every day of our journey. We are going to enjoy building the ship, sailing the high seas, and living in the promised land. We are not going to wait for the promised land to start having fun and being happy!

If addicts, myself included, are to experience true joy, it will not be because they have successfully controlled other people, places, and things, but rather because they have let the "old man" be "crucified" and have chosen to "walk in newness of life" (see Romans 6:4, 6). Truly one of the great blessings of sobriety is to be able to live for today.

All of this comes back to the topic of this chapter—faith and hope— but first addicts have to shed a few layers of selfishness. The irony is that, for now, they must be a little selfish—but in a different way than they are accustomed to.

I want to define faith—the only kind of faith that will keep an addict clean and sober. He or she may believe or even have a testimony of the reality of God. That's a good start, but it's not enough to work a miracle. Believe me, addicts need miracles. I should know. God is a God of miracles! If my personal testimony is not good enough—and it shouldn't be—then turn to pages 323 and 324 in the Topical Guide of your scriptures. You will find a full page of miracles listed in very fine print. I will list only two: "For behold, I am God; and I am a God of miracles; and I will show unto the world that I am the same yesterday, today, and forever; and I work not among the children of men save it be according to their faith" (2 Nephi 27:23). "God has not ceased to be a God of miracles" (Mormon 9:15).

In their hearts and minds, addicts cannot limit God's power to rescue *them*. Nor can they afford to displace His grace to other times and other people.

Elder Neal A. Maxwell said, "The failure to believe in a revealing God was especially basic. Some moderns who wish to distance themselves from God try placing His pavilion firmly in the past. By believing in such a disabled God, people can do pretty much as they please. It is then not many steps further to saying there is no God, therefore no law and no sin!" He goes on to point out the limited degree of faith of Laman and Lemuel. "Their enormous errors led to almost comical inconsistencies, such as Laman and Lemuel's believing that God could handle mighty Pharaoh and great Egypt's army at the Red Sea all right, but not a local Laban!" (Neal A. Maxwell, "Lessons from Laman and Lemuel," *Ensign* [November 1999]: 6).

I want to introduce a concept I call "proximate faith." Proximate means near or direct. It is not enough to believe that Jesus worked miracles during His mortal ministry. It is not enough to believe Moses was a prophet of God and President Monson is a prophet of God. It is not enough to believe that God will work a miracle for the guy sitting nearby in a recovery meeting! Everyone must come to know that God will work miracles for them!

Laman and Lemuel make good models for "half measures" and the "easier, softer way." They did not have a problem accepting Moses as a prophet or acknowledging that Moses could work a miracle on behalf of the children of Israel. They did not have a problem believing that Moses could speak to the waters of the Red Sea and that the waters would be divided, allowing their fathers to come through "out of captivity, on dry ground" (see 1 Nephi 4:2).

For Laman, Lemuel, and Nephi, this was a point of agreement. Nephi says to Laman and Lemuel, "Now behold ye know that this is true" (1 Nephi 4:3). Nephi uses this example to compare the similarity of their own situation to the situation of Moses and the children of Israel. But look at the difference in their faith. Laman and Lemuel murmur, wondering, "How is it possible that the Lord will deliver Laban into our hands? Behold, he is a mighty man, and he can command fifty, yea, even he can slay fifty; then why not us?" (1 Nephi 3:31) They could have drawn the comparison the other way, using the Lord as the common denominator. They could have said, "Behold, the Lord is mighty, and He can part the waters of the Red Sea and deliver the children of Israel;

then why not us?" Only Nephi has the faith to think that way. He says, "Let us go up; the Lord is able to deliver us, even as our fathers, and to destroy Laban, even as the Egyptians" (1 Nephi 4:3).

Many alcoholics, like me, have the same faith problem. They believe that the Lord can rescue others, bringing them "out of captivity" and onto "dry ground," but many lack the faith to believe that God will work the same miracle for them.

We can be certain the promises of the Lord are sure. He promises, "But if ye will turn to the Lord with full purpose of heart, and put your trust in him, and serve him with all diligence of mind, if ye do this, he will, according to his own will and pleasure, deliver you out of bondage" (Mosiah 7:33). What an incredible, marvelous promise! To clarify this and put it into context, here the Lord is talking about a bondage that is primarily physical, as the people of Limhi were in a physical bondage to the Lamanites.

Addicts' bondage, even though it may deal with a physical substance, such as alcohol, drugs, or pornography, is primarily a spiritual bondage. Remember the *Big Book* teaches that our "daily reprieve [is] contingent on the maintenance of our spiritual condition" (p. 85). No matter what our personal struggles are, addictions or otherwise, if we are truly seeking God's will for us, then we must ask ourselves, what is the Lord's timeline for deliverance? If we are asking to be delivered from the pain of affliction, then deliverance may not come in the near future. The Lord sometimes allows us to suffer through afflictions and adversity because those things allow us to grow spiritually. But if we are asking to be delivered from the effects of a destructive influence like alcohol, drugs, or pornography, then deliverance is imminent. How many more days do you think the Lord would have us drink, abuse drugs, or view pornography with their poisonous effects?

The Lord repeats His promise in another place. The scripture states, "But behold, he did deliver them because they did humble themselves before him; and because they cried mightily unto him he did deliver them out of bondage; and thus doth the Lord work with his power *in all cases* among the children of men, extending the arm of mercy towards them that put their trust in him" (Mosiah 29:20, emphasis added). Wouldn't you say "all cases" constitutes a fairly high percentage?

There is another extremely important concept. Faith is power. In *Lectures on Faith* the revealed attributes of God are clearly outlined. "Having said so much, we shall proceed to examine the attributes of God, as set forth in his revelations to the human family and to show how necessary correct ideas of his attributes are to enable men to exercise faith in him; for without these ideas being planted in the minds of men, it would be out of the power of any person or persons to exercise faith in God so as to obtain eternal life." (*Lectures on Faith*, Lecture Fourth, paragraph 3)

No wonder the phrase, "God as we understood Him," is repeated twice in the Twelve Steps. Understanding the attributes of God is one of the most important concepts mentioned in the Steps. In fact, there is probably nothing more important in all the Steps!

In *Lectures on Faith* six attributes of God are listed. The first two attributes are both mentioned in Step Eleven—namely knowledge and power. That is comforting to know, since those are the things to seek from God through prayer and meditation according to Step Eleven. But look at how the second attribute of God is mentioned: "Secondly—Faith or power" (*Lectures on Faith*, Lecture Fourth, paragraph 6). Faith is equated with power. Then a wonderful scriptural example is given. "Through *faith* we understand that the worlds were framed by the word of God" (Hebrews 11:3, emphasis added). According to Alma's discourse on faith and the word of God, if faith can grow into a sure knowledge so that our faith becomes dormant (see Alma 32:34), then faith, if centered in Christ, can produce both knowledge and power.

As Nephi read about Moses, Abraham, Isaac, Jacob, and many other ancient prophets, he gained an absolute testimony of the power of God. His faith became an absolute assurance that God will not only help those ancient prophets, but God will help *him* too. His attitude can be well summarized by four words, "The Lord is able" (1 Nephi 4:3). With that kind of proximate faith, Nephi has the trust and courage to exclaim, when faced with obtaining the brass plates from Laban, "Therefore let us go up; let us be strong like unto Moses; for he truly spake unto the waters of the Red Sea and they divided hither and thither, and our fathers came through, out of captivity, on dry ground" (1 Nephi 4:2).

Likewise, if an addict wants to come "out of captivity" from the bondage of alcohol, drugs, pornography, and other addictions, and end up on "dry ground," then he or she must have the same kind of faith and must believe in the simple ABCs of recovery as taught in the *Big Book*:

    a. "That we were alcoholic [or addicted] and could not manage our own lives."

    b. "That probably no human power could have relieved our alcoholism [or addiction]."

    c. "That God *could* and *would* if He were sought" (p. 60, emphasis added).

WHICH IS THE GREATEST MIRACLE?

As I explained previously, when I was only forty days sober, I checked into a nice hotel in Washington D.C. Upon searching the room for a phonebook to call AA, I instead found a drawer with about fifty full mini bottles of hard liquor. Though I fled the room and found an AA meeting, I had to return later that night.

As I entered the room, the compulsion to drink was overpowering. I could feel a wild, turbulent feeling entering my body, and a raging storm ensued in my soul. I was defenseless just like the *Big Book* warns.

I knew I could prevail against the urge no longer, and I kneeled down by the bed and breathed out a short, desperate prayer. Suddenly, I felt the strength go out of my body, the storm was stilled, and peace and calm prevailed for just a brief moment before I harmlessly collapsed on the bed and fell asleep.

I have read about the Lord's ministry in many scriptures many times. I have read how He calmed the tempest. He "rebuked the wind, and said unto the sea, Peace, be still. And the wind ceased, and there was a great calm" (Mark 4:39). I know He stilled the raging sea and quieted the tempest. One of the reasons I know is because He calmed the raging tempest inside my soul that night. When I felt turbulence deep down inside, and it felt like nothing could calm the storm, He quickly replaced it with peace and quiet, and love and hope.

Today I know that behind every physical manifestation of a miracle, there is something far greater. As great as it was for the Savior to open the eyes of the blind, cause the deaf to hear, and heal the sick, this was not His real mission. Behind every physical healing lies a far greater spiritual healing that represents His true mission.

Which is the greater miracle? Is it calming the raging sea and the turbulent storm or calming the turbulence of the inner soul? I am not sure I know the answer to this question, but here is something to think about. The physical elements always obey the Lord. During the creation process, "the Gods watched those things which they had ordered until they obeyed" (Abraham 4:18). But God gave man his agency and his own will. We do not always obey.

The miracles in an addict's recovery may not be as flashy as the calming of the storm, but they are just as real. The Twelve Steps are a program of miracles. I can promise full recovery, because the Lord already has. I simply repeat the promise: "But behold, he did deliver them because they did humble themselves before him; and because they cried mightily unto him he did deliver them out of bondage; and thus doth the Lord work with his power *in all cases* among the children of men, extending the arm of mercy towards them that put their trust in him" (Mosiah 29:20, emphasis added).

The Lord will work with and honor any amount of faith we have, even if it is just "a particle of faith" (Alma 32:27). As long as we all put forth some sincere effort, we will receive of God's grace, we will begin to see miracles, and our faith will be increased. I promise! Like the parable of the talents (see Matthew 25:14–29), the amount of faith we have in the beginning is not as important as what we do with that faith.

I consider the miracle of recovery to be as great as any miracle the Lord ever performed on earth. May all of us have the faith in our Savior to allow Him to save us.

hoist up the sails

Before launching a recovery ship, addicts need to hoist up the sails.
The sails are one of the most important components of the ship. They
will catch the wind and drive the ship. Remember that *wind* and *spirit*
are both *pneuma* in Greek (see *Strong's Exhaustive Concordance of the
Bible* #4151). The Spirit of the Lord will fill the sails, drive the ship, and
guide passengers safely to the promised land of recovery.

Everything needed for a recovery ship is found in Section 26 of the
Doctrine & Covenants. It is two verses long and reads:

> Behold, I say unto you that you shall let your time be
> devoted to the studying of the scriptures, and to preaching,
> and to confirming the church at Colesville, and to performing
> your labors on the land, such as is required, until after you
> shall go to the west to hold the next conference; and then it
> shall be made known what you shall do.

And all things shall be done by common consent in the
church, by much prayer and faith, for all things you shall receive by faith. Amen.

This may not sound like much but an entire addiction recovery program built around these verses would be a pretty good one. We have
covered many of these, but let's make a list of things for addicts to do in
their program from the above verses and discuss those needing further
explanation. The following list is written specifically for addicts, but
non-addicts can gain valuable knowledge and insights from the principles as well.

1. Mighty prayer.
2. Studying the scriptures. Become "devoted." For addicts, also study the *Big Book*. Treat your spirit as
   you do your body. If you eat food every day, make
   sure you give your spirit some spiritual nourishment every day too.
3. Proximate faith.
4. Attend Church meetings regularly and be at ninety Twelve-Step meetings in ninety days. Attend
   Twelve-Step meetings regularly after the ninety
   days. Liken "preaching" to sharing experiences,
   strength, and hope with other addicts at Twelve-
   Step meetings, and sharing experiences, strength,
   and hope with your brothers and sisters in the gospel at Church meetings.
5. See your bishop and get a sponsor (other than
   your bishop). Call your sponsor every day for
   the first while, and he or she can advise you as
   to when you can taper off. Don't think you can
   fire your sponsor just because you have long-term
   sobriety under your belt. If your sponsor doesn't
   strongly advise you to call regularly, or doesn't ever
   chew you out, or doesn't call you on your balo-
   ney, then go ahead and fire him or her, but find
   a new one who will help you work your program.

Meet with your bishop on a regular basis during early recovery. When you get to Step Five, do a thorough Fifth Step with your bishop. Go ahead and tell him everything, even if he doesn't ask in detail. Believe me when I say it's a lot easier to get everything out at once than it is to have to keep going back to your bishop like I've had to do. We will liken the phrase, "hold the next conference," to holding a daily conference with your sponsor. We will liken the phrase, "all things shall be done by common consent in the church," to the footnote for that phrase, which refers to the Topical Guide under the topic, "Sustaining Church Leaders." You sustain your bishop when you hearken to his inspired counsel. Don't think your bishop can't give you inspired counsel because he is not an alcoholic or an addict.

6. Work the Twelve Steps! They are numbered. "Hold a conference" with your sponsor to determine when you should work the next step. If you are attending the LDS Substance Abuse Recovery meetings, don't try to work a new step every week just to keep up with the missionaries' lessons. If you are having problems with a step, it is probably not *that* step you are having problems with. Go back and work the previous step, and "then it shall be made known what you shall do." Work with your sponsor and follow the Spirit. Remember, the Spirit is pushing your sails.

We will liken the phrase, "performing your *labors* on the *land*, such as is required," to *working* the "suggested" steps, which are required to stay clean and sober in the promised *land* of recovery. Remember, the *Big Book* states, "Here are the steps we took, which are suggested as a program of recovery" (p. 59). This makes a very simple equation. No Steps equals no program. No program equals no recovery. Those who were inspired to write the *Big Book* probably used the word *suggested* because alcoholics, myself included, are stubborn and rebellious by nature, and we don't like to be told we have to do something.

7. Get involved in service at your Twelve-Step meetings. If you go to AA, seek out service positions. Most of these have a recommended amount of sobriety, but work for those positions. Your spirituality and gratitude will be greatly enhanced as you lose yourself in service. If you go to the LDS meetings, then also look to serve that group. Look forward and work for the day when you can become a facilitator or even a missionary. It may seem farfetched right now, but be forewarned that miracles do happen in this program. None of us who are now serving in these positions thought it was possible for us when we first came into the program. If you simply "suit up and show up" at Church, you will probably be called to serve somewhere. This is the Lord's Church, and He believes in service! When He was here in mortality, His entire life was spent giving service. If you are called to serve in the Church, accept that calling and give it your best shot—even if you feel inadequate. Your bishop, who received your call from the Lord, probably felt inadequate when he was called too. The Lord will make you equal to the task as you serve Him. We will liken the phrase, "confirming the church at ___" (fill in the blank with the name of your hometown) to giving service to the Lord and to your fellowman. *Confirming* in this case means to help build up. That is what you do by giving service, and you will grow spiritually in the process.

Any addict who will make these seven principles the foundation of his or her recovery program will experience full recovery. We have already discussed prayer, scripture study, and faith in detail. I want to discuss briefly the other four principles.

MEETING ATTENDANCE

Attendance at both Church meetings and Twelve-Step meetings is a crucial part of recovery. We gain knowledge and power, as required for Step Eleven, in three vital areas.

Things We Gain from Attending Meetings

First, we can feel the Spirit. The Holy Ghost is a power source, and when we feel the Spirit, it becomes like wind in our sails. The interchangeability of the words *wind* and *spirit* in the Greek, and the Savior's comparison between the wind and the Spirit in the Gospel of John is a fascinating likeness.

When the Lord teaches Nicodemus about spiritual rebirth, He says, "The wind bloweth where it listeth, and thou hearest the sound thereof, but canst not tell whence it cometh, and whither it goeth: so is every one that is born of the Spirit" (John 3:8). The word *listeth* means to will, have in mind, intend, or to be resolved or determined (see *Strong's* #2309). In modern English we may say instead, "The wind has a mind of its own." The Holy Ghost likewise is our personal Liahona, telling us at every fork in the road, where we need to turn to be in harmony with the Lord's will for us. The Spirit is our connection to the mind of God. This is the essence of Step Three—"Made a decision to turn our will and our lives over to the care of God as we understood Him." The Holy Ghost becomes the link between us and the will of the Father. We cannot fully work Step Three without the Holy Ghost.

Second, you will hear some good AA wisdom. When I was just starting out, I remember hearing people say, "Fake it till you make it" or "It's not the quantity of your sobriety; it's the quality" or "First things first." I learned what SLIP stands for—Sobriety Lost Its Priority. I learned what a "dry drunk" was and what it meant to "white knuckle it." I heard profound wisdom. I heard people say things like, "If I don't take a drink today, I'll probably stay sober" and "If you want what I have, do what I do." I heard other alcoholics share that it was always the first drink that got them drunk. They would say that if you are an alcoholic, then being a little bit drunk is like being a little bit pregnant. You either are or you are not. You are either drunk or you are sober. There is no middle ground. Throughout my drinking career, I could never figure that one out. Was it my second or third six-pack that got me drunk? Was it my fourteenth or fifteenth mini bottle? After I passed out and woke up the next morning, I could never remember which one got me drunk. Today, I know how much I can drink. Today I consider it a good thing to know that I am an alcoholic. Today I know that only one drink separates me from the horrible, drunken world I lived in twenty years ago.

Third, we gain faith from attending meetings. When I first started attending AA, I would hear some people share about what I considered massive lengths of sobriety—ninety days! I even saw one guy receive a one-year medallion. I asked myself how anyone could stay sober for a whole year. Ninety days was unbelievable. I thought that these people had to be lying about their sobriety.

After a while, I began to see tears of gratitude and gleams of hope in their eyes. They all spoke of a higher power who somehow made them sober. A little place deep inside my heart confirmed to me that this was true. I could quickly see that sobriety was the most important thing in these peoples' lives, and I could see God work in peoples' lives. I could see miracles in the lives of some very ordinary people. My perception of God began to change. I could see that you didn't have to be a General Authority to receive the Lord's help. God's grace was not limited to only those who went to Church and had a temple recommend. I could see how the Lord had picked people up out of the gutter and made them into something special.

The more meetings you go to, the more miracles you get to hear about. Hearing other alcoholics and addicts share their experiences will increase your own faith and your trust in the Lord. Likewise, going to Church and hearing others share their experiences and their testimonies of the gospel will have a profound impact on your own testimony. You will gain a greater appreciation of the Lord's eternal plan for you. If you are new to the gospel or if you have been away from Church for a while, you will likely be surprised at how you are welcomed with open arms at Church by your brothers and sisters!

I remember the first time I went to Elders' Quorum after a long absence. There was a good brother there who raised his hand and said, "I just want to say how glad I am to see Brad back with us again!" It was truly a great feeling to be welcomed back into activity in my own ward and stake. I think you will find similar experiences.

MEETING WITH YOUR SPONSOR AND BISHOP

Talking with your sponsor and counseling with your bishop are also important parts of your recovery. I remember that first year of sobriety. Part of that "pink cloud" sobriety was an incredible feeling of gratitude that seemed to envelope my whole being. It sometimes felt like raw truth, and I knew it was real. I had not felt anything so wonderful for thirteen years. I learned to recognize those feelings as the influence of the Holy Ghost. I had driven Him away thirteen years ago and had made it impossible for Him to return to my life. I remember wondering whether Church members really appreciate what a wonderful gift it is to have the Spirit in their lives.

My first sponsor helped me by laying out his rules:

1. Get yourself to at least one meeting every single day for the first ninety days—always! It's not my responsibility to see that you get to a meeting—it's yours!

2. Never take a drink of whiskey without calling me first. (He always called it "whiskey," even though he knew I drank something else.) If you take that drink without calling, then you had better find yourself another sponsor.

3. You call me every single day! Have you got that?

4. Every morning when you get out of bed, get on your knees and ask your Heavenly Father to keep you sober today. At night before you go to bed, get down on your knees and thank your Heavenly Father for another day of sobriety. Pray any other

time of the day when you get thirsty. Then he said,
"I can talk to my Higher Power as I'm driving down
the road with my eyes wide open."

5. Get out your *Big Book* every day and read something out of it.

6. You never make any major decisions in your life
without discussing it with me first!

A sponsor will help you stay sober and work the Twelve Steps.

Your bishop is also important. He is your judge in Israel. He will help you work the steps of repentance, which will largely overlap the Twelve Steps. He will help you make your transition back into the Church and into the gospel. Don't confuse the role of your sponsor with the role of your bishop. Both of them will help you heal, but don't substitute one for the other. You need them both.

Your bishop holds the keys of the priesthood. May I suggest he also holds the keys to much of your recovery and future. Because he is en-titled to receive revelation from the Lord, he can see you for what you can become rather than what you presently are. As your judge in Israel, he sees you as a son or daughter of Jacob to whom all of the rights and blessings of the Abrahamic Covenant pertain. Your bishop can show you and guide you along the path to receiving the special blessings the Lord has in store for you!

I know that every bishop I have had since I started drinking knows that I am an alcoholic. Yet they do not see me that way. When my bish-op sees me at Church, he sees me as a fellow saint—as a son of God. Your bishop will help you overcome the limitations in your life that were placed there when you were active in your disease.

There is one more thing about bishops. Make sure you work through *your own* bishop. I know of some who have wanted to work with a bishop in another ward, or who have wanted to see a former bishop, or who have wanted to work through another active Church member. Some have sought for another bishop or other Church leaders because they think these other leaders are more experienced in addiction and recov-ery. Your own bishop holds the priesthood keys necessary for your own repentance and recovery.

WORK THE TWELVE STEPS

The next important concept is to work the Twelve Steps. They are numbered for a reason. It is vitally important for addicts to have a sponsor who serves as a mentor in helping them work through the steps. The sponsor will help them know when they are ready to move on to the next step.

I remember that first week of AA meetings. I looked through those steps and thought I could probably knock out all twelve steps in about two weeks. I was ready to tackle all twelve and be done with them, so I could move on with the rest of my life. It was that graduation mentality.

I thought I would only have to work Step Three one time. I thought that when I made the decision to turn my will and my life over to the care of God, the decision was a done deal. I could just move on to Step Four. But my sponsor said, "No way! You work the first three steps and get a good foundation first." I am glad I listened. Had I done it my way, I probably would have gone back out. Today, I work a 1 – 2 – 3 every day. Each morning I realize (Step 1) I am powerless, (Step 2) only God can restore me, and (Step 3) I will "let go and let God."

The help of a sponsor is vital in working the steps. And remember, these steps require a lot of practice. It is a lifelong pursuit, but well worth the time! I find I must work through all twelve steps for each addiction and each character defect I am trying to overcome.

SERVICE

The final concept is giving service. The Lord has said, "For whosoever will save his life shall lose it: but whosoever will lose his life for my sake, the same shall save it" (Luke 9:24). Besides being a great statement on self-will versus surrender, this is also a profound statement regarding service.

Addicts will actually find more power to overcome addictions as they lose themselves in serving others. There is a spiritual connection between being clean and giving service. James teaches the following: "Pure religion and undefiled before God and the Father is this, To visit the fatherless and widows in their affliction, and to keep himself un-spotted from the world" (James 1:27).

With these seven basic concepts as the foundation for a recovery program, the ship is complete. Addicts are ready to set sail for the prom-ised land of recovery and sobriety. They will still face fierce winds, rough storms, and turbulent waters. Nothing worthwhile ever comes easy. Nevertheless, they are prepared, this cannot be said of them: "Thy tack-lings are loosed; they could not well strengthen their mast, they could not spread the sail" (Isaiah 33:23).

Addicts can become "happy, joyous, and free" and "walk in newness of life" (Romans 6:4). They can "taste . . . of the goodness of Jesus" (see Mormon 1:15) and "have great views of that which is to come" (Mosiah 5:3). Life really can be sweet, rewarding, and delicious for them again. After being set free from the guilt of yesterday and the fear of tomorrow, they will have the opportunity to live for today. They can have the good life restored to them again. In true sobriety, they can have the promised blessings of eternity.

"wisdom to know the difference"

Most AA sobriety chips have a rather famous prayer on the back of them. It has become known as the "Serenity Prayer." AA members usually quote only the first verse of this prayer. They often end AA meetings by holding hands and reciting this verse. The prayer was penned by Reinhold Niebuhr, but its origin remains a point of controversy. The ideas expressed in the Serenity Prayer may have had their roots in early Christianity among the early Saints. Some historians have traced the basic concepts of the prayer back to Greek philosophers, including Aristotle.

The first verse of the Serenity Prayer is as follows:

> God grant me the serenity
> To accept the things I cannot change;
> Courage to change the things I can;
> And the wisdom to know the difference.

This is a beautiful and powerful prayer. When I can continually have this prayer in my heart, my sobriety and recovery are much deeper and more rewarding. It has been an integral part of my recovery. I am certain that this opinion would be unanimous among addicts in recovery. The Serenity Prayer represents total trust in God. It expresses our mind when we have fully turned it over to God. It is the epitome of Step Three: "Made a decision to turn our will and our lives over to the care of God as we understood Him."

Shortly after I met my wife—on one of our first dates—she pulled me aside and informed me that she was a genetic carrier of hemophilia, a bleeding disorder preventing the blood from clotting after blood loss or injury. It is a genetic disease in which the mother is not affected, but she passes the disease to a son, who will be affected by the disease.

I learned she had two brothers with the disease and had recently lost a nephew, a twelve-year-old boy who had died from complications after being infected with HIV as a result of some tainted blood products used to treat his hemophilia. One of her two brothers with the disease had also died. It scared me to death. I wanted to run away. The probability of potential children having the disease was 50 percent for males. There was also a 50 percent chance that a daughter would carry the disease.

A week or two later, I was on the freeway on my way to work. I still remember the exact location where a verse of scripture popped into my head. Back then my ability to quote, remember, or find important scriptures was average at best, but I knew that I had once heard or read a scripture stating that "perfect love casteth out fear" (1 John 4:18; see also Moroni 8:16). Even though we were not yet engaged, I knew I had a deep love for this special person, who became my wife a short while later. I knew my love was not perfect, and it still is not, but it grows stronger with each passing day. I knew at that moment the answer to my fear was love. Suddenly, I felt serenity. If for only a moment, I had complete trust in my God. I knew that whatever happened, if I would only do the right things, then everything would work out okay.

A few months later, we were married in the temple. Several months after that, a doctor told us that pregnancy would probably be impossible for us. But in spite of this medical evidence, a few months later we were given the wonderful news that a baby was indeed on the way.

I would like to be able to tell you that because I had already turned it over once, all of my fears were gone forever. But that would be a lie. Those fears became more real, and my worries increased. Was it a boy or a girl? If it was a boy, would he have hemophilia?

Early during this pregnancy, I had two vivid dreams. This is not normal for me. I rarely remember my dreams, and they are usually irrational or disjointed if I do remember them. In one dream I saw a nurse bringing a newborn baby boy to my wife in the hospital. In the other dream I saw my wife's nephew who had died from complications related to hemophilia. I had never seen him before since he had died just two months before I met my wife. I had seen photos of him when he was much younger. But in this dream, I recognized him immediately. He was running along a beach. He was tanned and looking very healthy and happy. He also appeared to be about fourteen or fifteen years of age. As he was running away from me, he turned around, gave me a radiant smile, and called me by name. The expression on his face gave me the impression that everything would be okay. He then turned and ran into the water.

I told my wife that I thought we were having a boy. She said she had had similar feelings. A couple of months after that, an ultrasound confirmed our feelings. It was a boy. The odds of having a son with hemophilia were 50-50. I thought about the dream of my wife's nephew. Did his reassuring look mean we would have a healthy baby boy? I thought about it often.

In the October 1995 general conference, Elder Richard G. Scott gave a wonderful talk entitled "Trust in the Lord." He addressed the adversities of life and how we can learn and grow from them. As I was listening to his talk on the radio, I had a profound feeling come over me that our son would indeed have some serious health-related challenges in his life. But I also knew, if just for that moment, that whatever happened would be the Lord's will. I knew the profound truth of the *Big Book of Alcoholics Anonymous* that "nothing, absolutely nothing, happens in God's world by mistake" (p. 417).

Thirteen days later, the doctors decided to deliver our son six weeks early. Some other problems had developed, and he weighed just over two pounds when he was born. Just minutes after his birth, he was hooked up to all kinds of tubes and wires to monitor his vital signs and keep him alive, if necessary. Despite his low birth weight, everything went exceptionally well. Just hours after birth, they drew blood to test for hemophilia. A nurse commented on how well his blood had clotted after the needle poke, but early the next morning, the lab results were completed, and our doctor gave us the bad news that he did indeed have severe hemophilia.

At first I asked myself those unanswerable questions that Elder Scott had counseled against—questions like, "Why me? Why did this have to happen to a sweet, innocent baby?" These are not good serenity questions.

The Holy Ghost had done all He could do to prepare me for this situation. I would have given or done anything to give my son a totally normal and healthy life, yet I was powerless. But I did notice one thing through all of this. My prayers became much more meaningful. I felt closer to my Heavenly Father. I relied on my Savior to a greater degree.

As I was going through this experience, and also at other times in my life, I was so grateful that I had had some experience with the Twelve Steps. I was glad I had some practice in turning it over to God. I hasten to add that I learn incrementally at the speed of pain. I can only take baby steps in this whole serenity thing. Just last week I came unglued at my dear wife for committing the gross crime of purchasing the wrong kind of chicken at the grocery store. When I shared about this in a AA meeting, everyone laughed at the silliness of it all. Serenity and sanity don't come easy for me and for most other addicts!

But every once in a while, I can have those serenity moments. I realize how fortunate I am to be sober. How blessed I am to have recovery. How grateful I feel to have a knowledge and testimony of the gospel of Jesus Christ. What a miracle it is to be delivered from bondage. Indeed, when I think of how blessed I really am, I wonder why I sweat the small stuff.

There are many things people are powerless over besides an addiction of choice. Here is a partial list:

Other people	Choices made by others
Other places	War and poverty
Other things	Crime
Acceptance by others	Social problems
Situations	Natural disasters
Health	Disease and accidents
Yesterday	Employment problems
Tomorrow	Death

The list could go on forever. Addicts and non-addicts alike could worry themselves sick over these things. They could jump in and try to control them all. But the real key to serenity is to have the wisdom and faith to understand which things they can really influence and which things they cannot, or, in other words, "wisdom to know the difference." For an addict, some of these problems may be of his or her own making—at least partially. Some of them result from wreckage of the past. Addicts may have damaged their health from alcohol and drugs. They may have caused problems with their employers. But some of these things happen to people who have never been addicted to alcohol, drugs, pornography, or other things.

The important thing about serenity is to realize that once we have done everything in our power to make things right, then we must accept those things we cannot change, and simply turn it over to God. Trusting God is the key to serenity. Today, whenever I allow myself to be guided and comforted by the Spirit, I realize that whatever God puts in front of me is for my own good and spiritual growth. I know a loving Father would not put one ounce of suffering in my life or anyone else's, if it were not necessary for spiritual progression.

Again, like any other principle in recovery, answers and role models are in the scriptures. Shadrach, Meshach, and Abednego understood that it was within their power to refuse to worship the golden image. Their behavior was not dependent upon the situation. They knew the outcome was not within their control, yet they trusted in the Lord. Shadrach, Meshach, and Abednego were miraculously saved from the flames of the fiery furnace (see Daniel 3). Abinadi was not (see Mosiah 17). Yet Abinadi knew he could finish his message and go on to gain his exaltation. When Alma and Amulek were imprisoned, the prison walls were rent in twain, and they walked free (see Alma 14). Joseph and Hyrum Smith did not walk out of the Carthage Jail. Yet they were all able to turn it over to God.

When Alma prayed for the apostate Zoramites, it may have been easier for him to pray that the Lord would simply fix them. He probably could have convinced the Lord that he was right. They certainly could have used some fixing. Instead, he prays for patience to endure, recognizing that the Lord is not going to take away their agency just so Alma can have an easier ride (see Alma 31:26–35).

Another important part of serenity is having proper priorities. One of the mighty changes in recovery is having a new set of priorities. Once upon a time, there was only one important thing in my life—getting my next drink. Today, my sobriety comes first, because that's the only way God can work in my life. Without my sobriety, all of my other priorities are gone.

Once again, Nephi is a great role model for serenity. After reading a chapter like 1 Nephi 17, it would be hard to believe that Nephi, Laman, and Lemuel are all on the same trip. Their perspectives are so different. Here is Nephi's perspective with an attitude of serenity:

> And so great were the blessings of the Lord upon us, that while we did live upon raw meat in the wilderness, our women did give plenty of suck for their children, and were strong, yea, even like unto the men; and they began to bear their journeyings without murmurings.
>
> And thus we see that the commandments of God must be fulfilled. And if it so be that the children of men keep the commandments of God he doth nourish them, and strengthen them, and provide means whereby they can accomplish the thing which he has commanded them; wherefore, he did

provide means for us while we did sojourn in the wilderness.
(1 Nephi 17:2–3)

What faith and perspective Nephi has. I call this a 100 percent guarantee of success. As long as the Lord commands it, it is His will. And as long as it is His will, He will give us the means whereby we can carry it out, much as it says in the Step Eleven prayer: "Sought through prayer and meditation to improve our conscious contact with God as we understood Him, praying only for knowledge of His will for us and the power to carry that out." The goal is to bring our will in-line with God's will. Nephi promises that the Lord will always give us the means to accomplish His will.

As we analyze the Serenity Prayer, we see two categories. We must accept the things we cannot change. We often summarize this to mean other people, places, and things. These are the things beyond our control.

There is one thing we can change. We, addicts in particular, must have courage to exert our influence over those things within our control. I have heard many in Twelve-Step meetings say, "I can change me." I submit that this may be an overstatement. It may be more accurate to say, "Only the Lord can change me." For me it is the pure truth to say that I could never quit drinking. It is also true that I didn't quit by myself. The adage is true: "But for the grace of God, there go I." I have a dear friend whom I respect and admire. He says he can change only one thing—his attitude. We do have our agency. We can choose to do the next right thing God puts in front of us, but, like Nephi, it may take the Lord to soften our hearts (see 1 Nephi 2:16).

If our contentment in life is based upon other people, places, and things, then we are not going to experience much serenity. With this in mind, let's look at Laman and Lemuel's perspective and its connection to other people, places, and things:

> We have wandered much *in the wilderness* [places], and
> we have suffered much affliction, hunger, thirst, and fatigue;
> and after all these sufferings we must perish *in the wilderness*
> [places] with hunger.
> And thus they did murmur against *my father* [other

people], and also against *me* [other people]; and they
were desirous to return again to *Jerusalem* [places].

And Laman said unto Lemuel and also unto the sons of
Ishmael: Behold, let us slay *our father* [other people], and also
our brother Nephi [other people], who has taken it upon him
to be our ruler and our teacher, who are his elder brethren. (1
Nephi 16:35–37, emphasis added)

Later they continue their tirade:

And *thou* [other people] art like unto *our father* [other
people], led away by the foolish imaginations of his heart;
yea, *he* [other people] hath led us out of the *land of Jerusalem,*
[places] and we have wandered *in the wilderness* [places] for
these many years; and our women have toiled, being big with
child; and they have borne children *in the wilderness* [places]
and suffered all things, save it were death; and it would have
been better that they had died before they came out of *Jerusalem* [places] than to have suffered these afflictions.

Behold, these many years we have suffered *in the wilderness* [places], which time we might have enjoyed *our possessions*
[things] and *the land of our inheritance* [places]; yea, and we
might have been happy. (1 Nephi 17:20–21, emphasis added)

It is quite apparent from these verses exactly what their attitude is.
Laman and Lemuel think that if they didn't have to deal with Nephi and
Lehi, and if they'd stayed in Jerusalem, and if they still had all of their
material possessions, they *might* have had a shot at happiness. You have
to wonder about those words, "we *might* have been happy." I doubt it.

Once again, this is one of the many great reasons for scripture study.
You can learn much about recovery from these models. We have role
models of serenity, like Nephi, and we have role models of disappointment and pride, like Laman and Lemuel.

There is one other very significant aspect of serenity. In sobriety
recovering addicts have the opportunity to live for today. They can enjoy the present. Too often in life, today is taken hostage by tomorrow
or yesterday. When I was out there running and gunning, I always felt

guilt and shame for yesterday and fear as I thought of tomorrow. I was torn in two directions every day.

There could not be a more poignant message of living for today than a quote from President Thomas S. Monson in the October 2008 general conference. He spoke of the musical entitled *The Music Man*. Professor Harold Hill, one of the principal characters, voices a concern: "You pile up enough tomorrows, and you'll find you've collected a lot of empty yesterdays." President Monson's profound counsel is to "find joy in the journey—now." He later added, "My brothers and sisters, there is no tomorrow to remember if we don't do something today" (Thomas S. Monson, "Finding Joy in the Journey," *Ensign* [November 2008]: 84).

I learned early on in AA that if I am worried about tomorrow or still living in yesterday, I am wasting today. While it is true that today's decisions will influence tomorrow, it is also true that I can't do anything about tomorrow yet. It is also a waste of time and energy to worry about yesterday. There is nothing I can do to change the past. The only thing I can have an influence on is the present. For addicts who don't have a great length of sobriety, take comfort in the fact that you only need to stay clean and sober today. In Twelve Step recovery everyone stays sober "one day at a time." When I just started out, I could not conceive of the idea of never taking another drink for the rest of my life. It seemed impossible. It was too much to bite off at once. But when I felt overwhelmed by this type of "stinking thinking," I realized that I didn't have to worry about staying sober the rest of my life. I only needed to stay sober today.

When I had been sober for about eight months, I ran into a friend on a Saturday afternoon. He said he hadn't seen me in the bar for a long time. I simply nodded. He then asked me if I would be going to the bar today for a few beers. I didn't feel like I should get up on my soapbox and lecture him or even state that I had sworn off drinking forever. I simply replied, "Not today."

After almost twenty years, it seems like a possibility that I could go the rest of my life without a drink. That doesn't mean I'm cured, but a top priority of mine is to die sober. I expect to do it. Today, drinking is not an option.

Life is truly happy as we learn to properly employ acceptance, courage, and wisdom. Faith and virtue produce courage, such that our confidence can "wax strong in the presence of God" (see D&C 121:45). The Holy Ghost can give us discernment to know whether we need acceptance or courage for any given moment.

the physical skateboard and the spiritual cadillac

We are all eternal, spiritual beings housed in mortal tabernacles of clay. Our final state is to receive an immortal, resurrected body, quickened (or made alive) by celestial glory (see D&C 88:28–29).

Our spiritual side seeks supernal fruits—"love, joy, peace, longsuffering, gentleness, goodness, faith, meekness, temperance" (Galatians 5:22–23). Our physical side, though limited and mortal, is powerfully impressive. Human eyes can discern light and color of over a million shades. The mind (on good days) has tremendous, rapid recall ability—better than the best computers. The body can repair and reproduce. It grows stronger with use (until you hit 50). The best machines cannot imitate the body. Our physical sides are incredible.

But as great as this is, the physical body will only seek two things in and of itself. The body only desires pleasure and seeks to avoid pain. Therein lies every addiction out there.

THE "GOD HOLE"

One of the most marvelous things about six-dimensional experiences (things discerned by the five senses and accompanied by the Holy Ghost) is that these experiences fill our souls. There is a popular term in Twelve Step recovery called the "God hole." It is that empty place in the center of our souls that we try to fill up with alcohol, drugs, food, sex, and many other things. We never get enough and are never satisfied. The empty hole remains in our souls.

Isaiah prophesied about this "God hole" as a major characteristic of the "last days," when "all the lands of the earth . . . . will be drunken with iniquity" (see 2 Nephi 27:1). He said:

> And all the nations that fight against Zion, and that distress her, shall be as a dream of a night vision; yea, it shall be unto them, even as unto a hungry man which dreameth, and behold he eateth but he awaketh and his soul is empty; or like unto a thirsty man which dreameth, and behold he drinketh but he awaketh and behold he is faint, and his soul hath appetite . . .
>
> For behold, all ye that doeth iniquity, stay yourselves and wonder, for ye shall cry out, and cry; yea, ye shall be drunken but not with wine, ye shall stagger but not with strong drink.
>
> For behold, the Lord hath poured out upon you the spirit of deep sleep. For behold, ye have closed your eyes. (2 Nephi 27:3–5; see also Isaiah 29:8–10).

I can relate to these verses. I drank enough booze to fill a lake, and yet I never got filled up. I always felt empty inside and wanted just one more drink! That's the "God Hole."

The Savior taught the people of Nephi and gave them a discourse similar to the Sermon on the Mount. In the Beatitudes He taught them, "And blessed are all they who do *hunger* and *thirst* after righteousness, for they shall be *filled* with the *Holy Ghost*" (3 Nephi 12:6, emphasis added). If we are filled with the Holy Ghost, we are truly satisfied and happy. Our souls are going to hunger after something, especially if we are addicts, so we might as well hunger after something we can obtain and something that fills our souls.

Let's look at a scripture in Helaman: "Nevertheless they did fast and pray oft, and did wax stronger and stronger in their humility, and firmer and firmer in the faith of Christ, unto the *filling their souls with joy and consolation*, yea, even to the purifying and the *sanctification* of their hearts, which *sanctification* cometh because of their yielding their hearts unto God" (Helaman 3:35, emphasis added).

Those who hunger and thirst after righteousness and keep the commandments are filled with the Holy Ghost. They enjoy the fruits of the Spirit. Unlike an addict's drug of choice, which only left an empty hole in the middle of his or her soul, fruits like joy and consolation make us happy and content.

In Lehi's vision of the tree of life, he exclaims, "And as I partook of the fruit thereof it *filled my soul* with exceedingly *great joy*; wherefore, I began to be desirous that my family should partake of it also; for I knew that it was *desirable above all other fruit*" (1 Nephi 8:12, emphasis added).

The Lord wants us to be filled with such fruit—love, joy, peace, and consolation. The verse in Helaman speaks of the purification and sanctification of our hearts. The word *sanctify*, especially in the Old Testament, means to consecrate, hallow, set apart, make holy or majestic, dedicate, or keep oneself apart and separate (see *Strong's Exhaustive Concordance of the Bible* #6942). It means much more than just to cleanse—as important as that is.

The Lord doesn't want to merely erase our sins and set us back to zero. We were born with a clean slate. He would rather fill us up with the good things of life. He would rather infuse us with righteousness (see Romans 4). He doesn't want to merely clean house and leave us empty.

Latter-day revelation teaches that "man is the tabernacle of God, even temples" (D&C 93:35). Paul says, "Know ye not that ye are the temple of God, and that the Spirit of God dwelleth in you? If any man defile the temple of God, him shall God destroy; for the temple of God is holy, which temple ye are" (1 Corinthians 3:16–17; see also 1 Corinthians 6:19–20).

The comparison of the body to the temple is quite interesting. Notice the scriptures do not say, "Know ye not that ye are the shrine of God?," or "Know ye not that ye are the monument of God?". A shrine would be like a memorial. It would be a place for people to come to look at and remember something, but it would be built primarily for display only. The Church could invest its resources into building shrines or memorials to help us remember God, but even the Church historical sites do not have such a narrow, singular purpose. Instead, the Church constructs temples all over the world.

Can you imagine the Church ever building a temple and making sure everything inside was clean, white, pure, and spotless, and then, after dedicating the temple, locking all of the doors to make sure nothing ever got inside to pollute it? Would the Lord want His house left empty, just in case He ever wanted to come to a solitary place to visit? Everything inside would stay clean and unpolluted certainly, but such an idea is absurd.

It is just as absurd to think that the Lord would want our bodies to be merely empty tabernacles. They are temples because the Spirit can dwell inside. Maybe the real cost of addiction is not just the fact that our tabernacles are defiled and polluted. Maybe the real cost of addiction has to do more with the wonderful things we kick out of our tabernacles, so our drug of choice (and that includes pornography and sexual addiction) can have an abode. The Lord would rather see us feast on the fruits of the Spirit.

A SKATEBOARD OR A CADILLAC?

One year for Easter, when I was a kid, I received a new skateboard. Back then the idea of a skateboard was revolutionary. Roller skates had been around for a long time, but skateboards were brand new. By today's standards, it was pretty plain. It was a simple, thin, rectangular block of wood with four metal wheels mounted on the bottom. We lived on a hill, so my sister and I would carry our skateboards to the top of the street and coast down the sidewalk in front of our house. We had a blast.

It did have its limitations, though. It could only go downhill. When we got to the bottom of the hill, we had to carry our skateboards back up the hill on our own power. We were exposed to the elements. If it was raining, it was hard to ride our skateboards, and on cold days, the wind chill was a little unbearable. Old skateboards were hard to steer. They wanted to go straight. If you came to a sharp bend in the sidewalk, you had to get off sometimes.

At the same time I received my skateboard, my grandpa had a beautiful '59 Cadillac Coupe de Ville. It had classic fins on the back. It had yellow paint. It was the first car I'd ever seen with power windows. My sister and I liked to play with the windows in the back seat. It had all the bells and whistles. The engine purred like a kitten as it glided down the highway. Grandma and Grandpa would take us for long rides in their Cadillac. I have great memories of that car.

My skateboard was a lot of fun, but Grandpa's Cadillac could do so much more. You could roll up the windows and turn on the heater if it was cold outside. It would go uphill and downhill. It had gears with a forward and a reverse. It had a radio, and you never needed to worry about falling off and getting road rash like you did on a skateboard. There was really no comparison between my skateboard and my grandpa's Cadillac.

The things I would cling to back in my drinking days remind me of that skateboard. In the early days, they were good for a few cheap thrills, but it was always a downhill ride. As my addictions got out of control, I could see there was no getting off the skateboard without crashing, and it was going to hurt when I hit bottom. Would I live to see another day? As my skateboard and my life ran out of control, it looked like I would hit a brick wall. Who would come to my rescue? Who could deliver me from that awful crash?

My life in recovery seems a little like that old Cadillac. It has been an uphill climb, but it has been an incredible ride. I have seen new vistas. I have gone places I never dreamed were possible. Twenty years ago, I hoped to poison myself quickly, because there was no other way out—or so I thought. Today I can "with surety hope for a better world" (Ether 12:4). When I put my own will firmly in the backseat, it is usually smooth sailing. I can feel safe and secure today, when I let the Lord do the driving.

THREE BAD TRADE-INS

I love to read Fourth Nephi in the Book of Mormon. For two hundred years, life is great for the people. They live in continual peace, and all things are common among them. It gives me great hope to know that you and I can live right and feel the love of God as it dwells in our hearts (see 4 Nephi 1:15). Fourth Nephi is such a beautiful story, and it's exciting to know it really happened that way.

Then the people cross over an invisible line. I've crossed over invisible lines too. I remember a time when I *thought* I had control of my life—when I thought I could control my drinking and quit whenever I wanted to. I just wasn't ready yet, and it was no big deal. I couldn't tell you the date when I crossed over that invisible line. I can remember 1983 and 1984—at least part of those years. I thought I had a grip on life. Drinking was still a rush, and life was still a big party, but by 1988, life was spinning out of control. The alcohol didn't work anymore; the emotional pain was flooding through, and I couldn't quit! The invisible line was somewhere in between those years.

The people in the Book of Mormon also crossed over an invisible line. We can't call them Nephites or Lamanites during this time because they didn't have any "-ites." "They were in one, the children of Christ, and heirs to the kingdom of God" (see 4 Nephi 1:17).

We don't know the exact time (though it was in AD 201) or even the root cause of their crossing over the line, but we know where it occurs in the Book of Mormon text. I have it labeled in my scriptures in the left margin on page 467 between verses 23 and 24 of Fourth Nephi. I have it labeled as "The Fall." This is the beginning of the downfall of the Nephite civilization.

Verse 23 reads, "And now I, Mormon, would that ye should know that the people had *multiplied*, insomuch that they were spread upon all the face of the land, and that they had become *exceedingly rich*, because of their *prosperity in Christ*" (emphasis added).

The people had been blessed according to the Abrahamic covenant. The Lord had promised Abraham, saying, "I will *multiply* thy seed as the stars of the heaven, and as the sand which is upon the sea shore"

(Genesis 22:17). The people were "rich, because of their prosperity in Christ."

There are two ways of looking at this scenario. First, they may have been blessed with material wealth because of their righteousness in keeping the commandments. Second, maybe it didn't matter to them how much money they had, because their real prosperity was in Christ. They were rich in blessings and grateful for what they had, and they focused on Christ, who was the source of their blessings. They realized that "he that hath eternal life is rich" (D&C 6:7), yet they didn't have to wait for the next life to be completely happy. The record says, "Surely there could not be a happier people among all the people who had been created by the hand of God" (4 Nephi 1:16). They were partakers of that sweet fruit of the tree of life, which is representative of the love of God (see 1 Nephi 11:21–25). They were "made free, and partakers of the heavenly gift" (4 Nephi 1:3).

Which of these two scenarios is true? Did they have the money in the bank, or did they have an attitude of gratitude? As I read the scriptures, I personally think they had both. Definitely, they were focused and had an eternal vision.

Let's review the attitude change in verse 24: "And now, in this two hundred and first year there began to be among them those who were lifted up in pride, such as the wearing of costly apparel, and all manner of *fine pearls*, and of the *fine things of the world*" (emphasis added).

In verse 23, the *fine things* were Christ and His gospel. In verse 24, the fine things are of the world. The focus has shifted from the spiritual to the physical. They traded in their spiritual Cadillac for a skateboard.

Another bad trade is found in the New Testament. A rich young man comes to the Savior with the question, "What shall I do that I may inherit eternal life?" It is certainly a great question and a worthy goal. Jesus responds with the answer:

> Thou knowest the commandments, Do not commit adultery, Do not kill, Do not steal, Do not bear false witness, Defraud not, Honour thy father and mother.
>
> And he answered and said unto him, Master, all these have I observed from my youth.

Then Jesus beholding him *loved* him, and said unto him, One thing thou lackest: go thy way, sell whatsoever thou hast, and give to the poor, and thou shalt have *treasure in heaven*: and come, take up the cross, and follow me.

And he was sad at that saying, and went away grieved: for he had great possessions. (Mark 10:17–22, emphasis added)

This was really not a trade. The young man had such a nice physical skateboard that he couldn't even *see* the spiritual Cadillac. But before we get too judgmental of this poor young man, we need to look at the requirement of the Lord. It is more than what it appears to be on the surface. It would have been more than merely selling his possessions and distributing the money to the poor.

The invitation at the end to "take up the cross" is really a rather large sacrifice. On another occasion the Savior said, "And now for a man to take up his cross, is to deny himself all ungodliness, and *every worldly lust*, and keep my commandments" (JST, Matthew 16:26; emphasis added). It is really the culmination of working Steps Three, Six, and Seven in their entirety. It is accomplished by taking our self-will, character defects, and all worldly lusts, and placing them on the altar of sacrifice to be surrendered to God.

Elder Bruce R. McConkie said the following of this rich, young man:

> And we are left to wonder what intimacies he might have shared with the Son of God, what fellowship he might have enjoyed with the apostles, what revelations and visions he might have received, if he had been able to live the law of a celestial kingdom. As it is he remains nameless; as it might have been, his name could have been had in honorable remembrance among the saints forever. (Bruce R. McConkie, "Obedience, Consecration, and Sacrifice," *Ensign* [May 1975]: 50)

The third example comes in the Book of Mormon, right after the birth of the Savior. The scriptures record:

> And it came to pass that thus passed away the ninety and fifth year also, and the people began to forget those signs and

wonders which they had *heard*, and began to be less and less astonished at a sign or a wonder from heaven, insomuch that they began to be *hard in their hearts*, and *blind* in their *minds*, and began to disbelieve all which they had *heard* and *seen*—

Imagining up some *vain* thing in their *hearts*, that it was wrought by men and by the power of the devil, to lead away and deceive the hearts of the people; and thus did Satan get possession of the *hearts* of the people again, insomuch that he did *blind their eyes* and lead them away to believe that the doctrine of Christ was a foolish and a vain thing. (3 Nephi 2:1–2, emphasis added)

This passage reveals the effect of a naturalistic philosophy or a *five-dimensional* experience—an experience perceived only by the five senses. There are some real problems with this.

First, five-dimensional experiences don't work. They do not promote faith or belief. They are not reliable sources to lead us to the truth, and, as in this scripture, can be doubted and forgotten. No wonder the Lord does not give a sign or miracle to everyone who merely asks.

Second, they can be misleading. In the Book of Mormon, Amalickiah uses five-dimensional experiences to create counterfeit evidence to intentionally deceive. He seizes the Lamanite kingdom by having one of his servants stab the king as the king comes out to greet Amalickiah. The servants of the king flee in fear, and Amalickiah uses this as evidence to convince the people that the servants of the king are guilty of murder. He even invites them to "come and see" the false evidence. The people do not see the truth—Amalickiah planned the murder from the beginning (see Alma 47).

The third problem with five-dimensional experiences is that we develop a tolerance to anything that is purely physical. When drinking and using, it takes more alcohol, more drugs, and harder pornography for addicts to reach the same effect. The same holds true for other forms of physical stimulation.

The people in Third Nephi had seen some pretty incredible things. They watched the sun go down and saw that it was still light throughout the night (see 3 Nephi 1:15, 19). They saw a new star appear (see

3 Nephi 1:21). But as they saw more signs, they became "less and less astonished at a sign or a wonder from heaven." After a while, we become numb to physical phenomena unless we have a witness from the Spirit. I find it truly amazing, yet I have seen it happen with myself and with others. We are able to totally discount experiences perceived with our own senses. Notice how these people in the Book of Mormon actually do not believe things they had actually seen with their own eyes and heard with their own ears!

The fourth problem is that five-dimensional experiences promote insanity. With the absence of the Spirit, vain imagination takes over. Addicts start to "imagine up" crazy ideas—like believing they can continue in their addictive behaviors and expect better results in the future. Remember, it is in Step Two, where they are restored to sanity and wholeness, because of their faith or belief in a power greater than themselves. It takes power to restore them and make them whole, and that power often comes through the Holy Ghost.

The fifth problem with five-dimensional experiences is that they cause our lives to lose focus and balance. The more emphasis we place on physical things, the more powerful and more important they become to us. After awhile, they consume us. We spend every waking moment thinking about physical things and satisfying the natural man.

Elder Neal A. Maxwell taught this concept powerfully. He said, "One of the best ways we can put 'off the natural man' is to starve him (Mosiah 3:19). Weakened, he is more easily dislodged. Otherwise, he insists on getting his ticket punched at every stop on the temptation train" (Neal A. Maxwell, "The Seventh Commandment: A Shield," *Ensign* [November 2001]: 78).

Alma taught a similar concept. He spoke to his son Helaman about Lehi and his family and their journey in the wilderness. He spoke of following the Liahona and about the spiritual principles of faith, obedience, and diligence. He said,

> Nevertheless, because those miracles were worked by small means it did show unto them marvelous works. They were slothful, and forgot to exercise their faith and diligence

and then those marvelous works ceased, and they did not progress in their journey;

Therefore, they tarried in the wilderness, or did not travel a direct course, and were *afflicted with hunger and thirst*, because of their transgressions. (Alma 37:41–42, emphasis added)

There are two ways of looking at these verses. One view is that they actually had less food and water because they were less righteous, and thus the Lord was not able to bless them as much. The other view is that they were heavily focused on physical things, and they were thinking less about spiritual things. As a result, their physical appetites and discomforts became more pronounced, and they noticed them more. Have you ever noticed on fast Sundays, how much hungrier you get in Church when the speakers are boring? Have you ever noticed how a headache becomes milder, if you are watching a good movie or reading a good book?

One of the best vehicles for taking us away from our physical afflictions and temptations is the Spirit. One of the changes that has happened to me in recovery is that if Church is boring me, I take responsibility for it. I realize now that it is not the speaker's responsibility to entertain me, rather it is *my* responsibility to learn what the Spirit would teach me.

This same principle of personal responsibility holds true for scripture reading and temple attendance. If I go to the temple and don't learn something new—that's my fault. I attend the temple regularly, and almost without exception, I learn something new every time. I used to get bored reading the scriptures, but somewhere along the line, they came alive and became exciting to me. Today, I get goose bumps one minute, and tears the next. The scriptures haven't changed. The difference is the Spirit.

If you are "afflicted with hunger" and a compulsion for the things of the flesh, or if you are "afflicted with thirst" and desire a drink, try some spiritual nourishment. I know the natural man inside me is alive and well, but I also know that when I am immersed in feasting on the scriptures, when I am empowered within the temple, and when I am engrossed in mighty prayer—then the appetites of the natural man are subdued to the point of forgetting.

There is one final point about the physical and spiritual realms. True spirituality does not squash the physical. "Spirit and element, inseparably connected, receive a fullness of joy" (D&C 93:33). We can't have the sacrament without physical bread and physical water. We can't have any ordinance in the Church without something physical in the likeness of something spiritual (see D&C 77:2). We can't have an infinite Atonement without "the precious blood of Christ, as of a lamb without blemish and without spot" (1 Peter 1:19). Indeed I believe we will never be so overjoyed as when we rise in the morning of the first resurrection with a perfect, celestial, and very physical body.

because jesus likes chocolate, you can have recovery

While I can't speak for the Lord's food preferences, I am sure He had His favorites. He probably had His favorite places to pray and meditate. He probably enjoyed good art and literature. He seemed to like the poetic style of Isaiah. He spoke of the "lilies of the field" and ate fish and honeycomb with His disciples (see Matthew 6:28; Luke 24:42).

Because He could see a rainbow, hear the chirping of birds, smell a rose, taste honey, and feel the cool breeze against His face, He can give the gift of recovery. Although He lived a perfect life, He experienced many of the same things you and I do. He felt the full range of human experience in Gethsemane. He suffered "temptations, and pain of body, hunger, thirst, and fatigue, even more than man can suffer" (Mosiah 3:7).

He knows how it feels to have a crown of thorns pressed harshly against His head. He knows how it feels to be scourged, spit upon, and have chunks of His beard ripped out of His face (see Matthew 27:29–

30; John 19:1–3; and Isaiah 50:6). He knows the awful hurt of ridicule and betrayal.

Because of the dual nature of Jesus Christ, addicts can have recovery. He inherited the immortal traits of a God from His Father, God the Father. Before His mortal birth, He was Jehovah. Abinadi taught that Christ is both the Father and the Son. He is the Father, "because he was conceived by the power of God" (Mosiah 15:3). He had power over death, which He inherited from His Father. During His mortal ministry, He plainly taught: "I lay down my life, that I might take it again. No man taketh it from me, but I lay it down of myself. I have power to lay it down, and I have power to take it again" (John 10:17–18).

This little tidbit of information means two things for addicts. First, the ante for their recovery and redemption was just raised by infinite proportions, because He didn't *have to* lay down His own life. He laid it down voluntarily because of His infinite love for us all. He certainly didn't have to atone for His own sins either. He didn't have any. Only pure love could motivate such an act.

The attributes He inherited from His Father mean something else for addicts. It means that the Atonement He wrought out is infinite in its scope (see D&C 76:69; Alma 34:10). It transcends every problem, temptation, addiction, pain, and adversity!

From His mother, Mary, He inherited the mortal characteristics common to all mankind. Abinadi refers to this side of His nature as "the Son." He is "the Son, because of the flesh" (Mosiah 15:3). That gave Him the capacity to lay down His life. It also gave Him the capacity to feel and experience firsthand every pain, temptation, and heartache that you and I could ever encounter.

His spirit was placed inside a mortal "tabernacle of clay," (Mosiah 3:5) so He could have the experiences of a mortal body—complete with passions, appetites, and feelings. That way, He could have the same challenges as you and I. But if that were not enough, He also had to battle Satan, who was working overtime to take Him down.

There are three temptations recorded in the Bible. After Jesus has been fasting forty days—He is physically tired and weak, and His appetites are at a peak—Satan comes to tempt Him. The first temptation is to turn stones into bread. That would be pretty enticing after a forty-day fast. The second temptation is to jump off the pinnacle of the temple. This could be quite alluring to an addict! It would provide a cheap thrill, a chance to show off a bit, and an opportunity to manipulate others. Angels would be called to the scene immediately to provide a quick rescue. Both of these temptations are enhanced by the pride factor—a character defect present in the Step Four moral inventories of many addicts. Satan prefaces both temptations with, "If thou be the Son of God." He often tries to get us to question our true identity.

The third temptation proves that Satan will try anything to lure us off the path of righteousness. For mere mortals, gaining all of the kingdoms of the world with all their power and glory would be an extremely powerful temptation. But does Satan realize to whom he is talking here? This is Jehovah in the flesh—the Creator of heaven and earth! Jesus could have called his bluff, but instead He merely dismisses him by saying, "Get thee hence, Satan: for it is written, Thou shalt worship the Lord thy God, and him only shalt thou serve" (see Matthew 4:1–11).

Every temptation we could ever face is within the realm of these three. They involve the instant gratification of physical appetites, the gratification of pride, and the lust for excitement, power, prestige, and wealth, but we can assume that this was not the end of temptation for our Savior. Here are some insightful scriptures:

And [Christ] shall go forth, *suffering* pains and afflictions and *temptations of every kind*; and this that the word might be fulfilled which saith he will take upon him the pains and the sicknesses of his people. (Alma 7:11, emphasis added)

For we have not an high priest which cannot be touched with the feeling of our infirmities; but was *in all points tempted like as we are*, yet without sin. (Hebrews 4:15, emphasis added)

These two passages of scripture teach a couple of great concepts. First, phrases like "temptations of every kind" and "in all points tempted" reveal that Jesus suffered and successfully overcame every single kind of temptation that we could ever be exposed to. We will not be able to teach Him anything new about temptation. Second, because Jesus was tempted in a manner similar to us, He has total personal empathy for our afflictions and struggles with temptation and compulsion.

These verses expose a big myth. That night on July 31, 1989, when I sat in my room and battled with the adversary, I was somewhat drawn in by Satan's propaganda as I listened to his lies. I felt as if he whispered to me, "Jesus could never understand what you're going through. He was never an alcoholic! He was too good to ever be tempted by anything. There's no way he can help you now!"

Many addicts have a preconceived idea that good people are never really tempted and don't know anything about temptation and that rebels like them are the only ones who truly understand temptation. This idea is totally false, and here is the flaw in the logic: C. S. Lewis once said the following:

> Only those who try to resist temptation know how strong it is. . . . You find out the strength of a wind by trying to walk against it, not by lying down. A man who gives in to temptation after five minutes simply does not know what it would have been like an hour later. . . . . Christ, because He was the only man who never yielded to temptation, is also the only man who knows to the full what temptation means" (C. S. Lewis, *Mere Christianity* [New York: HarperSanFrancisco, 1952], 142).

Latter-day scripture reveals that "The Son of Man hath descended below them all" (D&C 122:8). Jesus indeed suffered more than any man could suffer, and because He descended below all things and successfully overcame all things (see John 16:33), He is the supreme authority on overcoming every kind of temptation, trial, and addiction.

His power of deliverance does not stop there. He knows how to conquer sin from His own experience, and He knows the effects of sin from our experience. In Gethsemane, He felt and experienced the consequences of our transgressions and addictions. He suffered both in "body and spirit" (D&C 19:18). He knows how a hangover feels. He knows what it's like to wake up in the morning with that feeling of impending doom—to have the jitters from the inside out. He knows the clanging of the jail door as it slams shut behind one's back. He knows the hurt of having to tell one more lie in order to get one more fix. He knows "the weakness of man and how to succor them who are tempted" (D&C 62:1).

It is that very dual nature of Christ that will allow His grace to take full effect in each of our lives—addict or not. It will provide us with insight, strength, and ultimate victory in our desperate times of need. If the Savior were merely mortal and physical in nature, He would have great feeling and sympathy for our weakness and infirmities, but He would lack the spiritual knowledge and power to deliver us. If He were strictly spiritual in nature, He would have all knowledge, but He would have a difficult time getting down to our level and helping us get from point A to point B.

To demonstrate this idea, we will consider some fictional dialogues between an addict and a purely physical god, between an addict and a purely spiritual god, and between an addict and the Savior. I realize it is a contradiction of terms to have a mortal god, but we will do it anyway to make a point. God is not capitalized in the first two cases because these fictional gods do not represent the true nature of God as we understand Him (see Steps Three and Eleven).

DIALOGUE WITH A PURELY PHYSICAL GOD

Addict #1: I've just been busted again because I am addicted to meth. I've lost all of my material possessions and my job. Now my wife says she is going to leave me. I am sick all of the time. What can I do now?

Physical god: Boy, that's a tough one! You know, they didn't have those methamphetamines when I was on the earth. We didn't even know about such chemicals. I can sure sympathize though. I suffered through sickness too. And I can sure relate to that part about other people not understanding you. It seemed like everyone just rejected my message. Let me do some research, and I'll get back to you.

Addict #2: I can't seem to stay off those Internet porn sites! I live in shame. It's a secret life. I sometimes get so sick from viewing this filth, I want to throw up. I am always hiding from my wife and kids. I have to lie to stay in my addiction. Life is so awful!

Physical god: Sounds like a tough life for sure! I can sure understand your suffering. I don't have any answers, though. I always had enough willpower to stay away from places like that. Of course, we didn't have computers in my day, but I know life is full of suffering. Did you know they put a crown of thorns on my head? I wonder if your suffering is similar to mine.

DIALOGUE WITH A PURELY SPIRITUAL GOD

Addict #3: I am addicted to Internet pornography. I am always surfing the Internet to find harder and harder material. I can never get enough. It saps all of my strength and energy. How can I kick this habit?

Spiritual god: Are you telling me you can't just get up and walk away from this stuff? For heaven's sake, it's just a two-dimensional image coming out of a flat screen! It's not even real! I can't understand it. Is it the shape, the color, or just the perceived texture? Do you fixate over statues too? It's only flesh, after all! And flesh is merely the dust of the earth. What's your problem?

Addict #4: I guess I have to admit it—I'm an alcoholic. I've given my best effort to quit drinking, but I just can't do it. My wife's threatening to divorce me and kick me out of the house. I'm on the verge of losing my job. I'm sick and tired of being sick and tired all the time!

Spiritual god: Are you serious? Do you know what alcohol is? It's just a chemical! It consists of three elements—carbon, hydrogen, and oxygen. I can give you the chemical formula. It's CH_3CH_2OH. I could take out the carbon atoms and rearrange it a bit, and you would simply have plain water. You're willing to lose your family over three little elements? You're going to let a simple little chemical make your life totally unmanageable?

DIALOGUE WITH THE SAVIOR

Addict #5: My life is so messed up! I have so many addictions. I don't even know where to start. Sometimes I want to just give up. I will never be good enough to make it. How could my life ever be happy again?

The Savior: "Come now, and let us reason together . . . though your sins [and addictions] be as scarlet, they shall be as white as snow" (Isaiah 1:18).

"Ye cannot bear all things now; nevertheless, be of good cheer, for I will lead you along" (D&C 78:18).

"And after their temptations, and much tribulation, behold, I, the Lord, will feel after them, and if they harden not their hearts, and stiffen not their necks against me, they shall be converted, and I will heal them" (D&C 112:13).

"O all ye that are spared . . . will ye not now return unto me, and repent of your sins, and be converted, that I may heal you? Behold, mine arm of mercy is extended towards you" (3 Nephi 9:13–14).

"In the world ye shall have tribulation: but be of good cheer; I have overcome the world" (John 16:33).

"The Son of Man hath descended below them all" (D&C 122:8).

"He suffereth the pains of all men, yea, the pains of every living creature, both men, women, and children, who belong to the family of Adam" (2 Nephi 9:21).

"I will fight your battles" (D&C 105:14).

"Listen to him who is the advocate with the Father, who is pleading your cause before him—Saying: Father, behold the sufferings and death of him who did no sin, in whom thou wast well pleased; behold the blood of thy Son which was shed, the blood of him whom thou gavest that thyself might be glorified; Wherefore, Father, spare these my brethren that believe on my name, that they may come unto me and have everlasting life" (D&C 45:3–5).

"I say unto you, that as many as receive me, to them will I give power to become the sons [and daughters] of God, even to them that believe on my name" (D&C 11:30).

"And they shall be mine, saith the Lord of hosts, in that day when I make up my jewels; and I will spare them, as a man spareth his own son that serveth him" (Malachi 3:17).

"And he that receiveth me receiveth my Father; And he that receiveth my Father receiveth my Father's kingdom; therefore all that my Father hath shall be given unto him" (D&C 84:37–38).

"LET US . . . COME BOLDLY UNTO THE THRONE OF GRACE"

Remember the Apostle Paul said, "For we have not an high priest which cannot be touched with the feeling of our infirmities; but was in all points tempted like as we are, yet without sin" (Hebrews 4:15).

In ancient Israel, once each year on the Day of Atonement, a high priest entered the veil and into the Holy of Holies and made an atonement for all the children of Israel (see Leviticus 16). This was a type for Jesus Christ and His Atonement for us. But the high priest in ancient days could only imagine the pain and suffering of the children of Israel. He may have been sympathetic, but he could not experience their feelings. An ancient high priest of Israel would not have known how it feels to be an alcoholic or an addict unless he were an addict himself.

But the high priest of whom Paul speaks knows precisely how we are feeling every moment of every day of our lives. The Savior has such empathy, mercy, and infinite love that He will help each of us every single time we turn to Him. He has the power and ability to make us victorious in our individual quests to overcome the things of the world.

Consider this scripture from the Book of Mormon describing our Savior's Atonement:

> And he shall go forth, suffering pains and afflictions and temptations of every kind; and this that the word might be fulfilled which saith he will take upon him the pains and the sicknesses of his people.
>
> And he will take upon him death, that he may loose the bands of death which *bind* his people; and he will take upon him their infirmities, that his bowels may be filled with mercy, *according to the flesh*, that he may know *according to the flesh* how to succor his people according to their infirmities. (Alma 7:11–12, emphasis added)

As an alcoholic and addict and continual beneficiary of the Lord's grace, this is one of my absolute favorite passages of scripture. If this scripture were not true, I would not be alive and sober today.

This passage is quoted often in Church meetings, however, like many scriptures, we often do not read far enough. One day when I was reading this passage and feeling enlightenment from the Spirit, I became impressed with verse 13. The real impact of these three verses, for me at least, comes in the verse that follows: "Now the Spirit knoweth all things; nevertheless the Son of God suffereth *according to the flesh* that he might *take* upon him the sins of his people, that he might blot out their transgressions according to the *power of his deliverance*; and now behold, this is the testimony which is in me" (Alma 7:13, emphasis added).

In other words, the Savior could have gained knowledge through the Spirit to coach us and counsel us through our adversities without becoming mortal. He would have still had a perfect knowledge of our transgressions and their accompanying remedies. He could have still been our coach, watching from the sidelines, and He still would have been able to tell us how to play the game. But there would be two problems with this scenario. First, He would have lacked the actual experience necessary to play the game. He would never be an example for us to follow. We would never know how well He could do Himself, if He were put in the game. Second, the demands of justice and the penalties for sin would have never been satisfied. The bill would still be left unpaid.

Instead, our loving Savior willingly paid that debt. Then, and only then, could He call us His "jewels" (see Malachi 3:17; D&C 101:3). Because He redeemed us and bought us out of bondage with "the precious blood . . . as of a lamb without blemish and without spot" (1 Peter 1:19), He can now call us His "peculiar treasure" (Exodus 19:5). You don't think He is going to dump His treasure after paying such a staggering price, do you?

Instead of settling for an academic knowledge of our sins, pains, addictions, and sufferings, our Savior chose to place Himself right in the midst of our temptations and trials. Rather than a coach, He becomes our teammate in the game of mortal life.

Knowing He "will fight [our] battles" (D&C 105:14), "let us therefore come boldly unto the throne of grace, that we may obtain mercy, and find grace to help in time of need" (Hebrews 4:16). We need not be shy as we approach the throne of our King and ask for the miracle of recovery.

Because Jesus can taste chocolate, and because He descended below all things in Gethsemane, and because He overcame the world and the power of the flesh, you and I can taste those things in life most sweet and "most joyous to the soul" (1 Nephi 11:23). Sobriety is a pretty good deal, but it only comes by way of the Atonement. Because of the Atonement, "our old man is crucified," and we get to "walk in newness of life" (Romans 6:4, 6).

from bars to booths
to tabernacles to temples

In the August 2005 *Ensign*, President Gordon B. Hinckley challenged the members of the Church to read the Book of Mormon before the end of the year. He promised three things to those who took the challenge: "an added measure of the Spirit of the Lord, a strengthened resolution to walk in obedience to His commandments, and a stronger testimony of the living reality of the Son of God" (President Gordon B. Hinckley, "A Testimony Vibrant and True," *Ensign* [August 2005]: 3).

At the time I was just finishing my reading of the Doctrine and Covenants. I finished it during the month of August, and during the last week of August, I read the introduction and the prefacing material for the Book of Mormon. I planned to dive into First Nephi on September 1st. It was truly incredible to see so many people pulling out their copies of the Book of Mormon and reading along as I rode the bus each day.

When I feast on the word, I like to look at all of the cross-references and footnotes. I look up all the related verses. But I calculated that I would need to read five pages every day to finish the book by December

16, so I braced myself on September 1st and determined that I would read straight through without any stopping. I made it to page four. I got stuck on probably the shortest verse in the entire Book of Mormon: "And my father dwelt in a tent" (1 Nephi 2:15).

I felt impressed to look at the footnotes. There were five cross-references. I was fascinated with the first reference, Genesis 12:8, which appears in one of the chapters where the Abrahamic covenant is explained. The Lord tells Abraham to get out of his country and away from his kindred and from his father's house and go to a land that He would show him. The Lord then tells Abraham, "And I will make of thee a great nation, and I will bless thee, and make thy name great; and thou shalt be a blessing: And I will bless them that bless thee . . . and in thee shall all families of the earth be blessed" (Genesis 12:2–3). Abraham then took Sarah, his wife, and Lot, his nephew, and some others, and they journeyed toward Canaan. They took the "substance that they had gathered" (v. 5), which were probably just the bare necessities.

There is a strong parallel between this journey of Abraham and the journey of Lehi. The Lord commanded both to leave their native lands and go to lands of promise. Both traveled with meager substance, leaving everything else behind. Both dwelt in tents as they traveled through the wilderness.

As I was reading this cross-reference, I noticed that Abraham went to a "mountain on the east of Bethel, and pitched his tent, **having** Bethel on the west, and Hai on the east: and there he builded an altar unto the Lord, and called upon the name of the Lord" (see Genesis 12:1–8). I knew from reading chapters 28 and 31 in Genesis that *Bethel* means "House of God" in Hebrew (see Genesis 28:19 footnote a; 31:13; Bible Dictionary, "Bethel"; *Strong's Exhaustive Concordance of the Bible* #1008). I also noticed that Abraham went to a mountain and there pitched his tent. The word *mountain* or *mount* is often symbolic of the temple. He built an altar, suggesting sacrifices or covenants with the Lord, and he called upon the "name of the Lord." Why didn't it just say that he called upon the Lord? The *name* of the Lord implies power and priesthood blessings. The Lord also said to Abraham, "Behold, I will lead thee by my hand, and I will take thee, to put upon thee *my name*, even the Priesthood of thy father, and my power shall be over thee." Previously,

He said, "Abraham, Abraham, behold, *my name* is Jehovah, and I have heard thee, and have come down to deliver thee" (Abraham 1:16, 18, emphasis added).

How would you like a promise like that? How would you like the Lord to call you by name and say, "My name is Jehovah, and I have heard you, and have come down to deliver you from your bondage and addiction?" My message is that you absolutely *can* have a promise like this in your own recovery! You just need to continue in the journey of recovery until you find the places where you can receive a fullness of the Abrahamic covenant. Paul said, "And if ye be Christ's, then are ye Abraham's seed, and heirs according to the promise." Part of this covenant is baptism (see Galatians 3:27, 29).

My mind somehow went to the direction of Abraham's tent from Bethel or from the house of God. It was east of Bethel. I then asked myself, isn't that the direction the waters flowed from the house of the Lord in Ezekiel 47? I already knew what *Bethel* meant, but I didn't know what *Hai* meant, so I started turning to the Bible Dictionary. Remember that Abraham pitched his tent between Bethel and Hai. As I stuck my finger in the pages to turn to the Bible Dictionary, my finger went to Ezekiel 47—to the very page. I knew I was getting some divine assistance, so I stopped and looked at some verses. In Ezekiel 47, waters issue out from under the threshold of the house of the Lord. I noticed the following directional references in Ezekiel 47 (emphases in the following verses are mine):

> "Waters issued out from under the threshold of the house *eastward*" (v. 1)
>
> "The forefront of the house stood toward the *east*" (v. 1)
>
> "The utter gate by the way that looketh *eastward*" (v. 2)
>
> "The man that had the line in his hand went forth *eastward*" (v. 3)
>
> "These waters issue out toward the *east* country" (v. 8)

I had quite a few images floating around in my head. There was a mountain, a house of God, an altar, the name of the Lord, and living waters flowing eastward from the house of the Lord. When I do the math in my head, I come up with the following equation: Mountain +

House of God + Altar + Name of the Lord + Living Waters Flowing Eastward from the Lord's House = Temple. And at the center point of this well-defined site was a tent pitched by Father Abraham!

I just needed to find the meaning of *Hai* to complete the picture in my mind. I observed from footnote c in Genesis 12:8 that *Hai* and *Ai* mean the same thing. I continued to the Bible Dictionary and found that *Hai*, or *Ai*, means "heap of ruins" (Bible Dictionary, "Ai and Hai"; *Strong's* #5857).

For me, the bottom line of this whole scenario goes as follows: As addicts make their way in this journey from bondage to recovery, and as they wander in a strange, new wilderness, they find themselves somewhere between a "heap of ruins" (Hai) and the "House of God" (Bethel). The *Big Book of Alcoholics Anonymous* refers to that "heap of ruins" as the "wreckage of [their] past" (p. 164). Addicts must decide if they will continue on the journey to the promised land. They must decide if they are willing to make that trek to holy places where they can partake of the covenants of the Lord, and where they can enter into His house—His holy temple.

Some of them will settle for white-knuckle sobriety, wandering around in the wilderness of dry drunks. After a while, some of them will pass through the wilderness "hardly bestead and hungry . . . [and] when they shall be hungry, they shall fret themselves" (Isaiah 8:21), and some will go back out. Some of them, instead of pitching a tent, will try to build a permanent foundation somewhere between the "heap of ruins" of the past and the temple that lies in the future. I encourage those who have stopped to keep on going! The Lord will walk with you on your journey. Make that effort. It is worth it.

For Laman and Lemuel, the beach life, where they all pitched their tents by the seashore, was good enough. But Nephi chose to hearken to the voice of the Lord, so he "went up into the mountain and cried unto the Lord." There, in a temple-like experience, he received instructions to complete the rest of the journey. There, in the mountain, the Lord spoke to him, saying, "Thou shalt construct a ship, after the manner which I shall show thee, that I may carry thy people across these waters" (see 1 Nephi 17:5–8, 17–18).

"WE . . . JOURNEYED UNTO THE TENT OF OUR FATHER"

As I started over in my reading of the Book of Mormon, I paid careful attention to Lehi's packing list as he started out in his journey. The list of things he left behind includes his house, the land of his inheritance, his gold, his silver, and his precious things. The list of things he took with him includes his family, his provisions, and his tents (see 1 Nephi 2:4).

That latter list is a pretty short list. I am assuming that provisions would mean just the basic, necessary things to survive in the wilderness. But wouldn't the tents be part of those basic provisions? Passages in Nephi's account make it quite clear that they want to be brief in their description of temporal things (see 1 Nephi 6:3), so if Nephi wanted to be even more succinct, couldn't he have shrunken the list down to just family and provisions?

We know that if this list were fully itemized, it would have to be a pretty long list. They would need food, water, baggage, pack animals, blankets, bedding, clothing, tables, first aid supplies, equipment, tools, and many other things. We know that Nephi and his brothers packed bows and arrows since Nephi breaks his bow, and his brothers' bows lose their springs (see 1 Nephi 16:18–23). Why, then, the special attention to tents?

The word *tent* is used repeatedly in Nephi's account. Every time Nephi and his brothers "go up to Jerusalem" (see 1 Nephi 3:9–10; 7:3) and every time they "go down into the wilderness" (see 1 Nephi 4:34–38; 5:1; and 7:22), there is mention made of Lehi's tent.

It is important to note in this discussion that the words *up* and *down* probably have additional meaning besides going up or down in elevation. *Up* is usually coming unto the Lord or coming up into His presence. *Down* is often running away from the Lord or leaving His presence.

The brother of Jared went up to the top of the mount and asked the Lord to touch sixteen small stones to give light to the vessels. "The veil was taken from off the eyes of the brother of Jared, and he saw the finger of the Lord." The Lord then showed Himself unto the brother of Jared and said, "Because thou knowest these things ye are redeemed from the fall; therefore ye are brought back *into my presence*; therefore I show my-self unto you" (see Ether 3:1–13, emphasis added). Moroni summarizes the experience in a couple of verses:

"And the Lord commanded the brother of Jared to go *down* out of the mount *from the presence of the Lord*" (Ether 4:1, emphasis added).

"For it came to pass after the Lord had prepared the stones which the brother of Jared had carried *up into the mount*, the brother of Jared came *down out of the mount*" (Ether 6:2, emphasis added).

Jonah is another great example:

"But Jonah rose up to flee unto Tarshish *from the presence of the Lord*, and went *down* to Joppa; and he found a ship going to Tarshish: so he paid the fare thereof, and went *down* into it, to go with them unto Tarshish *from the presence of the Lord*" (Jonah 1:3, emphasis added).

In the next chapter, after spending three days in the "belly of hell," Jonah has a more repentant attitude and remarks, "Yet I will look again toward thy holy temple." He also says, "Yet hast thou brought *up* my life from corruption, O Lord my God" (Jonah 2:2, 4, and 6; emphasis added).

It is probable that this language of "going *up* to Jerusalem" and "go-ing *down* into the wilderness," has reference to the temple. The temple was in Jerusalem. They would go *up* to the city where the temple was lo-cated, and, as they were leaving Jerusalem, they would go *down* into the wilderness. The main purpose of the temple is to prepare us to return to the presence of God and become redeemed from the Fall.

The account of King Benjamin tells us that the people gathered themselves together "to go *up* to the temple" (Mosiah 1:18, emphasis added). In Mosiah 2:5, the people "came *up* to the temple," and they "pitched their *tents* round about." Once the people are assembled, King Benjamin says, "I have not commanded you to come *up* hither to trifle with the words which I shall speak" (Mosiah 2:9, emphasis added).

We return now to the discussion of Lehi's tent. After slaying Laban and securing the brass plates, Nephi makes an oath with Zoram, La-ban's servant: Nephi and his brothers will spare his life and allow him to be a "free man," if he will "go down" into the wilderness with them. The scripture records, "And it came to pass that we took the plates of brass and the servant of Laban, and departed into the *wilderness*, and journeyed unto the *tent* of our father" (see 1 Nephi 4:32–38). Nephi could have said, "We journeyed back to our father" or "We went back to camp" or "We returned from Jerusalem."

When the brothers go back to Jerusalem the second time to convince the family of Ishmael to join them, it is the same type of narration. Nephi says, "And after I and my brethren and all the house of Ishmael had come *down* unto the *tent* of my father, they did give thanks unto the Lord" (1 Nephi 7:22). Why the continued references to tents?

In Hebrew there are unique writing styles that are different from English literary styles. In English, we often use a thesaurus to vary our word usage. We would not want to use the same words over and over again, but in Hebraic writing, using of the same word repeatedly is a common style.

Jewish philosopher Martin Buber (1878–1965) discovered a textual style called *Leitwort* that was used in the Bible. It is a German word meaning "leading word." It refers to the repeated usage of a word that suggests a central theme. The fact that this Hebraic literary style appears often in the Book of Mormon, along with other Hebraic styles such as chiasmus, is an additional witness to the prophetic calling of Joseph Smith.

It appears that the word *tent* is a Leitwort, symbolically suggesting a forerunner to the temple. Of Nephi's twenty-three references to a tent, just over half of them have the words *journey, travel,* or *wilderness* nearby. Another form of the word *wilderness* is *bewildered*. The wilderness symbolizes a state of apostasy, confusion, or uncertainty. It is often a transitory state where we are seeking communion with the Lord. We must rely on the Lord to lead us through an uncharted wilderness. The tent becomes a makeshift dwelling in a hopefully temporary wilderness while we are en route to the promised land. We sometimes deliberately go into the wilderness to get away from the hustle and bustle of everyday life, so we can be in communion with God.

Some of the references to tents are of particular interest. Lehi sees a vision of the tree of life in 1 Nephi 8. He has a temple-like experience as he sees concourses of people "pressing forward" (vv. 21, 24, and 30) on a path to arrive at the tree of life and partake of the fruit, which represents the love of God (see 1 Nephi 11:21–25). In the very first verse of the following chapter, Nephi comments that "all these things did my father *see*, and *hear*, and *speak*, as he dwelt in a *tent*, in the valley of Lemuel, and also a great many more things, which *cannot be written* upon these plates" (1 Nephi 9:1, emphasis added). Lehi had a six-dimensional, temple-like experience.

In 1 Nephi 10, Lehi prophesies of the Babylonian captivity, John the Baptist, the mission of the Messiah, the apostasy of the Jews, the Nephites and the Lamanites in the promised land, and the scattering and gathering of Israel. Then, a similar comment is made: "And all these things, of which I have spoken, were done as my father dwelt in a *tent*, in the valley of Lemuel" (1 Nephi 10:16, emphasis added). After Nephi has a similar vision and sees the tree of life, the mission of the Savior, and many other marvelous things, he makes a similar comment in 1 Nephi 16:6. It seems that whenever Lehi or Nephi has a temple-like experience, they make sure the reader knows they were dwelling in a tent at the time.

Nephi eventually arrives in the promised land of America, but he and his people had not reached their final destination. The Lord warns Nephi to run from Laman and Lemuel, who were plotting his death, and "flee into the *wilderness*" with all those who would go with him. Nephi says, "And we did take our *tents* and whatsoever things were possible for us, and did *journey* in the *wilderness* for the space of many days. And after we had *journeyed* for the space of many days we did pitch our *tents*" (see 2 Nephi 5:5–7, emphasis added).

Nephi does not mention the word *tent* in his own narration again. There is an excellent reason for this. In the same chapter, he constructs a temple after the manner of Solomon (see 2 Nephi 5:16). The only other tent reference in Second Nephi is an Isaiah chapter; and Isaiah makes it perfectly clear that you will never see a tent—or a temple—anywhere in Babylon (2 Nephi 23:20).

The motif of a tent served its purpose well, but there is now a temple in their midst. They have also arrived in the promised land—the land of their inheritance.

"ENLARGE THE PLACE OF THY TENT"

The imagery of the tent has its counterpart in the Old Testament. Isaiah draws a similar likeness: *"Enlarge* the *place* of thy *tent,* and let them stretch forth the *curtains* of thy *habitations;* spare not, lengthen thy cords and strengthen thy stakes" (3 Nephi 22:2, emphasis added; see also Isaiah 54:2).

There are several key words here. The word *habitation* in the original Hebrew means dwelling-place, tabernacle, or tent. In fact, the most common usage means tabernacle (see *Strong's* #4908).

The word *curtain* also has some interesting applications. As the Second Coming is foretold in Section 88 of the Doctrine & Covenants, "there shall be silence in heaven for the space of half an hour; and immediately after shall the *curtain* of heaven be unfolded . . . and the face of the Lord shall be *unveiled"* (D&C 88:95, emphasis added). A curtain in this context could have reference to a veil. Notice that with this curtain being unfolded, the presence of the Lord is revealed. Remember, the primary purpose of the temple is to prepare us to come back into the presence of God.

The image of an *enlarging* tent could be symbolic of not only the growth of the kingdom of God in the last days, but it could also have reference to our own personal growth as individuals—for addicts, particularly growth in recovery. In the spirit of the *Big Book,* addicts absolutely believe in "spiritual progress" (p. 60) and making a progressive journey through the wilderness and toward the promised land.

The tent Isaiah speaks of is actually transformed into a palace fit for a king. Notice Isaiah's description of the kingdom near the end of the same chapter: "Behold, I will lay thy stones with fair colors, and lay thy foundations with sapphires. And I will make thy windows of agates [precious stones, possibly rubies; see *Strong's* #3539], and thy gates of carbuncles [gems that sparkle; see *Strong's* #688], and all thy borders of pleasant stones [decorative stones and gems]" (3 Nephi 22:11–12; see also Isaiah 54:11–12).

Latter-day scripture reveals a similar image of transformation from a simple beginning to a magnificent palace. The Prophet Joseph Smith was "called . . . to make a solemn proclamation of [the] gospel, and of this stake which I [the Lord] have *planted* to be a cornerstone of Zion, which shall be *polished* with the *refinement* which is after the similitude of a *palace*" (D&C 124:2, emphasis added).

This is beautiful imagery. The word *planted* suggests that it grew from a small seed to something marvelous. It is fit to become the dwelling-place for the King of kings. The word *place* in this Isaiah reference ("Enlarge the *place* of thy tent") is another Leitwort. The repeated use of the word *place* in the scriptures is also symbolic of the temple or a holy *place*. Some examples follow.

In Exodus 3, Moses comes to the "mountain of God." The Joseph Smith Translation corrects verse 2, and changes the phrase "angel of the Lord" to "presence of the Lord." The change makes a drastic difference because now it is clear that Moses went up on a mountain and came into the presence of the Lord. He saw "a flame of fire out of the midst of a bush . . . and the bush was not consumed." The Lord called to Moses saying, "Moses, Moses. And he said, Here am I." Then the Lord said:

> Draw not nigh hither: put off thy shoes from off thy feet, for the *place* whereon thou *standest* is holy ground.
>
> Moreover he said, I am the God of thy father, the God of Abraham, the God of Isaac, and the God of Jacob. And Moses hid his face; for he was afraid to look upon God.
>
> And the Lord said, I have surely seen the affliction of my people which are in Egypt, and have heard their cry by reason of their taskmasters; for I know their sorrows;
>
> *And I am come down to deliver them out* of the hand of the Egyptians, and to bring them up out of that land unto a good land and a large, unto a land flowing with milk and honey." (Exodus 3:1–8, emphasis added)

Moses inquired of the Lord saying:

> Behold, when I come unto the children of Israel, and shall say unto them, The God of your fathers hath sent me unto you; and they shall say to me, What is his name? what shall I say unto them?

> And God said unto Moses, I AM THAT I AM: and he
> said, Thus shalt thou say unto the children of Israel, I AM
> hath sent me unto you. (Exodus 3:13–14)

In this temple-like experience, the Lord tells Moses that the *place* whereon he is standing is holy ground. Moses is at the "mountain of God." Most of the prophets' temple-like experiences take place on a mountain. The Lord then promises to deliver the children of Israel out of bondage—away from their taskmasters. He also promises to bring them into a "good land . . . flowing with milk and honey." Moses acknowledges that the children of Israel will want to know the name of the Lord. The Lord reveals Himself as the great I AM. Jesus, in His own mortal life, reveals Himself as the Messiah to the Jews by saying, "Verily, verily, I say unto you, Before Abraham was, *I am.*" The Jews got the message. They picked up stones to throw at Him (see John 8:58–59).

In our dispensation, the Lord revealed that "the city New Jerusalem shall be built by the gathering of the saints, beginning at this *place*, even the *place* of the *temple*, which *temple* shall be reared in this generation" (D&C 84:4, emphasis added). The Lord has also said, "Wherefore, stand ye in holy *places*, and be not moved" (D&C 87:8, emphasis added).

In the Book of Mormon, Nephi made Zoram an extraordinary promise: "Therefore, if thou wilt go down into the wilderness to my father thou shalt have *place* with us." Nephi then said, "And it came to pass that Zoram did take courage at the words which I spake" (1 Nephi 4:34–35). Zoram knows he is leaving Jerusalem—the city of the temple—but he can "take courage" in the fact that he is on a journey to the promised land, and he will yet see the temple again. Notice the interesting order of the names Nephi lists as those who went with him into the wilderness to the land of Nephi: "Wherefore, it came to pass that I, Nephi, did take my family, and also Zoram and his family, and Sam, mine elder brother and his family, and Jacob and Joseph, my younger brethren, and also my sisters, and all those who would go with me" (2 Nephi 5:6). Zoram gets mentioned even before Nephi's brothers and sisters. Zoram was promised that by making the journey to the promised land, he would have the opportunity for temple blessings. In the very same chapter where Nephi takes Zoram and the others into the wilderness, he constructs a temple after the "manner . . . of Solomon," precisely ten verses later (see 2 Nephi 5:16).

Let's look at one more example, though there are several others.

In chapter 5 of Alma, Alma delivers one of the most beautiful discourses ever given. He raises the question, "Do you look forward with an eye of faith, and view this mortal body raised in immortality, and this corruption raised in incorruption, to stand before God to be judged according to the deeds which have been done in the mortal body?" To stand before God would certainly mean that one is in His presence. He continues, "I say unto you, can ye look *up* to God at that day with a pure heart and clean hands? I say unto you, can you look *up*, having the image of God engraven upon your countenances?" (Alma 5:15, 19, emphasis added). A pure heart and clean hands are temple criteria given in Psalms 24:3–4: "Who shall *ascend* into the *hill* [mountain or temple] of the Lord? or who shall *stand* in his holy *place*? He that hath clean hands, and a pure heart; who hath not lifted up his soul unto vanity, nor sworn deceitfully" (emphasis added).

To "[swear] deceitfully" in this case does not necessarily mean to use swear words or profane language. Rather it means to not faithfully keep covenants—to not honor our word. It is interesting that the set of questions given by the Psalmist and the similar set of questions given by Alma both sound like interview questions for a temple recommend.

The use of the word *garment* is also repeated several times in Alma 5. Some examples are:

> There can no man be saved except his *garments* are washed white; yea, his *garments* must be purified until they are cleansed from all stain, through the blood of him of whom it has been spoken by our fathers, who should come to redeem his people from their sins.
>
> And now I ask of you, my brethren, how will any of you feel, if ye shall *stand* before the bar of God, having your *garments* stained with blood and all manner of filthiness? Behold, what will these things testify against you? (Alma 5:21–22, emphasis added)

> Have ye walked, keeping yourselves blameless before
> God? . . . That your *garments* have been cleansed and made
> white through the blood of Christ, who will come to redeem
> his people from their sins? (Alma 5:27, emphasis added)

There are a couple of significant things here. First, Alma was clearly a jurist. Remember that Alma was "appointed to be the first chief judge" over the people of Nephi (see Mosiah 29:42). Consider his reference to the evidence of the stained garments, and how those clean or unclean garments would be used as testimony at the judgment bar of God.

Second, he mentions twice the process of having one's garments "washed white" through the blood of Christ. Besides the word *garment* there is another temple connection here. The Lord has stated:

> Behold, I will send my messenger, and he shall prepare
> the way before me: and the Lord, whom ye seek, shall sud-
> denly come to his *temple*, even the messenger of the *covenant*,
> whom ye delight in: behold, he shall come, saith the Lord of
> hosts. But who may abide the day of his coming? and who
> shall *stand* when he appeareth? for he is like a refiner's fire,
> and like *fullers' soap*. (Malachi 3:1–2, emphasis added)

The work of the fullers was to "cleanse garments and whiten them." Their abrasive soap was made of "salts mixed with oil" (Bible Dictionary, "Fullers"). Salt is a token of the covenant (see Matthew 5:13, footnote a; Leviticus 2:13; and Numbers 18:19). Gethsemane means "oil press" (*Strong's #1068*), and thus oil becomes symbolic of the Atonement. The Atonement was performed in the garden of the "oil press" and "great drops of blood" (Luke 22:44) were pressed out of our Savior's body.

Our own garments are "washed white" as we accept the Atonement of Jesus Christ and make it operative in our personal lives and as we keep covenants made in holy *places*.

In the middle of this beautiful, temple-laced sermon, Alma asks, "Behold, my brethren, do ye suppose that such an one can have a *place* to sit down in the kingdom of God, with Abraham, with Isaac, and with Jacob, and also all the holy prophets, whose *garments* are cleansed and are *spotless, pure and white?*" (Alma 5:24, emphasis added).

There is the word *place* again—used in another temple-like setting. It is in the temple where we receive the promises given to Abraham, Isaac, and Jacob. In latter-day revelation—just after the Lord revealed the law pertaining to the new and everlasting covenant of marriage— He then said, "Go ye, therefore, and do the works of Abraham; enter ye into my law and ye shall be saved. But if ye enter not into my law ye cannot receive the promise of my Father, which he made unto Abraham" (see D&C 132:19, 32–33).

The path that leads to the temple is the path we all must strive for and the *place* for an addict's recovery. The Hebrew word for *tent* is *ohel*, and it means covering, dwelling-place, home, tabernacle, or tent (see *Strong's* #168). The tent is a symbol—not the ultimate destination.

"I MADE THE CHILDREN OF ISRAEL TO DWELL IN BOOTHS"

According to the law of Moses, there were three times each year when every male of the covenant was commanded to "appear before the Lord . . . in the *place* which he [the Lord] shall choose." The three times were at the Feast of Unleavened Bread, the Feast of Weeks, and the Feast of Tabernacles (see Deuteronomy 16:16; Exodus 23:17).

The Feast of Tabernacles, or Ingathering, was considered to be the "greatest and most joyful of all." It eventually became known as simply "the feast" (see John 7:37). The Bible Dictionary states, "The events celebrated were the sojourning of the children of Israel in the wilderness and the gathering-in of all the fruits of the year" (Bible Dictionary, "Feasts"). There were two significant parts to this celebration—the celebration of a newfound life in the wilderness and a celebration of thanksgiving for the bounteous harvest at the end of the year. Both parts of this celebration have their counterparts in recovery from addiction. There is newfound sobriety and a new life for those addicts who venture into an uncharted recovery wilderness. It is a time for the discovery of new emotions and feelings. Many in recovery refer to this early sobriety as "pink cloud sobriety"—they acknowledge feeling as if they are floating around on a pink cloud and wandering around in a new wilderness of adventure.

They must remember why they are wandering around in this new wilderness. It is because they have been delivered by the hand of the Lord out of the land of Egypt—or "out of the house of bondage." The Lord said, "I am the Lord thy God, which have brought thee out of the land of Egypt, out of the house of bondage" (Exodus 20:2). The central message for the addict, as it relates to the Feast of Tabernacles, is that this is a major celebration of thanksgiving for the fact that the Lord, the Great I AM, has delivered him or her out of bondage. Alma aptly describes the scene of deliverance in Alma 36, and he likens it to his own recovery and spiritual rebirth:

> I will praise him forever, for he has brought our fathers out of Egypt, and he has swallowed up the Egyptians in the Red Sea; and he led them by his power into the promised land; yea, and he has delivered them out of bondage and captivity from time to time.
>
> Yea, and he has also brought our fathers out of the land of Jerusalem; and he has also, by his everlasting power, delivered them out of bondage and captivity, from time to time even down to the present day; and I have always retained in remembrance their captivity; yea, and ye also ought to retain in remembrance, as I have done, their captivity." (Alma 36:28–29)

There is the early, pink cloud sobriety, and there is the more seasoned recovery, which is a gathering or an inventory of all the Lord has restored to those in sobriety. It is an attitude of gratitude—a time of thanksgiving for all the blessings of the Lord. This Ingathering, or feast of thanksgiving, has its ties to our own Thanksgiving celebration. Many historians and scholars believe that the pilgrims used the Feast of Tabernacles as the Biblical basis for the first Thanksgiving feasts. Both celebrations would have been in the autumn, at the end of the harvest season.

The timing of the Feast of Tabernacles has its connections with the Sabbath. The Lord said, "The fifteenth day of this *seventh month* shall be the feast of tabernacles for *seven* days unto the Lord." He further said, "Also in the fifteenth day of the *seventh* month, when ye have gathered in the fruit of the land, ye shall keep a feast unto the Lord *seven* days: on the first day shall be a *sabbath*, and on the eighth day shall be a *sabbath*" (Leviticus 23:34, 39, emphasis added). In ancient Israel, a Sabbath was observed not only every seven days, but also in the seventh month and every seventh year. These seventh days, months, and years were "consecrated to the Lord" (see Bible Dictionary, "Sabbatical Year").

The characteristic feature of the Feast of Tabernacles, and from whence it gets its name, is the practice of dwelling in booths. The Lord said, "And ye shall keep it a feast unto the Lord *seven* days in the year. It shall be a statute for ever in your generations: ye shall celebrate it in the *seventh* month. Ye shall dwell in booths *seven* days; all that are Israelites born shall dwell in booths" (Leviticus 23:41–42, emphasis added). Again, there is a Sabbath connection and a connection with the symbolism of the number seven. Remember, the number seven represents completeness or perfection. In an eternal quest for perfection, all are on a journey of spiritual progress. There is some irony here. A booth is not a perfect dwelling-place, and yet the children of Israel were commanded to dwell in the booth for *seven* days, representing perfection.

Recovery is similar. No one works a perfect program. The *Big Book* says, "No one among us has been able to maintain anything like perfect adherence to these principles." Yet addicts must be "willing to grow along spiritual lines" (p. 60). Makeshift booths in the wilderness are far from a firm foundation. That is why they must rely "wholly upon the merits of him who is mighty to save" (2 Nephi 31:19). It is not personal perfection, but rather being "perfect in Christ" (Moroni 10:32–33) that will see addicts to the completion of their journey.

Let's look at some more of the language surrounding the Feast of Tabernacles. The Lord said that this celebration should be observed and remembered, "That your generations may know that I made the children of Israel to dwell in booths, when I brought them out of the land of Egypt: I am the Lord your God" (Leviticus 23:43). He reminds us again that He is the Great "I AM"—the God of Abraham, Isaac, and Jacob.

Whenever addicts see the word *Egypt* in the scriptures, they should think of bondage. There is nothing inherently bad about Egypt as a place or country; it just happens to be the place where the children of Israel were in bondage. When the Lord revealed Himself as the Great

I AM to Moses, he said, "I have surely seen the affliction of my people which are in Egypt, and have heard their cry by reason of their taskmasters; for I know their sorrow; And I am come down to deliver them out of the hand of the Egyptians, and to bring them *up* out of that land unto a good land . . . flowing with milk and honey" (Exodus 3:7–8, emphasis added).

Addicts' personal places of bondage may have had different settings. My own bondage began in the great and spacious building on the floor of vain imagination in the denial suite. It was later found in smoky, dingy, and dimly lit bars. Eventually it shrunk to the confines of my compact car as I sat inside drinking all alone at 3 a.m. in the middle of January. My drinking had gone from pleasurable recreation (so I believed in denial) to a painful compulsion. I felt as though I had a taskmaster over me, telling me I had to keep drinking. I was obedient because I felt like I would die otherwise. Little did I realize, that I had died spiritually long ago.

The Lord also said, "And thou shalt *rejoice before* the Lord thy God, thou, and thy son, and thy daughter . . . in the *place* which the Lord thy God hath chosen to *place his name* there. And thou shalt remember that thou wast a *bondman* in *Egypt*. . . . Thou shalt observe the feast of tabernacles seven days" (Deuteronomy 16:11–13, emphasis added). Footnote a in verse 12 tells us that the word *bondman* means slave. For addicts, drugs of choice become taskmasters, and they become slaves to them.

Remember that the Feast of Tabernacles was the "most joyful" of all feasts (see Bible Dictionary, "Feasts"). Indeed, once the Lord has delivered someone from the bondage of addiction, he or she really does have cause to celebrate and be joyful! Of course, I'm talking about the righteous kind of celebration with joy and gratitude being given to the Lord—not the stinkin' thinkin' kind of celebration where an addict gets a little sobriety, and his or her internal "committee" says it's okay to go back out and "celebrate" just one more time.

That is what the Feast of Tabernacles was all about. It was a joyful celebration of deliverance from bondage. I would call it a celebration of sobriety and recovery.

In the Book of Nehemiah, it was a double celebration. The children of Israel had now been delivered out of bondage twice. They were delivered out of Egypt in the days of Moses (see Exodus 14), and they have just come out of Babylonian captivity. Notice the language in Nehemiah: "And all the congregation of them that were come *again* out of the *captivity* made booths and sat under the booths" (Nehemiah 8:17, emphasis added). This is clearly the Feast of Tabernacles. A previous verse states, "And they found written in the law which the Lord had commanded by Moses, that the children of Israel should dwell in booths in the *feast of the seventh month*" (Nehemiah 8:14, emphasis added). Verse 17 also points out, "And there was very great gladness." The same holds true for addicts. Each of them has a special time of year to celebrate a sobriety birthday. Mine is July 31st. They celebrate and express gratitude to the Lord for their deliverance from bondage.

Now let's look at the booths themselves. The Lord said, "And ye shall take you on the first day the boughs of goodly trees, branches of *palm* trees, and the boughs of thick trees, and *willows* of the *brook*; and ye shall rejoice before the Lord your God seven days" (Leviticus 23:40, emphasis added). In the celebration described in Nehemiah, the people were told to "Go forth unto the *mount*, and fetch *olive* branches, and *pine* branches, and *myrtle* branches, and *palm* branches, and branches of thick trees, to make booths, as it is written" (Nehemiah 8:15, emphasis added).

Notice they were not commanded to make strong roofs made of asphalt shingles, tarpaper, or even something that would hold out the rain, like thatch. In fact, the meal at the Feast of Tabernacles is not supposed to begin until the third star in the sky can be seen through the roof of the booth. If you can see stars through the top, then you can get rained on too. The booth is a temporary, makeshift, and flimsy dwelling, yet this was the most joyous celebration of the year in ancient Israel. What is the message here?

First, for addicts, myself included of course, the journey of recovery is not finished yet. We are still wandering around in a newfound wilderness. For now, we are dwelling in booths en route to something far better. Lehi and his family traveled in tents as they sojourned in the wilderness, but as soon as Nephi and his people arrived in the land of Nephi, they constructed a temple and buildings (see 2 Nephi 5:15–17).

The second lesson is that we are fallen, mortal beings. King Benjamin begins his address to his people by saying, "I have not commanded you to come up hither that ye should fear me, or that ye should think that I of myself am more than a mortal man. But I am like as yourselves, subject to all manner of infirmities in body and mind." He also draws an analogy later in the sermon by saying, "And ye behold that I am old, and am about to yield up this *mortal frame* to its mother earth" (Mosiah 2:10–11, 26; emphasis added). A mortal frame, made of the dust of the earth, could be likened to a booth that has a framework of tree branches, which also grew out of their mother earth. However, King Benjamin finishes his address by saying:

> Therefore, I would that ye should be *steadfast* and *immovable*, always abounding in good works, that Christ, the Lord God Omnipotent, may seal you his, that you may be *brought to heaven*, that ye may have everlasting salvation and eternal life, through the wisdom, and power, and justice, and mercy of him who created all things, in heaven and in earth, who is God above all" (Mosiah 5:15, emphasis added).

To make matters worse for some of us—besides being mortal, we are addicts, subject to sickness, weakness, tribulation, leaky roofs, temptation, *and* relapse. For us, like a flimsy booth, our lives and our sobriety are fragile. One drink, one drug, or one little peek at pornography could land us back in Egypt, Babylon, or jail. But similar to King Benjamin's promises, if we are willing to "bind [ourselves] to act in all holiness" (D&C 43:9) before Christ, the Lord God Omnipotent, we will be brought to the promised land of recovery, and we will eventually receive eternal life.

As addicts symbolically journey through the wilderness in their booths, they can see the stars through the holes in the roof, and they may have a little rain fall on them. They are exposed to the elements— the heat, cold, wind, and bad weather—yet they can travel like Abraham. They may almost hear a voice saying, "My name is Jehovah, and I know the end from the beginning; therefore my hand shall be over thee." As they sit under a booth with a faulty roof, they can take comfort, like Abraham, in knowing that "eternity [is their] covering and [their] rock and [their] salvation, as [they journey]" (see Abraham 2:8, 16).

In such humble dwellings, I am reminded that "no flesh . . . can *dwell* in the presence of God, save it be through the merits, and mercy, and grace of the Holy Messiah, who layeth down his life according to the *flesh*, and taketh it again by the power of the Spirit" (2 Nephi 2:8, emphasis added).

Looking again at the elements of the feast in Leviticus 23:40, *palm* branches and *willows of the brook* are gathered for this celebration of rejoicing.

The palm branches represent Christ's triumphal victory over death, hell, and bondage. When Jesus made His triumphal entry into Jerusalem less than a week before His death, the people "took branches of *palm* trees, and went forth to meet him, and cried, Hosanna: Blessed is the King of Israel that cometh in the name of the Lord" (John 12:13, emphasis added). For addicts, the spiritual message behind the palm branches is that they must put Christ at the center of their recovery if they want to be victorious in their battles against addiction. For non-addicts, Christ must be at the center of their lives.

The "willows of the brook" were used to make a canopy over the altar. Every morning of the feast, there was a procession to the Kidron Valley where the willows were gathered. These willows would have been watered by the Gihon Spring, particularly before the time when Hezekiah had a tunnel built that diverted the water inside the walls of Jerusalem to the Pool of Siloam. The name Gihon means to gush out or burst forth (see *Strong's* #1521). This would be "living water"—like a "well of water springing up into everlasting life" (John 4:10, 14). Like the willows grown in the Kidron Valley, everyone's spiritual growth depends on how completely they turn to the Savior—the source of "living water."

In Nehemiah, the people were commanded to "go forth unto the *mount* [symbolic of the temple] and fetch *olive* branches, and *pine* branches, and *myrtle* branches, and *palm* branches. . . to make booths, as it is written" (Nehemiah 8:15).

Let's look at the symbolism here.

The Olive Branch

Gethsemane means "oil press" (see *Strong's* #1068). The Garden of Gethsemane was situated on the slope of the Mount of Olives. Pure olive oil would be produced by such an "oil press." The olive branches represent the Atonement of our Savior as He suffered in Gethsemane. It is that very Atonement that delivers all of us from bondage and makes recovery possible. Pure olive oil is used in priesthood blessings for the healing of the sick. Thus, the olive branches become symbolic of the healing power of the Atonement of Christ.

The Pine Branch

This branch also has a Gethsemane connection. The name Gethsemane comes from two Hebrew words—*gath* (meaning press or a vat) and *shemen* (meaning oil or ointment; see *Strong's* #1660 and #8081). The original Hebrew word for pine is *shemen*. *Shemen* can also mean fatness, a substance used for anointing, or a fruitful land or valley. Thus, a pine or *shemen* branch could also represent the blessings of fruitfulness and prosperity according to the Abrahamic covenant. It can also be symbolic of the ordinance of anointing. Like the olive branch, it represents the healing balm of the Atonement.

The Myrtle Branch

The myrtle shrub or tree is actually an evergreen tree. When I think of an evergreen tree, I think of a tree that will endure the harsh weather and cold storms. It is something that lasts forever, unlike an addict's drug of choice, which only brings fleeting pleasure and is always followed by constant compulsion and severe suffering. Addicts can experience a lasting "peace of conscience" (Mosiah 4:3), which would have been inconceivable when they were in the throes of addiction.

The Palm Branch

The palm branch represents the assurance of triumph over temptation and addiction. Paul said, "But thanks be to God, which giveth us the victory through our Lord Jesus Christ" (1 Corinthians 15:57).

Like everything else in the law of Moses, the hypothetical and symbolic booths in the wilderness of sobriety are composed of elements that point souls to Christ (see Jacob 4:5). There may be a hole in the roof, but nevertheless, the shelter from the storms of life and the raging world of addiction is pretty secure with eternity as "our covering and our rock and our salvation" (Abraham 2:16).

LIBATION AND LIGHT

This was perhaps the most joyous part of the Feast of Tabernacles. The Bible Dictionary states, "Of this [the tradition of drawing water from the Pool of Siloam and its libation on the altar] it was said that he who has not seen the joy of the drawing of water at the Feast of Tabernacles does not know what joy is" (Bible Dictionary, "Feasts").

The tradition included a daily procession to the Pool of Siloam. Music and trumpet sounding were part of the celebration. The priest, who led the procession, would come in through the Water Gate with a pitcher of water. The water was poured into a receptacle on the altar. You can see the Pool of Siloam and the Water Gate on map 12 of your scriptures. Perhaps the latter-day reference of those who are called to preside over us—"He that is ordained of me shall come in at the gate and be ordained" (D&C 43:7)—has reference to a similar gate (like the Water Gate), enabling us to plainly discern those who have been called and *sent* forth to link us with the "true vine" of Christ (see John 15:1). You will also notice that the temple is in close proximity to the Pool of Siloam and the Water Gate.

This water libation represents both sacrifice and communion with the Lord. It represents sacrifice as precious water is poured on the altar of sacrifice. The Feast of Tabernacles comes right before the rainy season in Israel. Water is necessary to soften the soil so the ground can be plowed in advance of spring planting. Thus, this ritual becomes a symbol of sacrifice and is a leap of faith. The people must wait for more rain.

With our Savior's mortal ministry and Atonement, the law of Moses was fulfilled, and this feast was no longer required. However, it took on additional meaning as He was careful to always attend the three required feasts. It was on the last day of the Feast of Tabernacles that Jesus said, "If any man thirst, let him come unto me, and drink. He that believeth on me, as the scripture hath said, out of his belly shall flow rivers of *living water*" (John 7:37–38, emphasis added; see also v. 2; 4:10–14). Thus, this "living water" also represents communion with Christ.

Anyone like me who drank gallons and gallons, trying to fill up the perpetual "God hole," yet always needing just one more drink, can celebrate and be joyous that the "living water" of the Savior really will fill them up, so they never become thirsty again. When you buy "living water," you are really buying a "well of water springing up into everlasting life" (John 4:14). No wonder Jacob and Isaiah say, "Come, my brethren, every one that thirsteth, come ye to the waters" (2 Nephi 9:50; see also Isaiah 55:1).

The water drawn from the Pool of Siloam is laced with covenant and temple implications. The water originates at the Gihon Spring. It then runs through Hezekiah's Tunnel and is brought within the city walls to the Pool of Siloam.

Solomon was anointed king of Israel with a "horn of oil out of the tabernacle" at the Gihon Spring. He rode to Gihon on King David's mule (see 1 Kings 1:38–39,45). This became a sign or a symbol for the king in Israel. The king always rode a mule. It established the pattern for the Savior when He made His triumphal entry into Jerusalem amid palm branches and "sitting on an ass's colt" as the people cried out, "Blessed is the King of Israel that cometh in the name of the Lord" (see John 12:13–15). At the waters of the Gihon Spring, one could be anointed to become a king or a queen in Israel.

The water from this spring runs into the Pool of Siloam, where it is drawn to be poured on the altar. These waters are referred to as the "waters of Shiloah" in the Old Testament. Isaiah said, "Forasmuch as this people refuseth the waters of Shiloah that go softly . . . behold, the Lord bringeth up upon them the waters of the river, strong and many." In other words, since these people reject the waters of Shiloah, which go softly and have a gentle, healing effect upon the soul, they are left with a strong current of a river that runs out of control and goes over the bank. Some addiction language appears later in the chapter when it is prophesied that "many among them shall stumble and fall, and be broken, and be snared, and be taken" (see 2 Nephi 18:6–8, 15). The imagery of a raging river that sweeps away everything in its path is an accurate likeness to the dangerous current of addiction.

The Pool of Siloam is the site where Jesus healed a man who was born blind. This miracle was performed on the Sabbath, which gives it an additional connection to the Feast of Tabernacles. "[Jesus] spat on the ground, and made *clay* of the spittle, and he *anointed* the eyes of the blind man with the *clay*, And said unto him, Go, *wash* in the pool of Si-loam, (which is by interpretation, Sent.) He went his way therefore, and *washed*, and came seeing" (see John 9:1–14, emphasis added).

King Benjamin prophesied that "the Lord Omnipotent who reigneth . . . shall come down from heaven among the children of men, and shall dwell in a *tabernacle of clay*" (Mosiah 3:5, emphasis added). The clay be-comes symbolic of our fallen, carnal, earthy, and mortal state. It is as if the Savior is telling this man that he must be able to wipe away the film of mortal existence. If he can see past the earthy and the sensual, then he can see into the eternities and have eternal vision. But first, he must wash away the carnal and sensual elements.

There are two ordinances involved here—a washing and an anoint-ing. Through the proper authority and priesthood ordinances, the man is able to come away seeing.

The irony here is that those who see well physically are spiritually blind, and he who was physically blind has 20/20 spiritual vision. Sometimes this physical world can be devilish and degrading, and sometimes it is just carnal, temporal, and distracting. In either event, it can impair our spiritual acuity. Jesus said, "I am come into this world, that they which see not might see; and that they which see might be made blind" (John 9:39).

Like the blind man at the Pool of Siloam, the spiritual insights gained in recovery are greatly enhanced by priesthood ordinances, administered by those having proper priesthood authority, and by the making and keeping of sacred covenants in sacred places. The blind man received an *anointing* and a *washing*. John's record makes it perfectly clear that there are ordinances and commissioned authority at work here. Notice the ac-count does not say that Jesus rubbed some mud on the blind man's eyes and told him to rinse it off with something. It specifically says *anointed* and *washed*, and the man was directed to a particular pool.

Even the name of the pool is significant. It is seldom in the scrip-tures that we get a direct translation from a Hebrew word given right in the text. It is probably inserted here for emphasis. The Hebrew word is *Shiloah*, and it means *sent*—just like the narration states (see *Strong's*

#7975). Notice that the word *Sent* is capitalized, perhaps suggesting a name or title. The Greek New Testament word for *Sent* is *apostello*. It is from the same word as the English word *apostle*. It basically means to receive a mission call and to be sent away to an appointed place for a specific calling. It can also mean to be set at liberty (see *Strong's #649*). This latter definition is especially appealing to the addict.

Our apostles and prophets and others who are called and appointed were prepared, chosen, and foreordained before coming to this earth. They "*stood* in the [council] of the Lord" (Jeremiah 23:18, emphasis added. The word *counsel* is changed to *council* . The original Hebrew word *cowd* can be translated to either *council* or *counsel*; see *Strong's #5475*; see also Abraham 3:23). They were prepared, called, foreordained, and *sent* forth to be "special witnesses of the name of Christ in all the world" (D&C 107:23) and to hold priesthood keys necessary to perform saving ordinances.

Because these critical priesthood keys have been restored to the earth through the Prophet Joseph Smith, we can receive the blessings of priesthood ordinances. These keys have been conferred upon stake presidents, bishops, and other Church leaders. As we hearken to the counsel of our Church leaders, we can have spiritual insights and be able to see things we could not see before. Priesthood ordinances such as baptism and temple ordinances help us wash away the muddy and the mundane things from our eyes, so we can see with new vision, clarity, and perspective.

"I AM THE LIGHT OF THE WORLD"

Our Lord made two statements regarding the ceremonies at the Feast of Tabernacles. The first had to do with living water. He said, "If any man thirst, let him come unto me, and drink. He that believeth on me, as the scripture hath said, out of his belly shall flow rivers of living water" (John 7:37–38).

The second statement appears in the next chapter, as Jesus said, "I am the light of the world: he that followeth me shall not walk in darkness, but shall have the light of life" (John 8:12; see also Bible Dictionary, "Feasts").

During the Feast of Tabernacles, four large golden candelabras were used to light the temple courts. Each lamp stand had four bowls, which were filled with oil. The light from these candelabra was supposed to permeate every court and corner in Jerusalem.

The symbolism is clear. The light of the Savior should penetrate every aspect of our lives, no matter who we are and no matter what temptations we are struggling with. Individual recovery programs for addicts must be built upon the foundation of rigorous honesty. There can be no dark alleys with sickly secrets.

As we look forward to the Second Coming, we need to make sure our light does not go out. Remember the parable of the ten virgins. It would be awful to be in the same predicament as the five foolish virgins, who let their lamps go out because they failed to take oil with them when they waited for the Bridegroom. The foolish virgins pleaded with the wise, saying, "Give us of your oil." The wise answered by saying that it doesn't work that way. They said, "Go ye rather to them that sell, and buy for yourselves" (see Matthew 25:1–13).

We must look to the "true Light, which lighteth every man that cometh into the world" (John 1:9). In our dispensation the Lord has said, "The glory of God is intelligence, or, in other words, *light* and truth. *Light* and truth forsake that evil one" (D&C 93:36–37, emphasis added). They also keep addicts clean and sober.

There is a link between *light* and *truth* as explained in D&C 93 and Step Eleven: "Sought through prayer and meditation to improve our conscious contact with God as we understood Him, praying only for *knowledge* of His will for us and the *power* to carry that out" (emphasis added). What we are really praying for is God-like intelligence. In our modern vocabulary, we use the words *light* and *power* almost interchangeably. Light is a source of energy or power. The lights go out when the power goes out. Truth is defined as "knowledge of things as they are, and as they were, and as they are to come" (D&C 93:24). In Step Eleven, addicts pray for knowledge of God's will for them and power to carry it out. Light equals power, and truth equals knowledge.

After the Lord rescued the house of Israel from bondage, a clear pattern of progression was established. He commanded them to dwell in flimsy booths for seven days. Then He gave them ordinances to be performed in the tabernacle, a portable temple. The tabernacle had a candlestick, reminding them of the Light of Christ (see Exodus 25:31; 27:20). It had a table of shewbread, a forerunner to the sacrament, suggesting His presence (see Bible Dictionary, "Shewbread"). Within the veil was the ark of the covenant, and upon its lid was the mercy seat. It was "God's throne in Israel" (see Bible Dictionary, "Tabernacle"; Exodus 25:22).

At the time of Solomon, a permanent temple was established. "The glory of the Lord had filled the house of the Lord" (1 Kings 8:11). Solomon offered the dedicatory prayer for the new temple during the Feast of Tabernacles (see 1 Kings 8:2).

Jehovah, the Great I Am, had taken His people from bondage, to booths, to a tabernacle, and finally to a temple. May we go and do likewise.

hands filled with sweet incense and clear stones

Once each year on the Day of Atonement, the high priest would enter the tabernacle to perform a series of atonements. These were a type of the true and infinite Atonement of Jesus Christ. Let us examine this day of fasting in ancient Israel. The process involves much ritual and is quite interesting. It is described in Leviticus 16.

This is also where the term *scapegoat* originated. The high priest would cast lots on two goats. One would be sacrificed for a sin offering, and the other (the scapegoat) would be sent away into the wilderness, where it would carry away the sins of the people into a "solitary land" (see Bible Dictionary, "Fasts"; see also Leviticus 16:8–10). I think you would agree that this is an interesting way to work Step Seven: "Humbly asked Him to remove our shortcomings." Personally, I would only trust the Lord to remove my sins! Alma said to his son Corianton, "Behold, I say unto you, that it is he [Christ] that surely shall come to take away the sins of the world" (Alma 39:15; see also John 1:29). I'm not going to trust a goat in the desert to take away my character defects. But I *will* trust the Lord!

In Leviticus 16: 12–13, a very meaningful ordinance is performed by the high priest: "And he shall take a censer [shovel] full of burning coals of fire from off the altar before the Lord, and his *hands full* of sweet incense beaten small, and bring it within the vail: And he shall put the incense upon the fire before the Lord, that the cloud of the incense may cover the mercy seat that is upon the testimony, that he die not" (emphasis added).

These two verses are loaded with meaningful symbolism. The burning coals are purifiers, which burn away sin and impurities. It is reminiscent of Isaiah's calling, when he said:

> Woe is me! for I am undone; because I am a man of unclean lips, and I dwell in the midst of a people of unclean lips: for mine eyes have seen the King, the Lord of hosts.
>
> Then flew one of the seraphims unto me, having a *live coal* in his hand, which he had taken with the tongs from off the altar:
>
> And he laid it upon my mouth, and said, Lo, this hath touched thy lips; and thine iniquity is taken away, and thy sin purged. (Isaiah 6: 5–7, emphasis added)

After Isaiah had been cleansed from sin, he had the courage to answer the Lord's call to serve as a messenger by saying, "Here am I; send me" (Isaiah 6:8).

In Step Six, "Were entirely ready to have God remove all these defects of character," addicts become willing to lay aside their sins and place them on the altar of sacrifice, allowing them to be consumed by fire. Scriptural passages like 3 Nephi 9:20, which speak of a baptism of fire and of the Holy Ghost, also refer to the cleansing power of the Spirit, which sanctifies us from all unrighteousness. The sanctifying power of the Holy Ghost is tied to priesthood ordinances. This Mosaic ordinance, performed by a high priest of the Aaronic order—which is not the same as the office of high priest in the Melchizedek Priesthood—is an example of the connection between the sanctifying influence of the Holy Ghost and priesthood ordinances.

As we enter the waters of baptism, and as we partake of the sacrament, we have the promise of the Lord that we will "always have his Spirit to be with [us]" (D&C 20:77). The influence of the Spirit is a great cleanser and sanctifier in recovery. Those who obtain the priesthood and magnify their callings are also "sanctified by the Spirit unto the renewing of their bodies" (D&C 84:33). That is a marvelous promise, especially if your body has become contaminated with alcohol, drugs, or pornography. I should point out that repentance is a prerequisite for these blessings and ordinances.

The burning coals, which purge our uncleanness, are taken from the altar of sacrifice. This suggests that we must be willing to give away our sins and character defects, and place them on the altar of sacrifice. The phrase "before the Lord" in Leviticus 16:12 implies that our sacrificial offering is presented perpetually and placed in front of, or in the presence of, the Lord (see *Strong's Exhaustive Concordance of the Bible* #6440). We can do this in the form of prayer as our pleas to have our shortcomings removed ascend upward into the ears of the Lord. Such sincere prayer is also symbolized by a cloud of smoke from the burning incense as it ascends upward into heaven (see Revelation 5:8; 8:3).

Besides the burning coals, the high priest carried incense into the Holy of Holies. The above verse in Leviticus 16 states that the incense was brought "within the vail." Thus, we can see that it is brought into the Holy of Holies, or the most sacred part of the tabernacle, which contained the mercy seat, or God's throne in Israel, and was where He would come to commune with His people. This should give us insight into the sacred nature of the incense.

The high priest fills *both* of his hands with "sweet incense." You will notice that *hand* is plural in verse 12. The Bible Dictionary emphasizes this point by stating that the high priest would take "a censer full of live coals from off the brazen altar with *two handfuls* of incense into the Holy of Holies" (Bible Dictionary, "Fasts," emphasis added). To only take one handful, would be a "half measure," which "avails us nothing." This becomes something greater than what has been offered in the past. This is not merely unloading some excess baggage or dumping off some of our sins. The hands filled with incense represent the very best we can offer to the Lord.

In a sense, we are exposing our hearts and baring our souls. Remember, the cloud of incense ascends toward heaven, as a prayer. The restoration of the gospel began with just such an offering. As Joseph Smith knelt in the Sacred Grove, he "began to offer up the desires of [his] heart to God" (Joseph Smith—History 1:15). Precious incense carries the seeds of communion with God.

It's not just any gift. Incense was imported from Arabia (see Bible Dictionary, "Frankincense"). One coming from afar to give praises to the Lord would only bring the most precious gifts. Frankincense is one of the ingredients in the holy incense. It was a gift worthy to be given to Jesus when He was a young child (see Matthew 2:11). The account in Leviticus 16 makes it clear that this is "sweet" incense. It is a highly valued gift.

This precious offering is even greater than that in Step Seven: "Humbly asked Him to remove our shortcomings." If you think it sounds like consecration, you are absolutely right! In fact, the Hebrew word for consecration literally means "to fill the open hand." It is actually a combination of two words—*male*, meaning "to fill," and *yad*, meaning "open hand" (see *Strong's* #4390 and #3027). In Hebrew there are two words for hand: *yad*, the open hand, and *kaph*, the closed hand (see *Strong's* #3709). This is the "open hand," indicating power, means, strength, or direction.

As the high priest fills his hands with precious incense, an act of consecration is literally being performed. He is bringing both his best and the most he is able to carry within the veil.

Even though we give our all in consecration, nothing is lost. I believe as we come before the Lord to make an offering we carry in our puny hands a very finite amount, although it may be all we have. But like our 10-percent tithe, the Lord returns the favor by opening the windows of heaven, and pouring out a blessing so great that there shall not be room enough to receive it (see Malachi 3:10). Each of us could say, "My cup runneth over" (Psalm 23:5). I believe that over time, the Lord gives us a bigger cup and bigger hands to hold the bigger blessings.

The Lord goes well beyond "filling the hand." He gives blessings that meet or exceed our capacity to receive them. As Jesus visited the Nephites and prayed for them, "so great was the joy of the multitude that they were overcome." But Jesus was not overcome. He was able to stand on His feet and bid the multitude to arise. As we become more like Him, our capacity for joy is increased (see 3 Nephi 17:18–20).

Returning to Leviticus 16, the great reward for living the law of consecration is set forth. As the high priest brings the censer of burning coals and his handfuls of sweet incense within the veil, he casts the incense upon the fire. A cloud of smoke covers the mercy seat, allowing him to feel of the presence of the Lord without being consumed by His glory (see Leviticus 16:13).

We have a similar promise in our day. When the Lord Jehovah appeared in the Kirtland Temple, He said, "For behold, I have accepted this house, and my name shall be here; and I will manifest myself to my people in mercy in this house" (D&C 110:7). The throne of God in ancient Israel was called the mercy seat. I know He still manifests Himself in mercy in His house.

Each day we must all consider our offering unto the Lord. Will we come before Him with our hands filled, so that He can pour out blessings upon us? Will we let Him fill our souls with everlasting joy?

My own feeble attempts often fall short, yet I know I have been blessed beyond measure as I try. I would have to say that the greatest blessing of recovery is to have communion with the Lord. As my prayers ascend like a cloud of burning incense, I know that He hears them. In return, He sends the sweetness of His Spirit and fills my soul. How great it is to feel of His love and tender mercy.

BEATEN SMALL, BEATEN WORK, BEATEN FOR THE LIGHT

Each of us must fill our hands and come before the Lord in a consecrated effort. As we do so, our gift to the Lord will be polished and refined. The Lord has said, "For he [the Lord] is like a refiner's fire, and like fullers' soap: And he shall sit as a refiner and purifier of silver: and he shall purify the sons of Levi, and purge them as gold and silver, that they may offer unto the Lord an offering in righteousness" (Malachi 3:2–3). The Lord as a Refiner of silver sits and watches the metal, until He sees His own reflection in the polished work. The best gift you can give the Lord will be yourself—"that when he shall appear we shall be like him, for we shall see him as he is . . . that we may be purified even as he is pure" (Moroni 7:48).

This is not an easy process. It takes heat and time to refine precious metals. The impurities must be burned away. Adversity will come. The Lord declares to the house of Israel, "I have refined thee, I have chosen thee in the furnace of affliction" (1 Nephi 20:10; see also Isaiah 48:10).

We are all somewhat like that precious incense being carried by the high priest within the veil. We, like the incense, are "beaten small" (Leviticus 16:12). We may at times feel beaten up or worn down, but it's all part of the refining process.

This process of becoming refined (or beaten) can be summarized by the Twelve Steps. They can be broken down as follows:

Steps 1–3 "Beaten small"

Steps 4–10 "Beaten work"

Steps 11–12 "Beaten for the light"

Beaten Small

"And he shall take a censer full of burning coals of fire from off the altar before the Lord, and his hands full of sweet incense *beaten small*, and bring it within the vail" (Leviticus 16:12, emphasis added).

In Step One, "We admitted we were powerless over alcohol [or other addictions of choice]—that our lives had become unmanageable," addicts admit their powerlessness, or smallness before the Lord. They have been beaten up and thoroughly defeated in the game of life. In recovery, we often speak of a "higher power." Some in the Church are offended by such a reference to Deity, but I needed just such a starting point in recovery. Even though I was a returned missionary and thought I knew the gospel, my concept of God was awfully messed up!

I always thought that God wanted me to control my own destiny. He'd given me a brain after all, but as I entered the rooms of Alcoholics Anonymous, I could see there were things in life that were bigger than me. Alcohol was one of them. A simple, chemical substance could control my whole life. I was obsessed with drinking every waking moment. Alcohol was one thing higher than me. I needed to find a power that was stronger and higher than alcohol. As I thought about it, I felt very small.

Next, I needed Step Two: "Came to believe that a Power greater than ourselves could restore us to sanity." Could I dare hope for such a thing? What if my dreams were crushed by some harsh reality that I could never be rescued from my world of drunkenness? Could He? Would He? My whole future was in His hands. I felt even smaller. Sanity and spiritual wholeness were such long shots to me.

What I really needed was Step Three: "Made a decision to turn our will and our lives over to the care of God as we understood Him." Then in a closed room on a Wednesday night with a bunch of drunks, I counted the cost. It was staggering. There had to be an "easier, softer way." Would I have to give Him my whole life? Would I have to surrender my will to let it become "swallowed up in the will of the Father?" (Mosiah 15:7) My will looked very, very small, yet it loomed so big.

The process of being "beaten small" (Leviticus 16:12), can either turn us bitter or sweet, like the incense. In the Book of Mormon we read, "Many had become hardened, because of the exceedingly great length of the war; and many were softened because of their afflictions, insomuch that they did humble themselves before God, even in the depth of humility" (Alma 62:41).

In the end, there are two kinds of smallness—smallness of character and smallness before the Lord that will bring us down to the "depth of humility." We get to pick.

Beaten Work

The Lord commanded Moses: "And thou shalt make a candlestick of pure gold: of *beaten work* shall the candlestick be made" (Exodus 25:31, emphasis added).

We can have all the humility and all the faith we want, and we can be totally willing to get down on our knees and surrender ourselves to God, but there comes a time when we must get up off our knees and go to work. Some of the steps are paired together. There is a willingness step, followed by an action step. Steps Six and Seven go together. In Step Six we "were entirely ready to have God remove all these defects of character." Then in Step Seven we "humbly asked Him to remove our shortcomings." Steps Eight and Nine also go together. In Step Eight we "made a list of all persons we had harmed, and *became willing* to make amends to them all" (emphasis added). Then in Step Nine we "made direct amends to such people wherever possible, except when to do so would injure them or others."

Recovering addicts will agree with me when I say, Steps Four through Ten are work. It is work to make a searching, written moral inventory. Especially when you have as many character defects as I do. It's not always easy for addicts to pick up the telephone and call their sponsor. It may be even harder for them to pick up the same telephone and make an appointment with their bishop to do a Fifth Step! It is a difficult thing for them to get down on their knees and plead with Heavenly Father to take away their shortcomings. It takes great effort to make a list of those they have harmed, and even then the work has only begun. They must track down all those people and attempt to make amends with them. Some will not be ready, and they may need to revisit them later. Each day it is important to do a mini-inventory. When they are wrong, they choke out two of the hardest words to say in the English language—"I'm sorry."

But each time addicts work through the steps, they are polished and refined just a bit more. It may feel like they are taking a beating, but they come out a little shinier, and they sparkle a little brighter with the afflictions the Lord sees fit to impose upon them. The same could be said of anyone struggling through adversity. Our feeling small, or our humility you could say, makes us realize how dependent we are on God's grace. None of us would be forgiven, and, in an addict's case, sober without the Lord's enabling power. Alone, we are still pretty small, but we also know that "by small means the Lord can bring about great things" (1 Nephi 16:29). Remember Ammon's words, "I will not boast of myself, but I will boast of my God, for in his strength I can do all things" (Alma 26:12).

Beaten for the Light

The Lord said to Moses, "Command the children of Israel, that they bring unto thee pure oil olive *beaten for the light*, to cause the lamps to burn continually" (Leviticus 24:2, emphasis added).

As previously discussed, pure olive oil is symbolic of the Atonement. Our Lord felt the weight of the whole world pressing down on Him in the Garden of Gethsemane. He was the only one who could perform such an atonement since He is the only one who was 100 percent pure. Spiritually speaking, there is only one place to go for pure olive oil. The healing balm of pure olive oil was bought and paid for in Gethsemane.

If we, addicts and non-addicts, want our lamps to burn brightly and continually, we must turn to our Savior and His Atonement. In order to make the Atonement operative in our lives, we must keep the Lord's commandments and partake of the power of sacred ordinances. As we make and keep covenants with the Lord, we will feel a new source of power flow into our personal lives.

A brightly burning lamp produces both knowledge and power—the two things addicts seek in Step Eleven: "Sought through prayer and meditation to improve our conscious contact with God as we understood Him, praying only for *knowledge* of His will for us and the *power* to carry that out." A good lamp illuminates the path before everyone. We are able to see and discern new spiritual insights, which were previously hidden in the dark. Our "mind[s] . . . begin to expand" (Alma 32:34).

A brightly burning lamp produces heat, energy, and power. It gives new life. It sustains us through adversity and gives addicts strength to work the Steps. It restores us to sanity and spiritual wholeness (see Step Two).

In Step Twelve, "Having had a spiritual awakening as the result of these steps, we tried to carry this message to alcoholics [or addicts], and to practice these principles in all our affairs," recovering addicts awake unto God. Alma describes his awakening by saying, "And oh, what joy, and what marvelous light I did behold; yea, my soul was filled with joy" (Alma 36:20). When one experiences such joy, there is a desire to share that newfound joy and "newness of life" (Romans 6:4) with others.

Regardless of our current struggles, we can become a light unto others. One of the great joys for an addict in recovery is to see how many are attracted by the light. Those addicts may become an instrument in the hands of God to help others and carry the message. It is humbling to realize it is not our own light we project to others. Jesus said, "Therefore, hold up your light that it may shine unto the world. Behold I am the light which ye shall hold up—that which ye have seen me do" (3 Nephi 18:24).

HANDS FILLED WITH "SMALL STONES . . . WHITE AND CLEAR"

I think this is one of the most fascinating stories in all of scripture. Its setting makes it even more appealing. The brother of Jared came forth at the time of the Tower of Babel (see Ether 1:33). The people at this time were attempting to "build . . . a tower, whose top may reach unto heaven," (Genesis 11:4) and thereby come into the presence of God. Genesis 11:6 suggests this is vain imagination, and the *Big Book of Alcoholics Anonymous* would call it "self-will run riot" (p. 62).

The story of the brother of Jared is a classic example of the balance between grace and works. Those who participated in building the Tower of Babel thought they could get into heaven on the basis of their own works—literally. The brother of Jared takes a different approach.

Instead of attempting to solve the problem of getting back into the presence of God by building a tower and relying upon his own works and abilities, the brother of Jared relies on the power of the Lord to overcome his fallen state. "The Lord showed himself unto [the brother of Jared], and said: Because thou knowest these things ye are redeemed from the fall; therefore ye are brought back into my presence; therefore I show myself unto you" (Ether 3:13). The brother of Jared was able to accomplish what others had tried to accomplish by building a tower.

Let's look at how he was enabled to come back into the presence of the Lord. First, instead of trying to build a high object, the brother of Jared used a high object that had already been created by the Lord. The brother of Jared "went forth unto the mount, which they called the mount Shelem, because of its exceeding height." In the mount he "did molten out of a rock sixteen small stones . . . and he did carry them in his *hands* upon the top of the mount" (Ether 3:1, emphasis added).

This demonstrates a balance between grace and works. It is not "self-will run riot," like the tower of Babel where the attitude is, "Hey, I can just build my own tower to heaven!" Nor does the brother of Jared sit at the bottom of the mount, waiting for the Lord to come down. He climbs to the very top, and when he has run out of mountain, he realizes that that is as far as his own works can carry him. He must then rely on the Lord to bridge the gap, knowing that His grace is sufficient to do so (see Ether 12:27; 2 Cor. 12:9).

Like the high priest on the Day of Atonement, the brother of Jared has both hands filled. Thus, this also becomes an act of consecration, or "filling the hand" (see Strong's #4390 and #3027; also Bible Dictionary, "Priests"). The word hand is plural once again. Like the high priest, the brother of Jared is carrying something small, refined, and precious in his hands. Like the high priest, he enters "within the veil" (Ether 3:20; see also Leviticus 16:12). But unlike the high priest, the brother of Jared comes directly into the presence of the Lord. It is not merely symbolic, and he doesn't need a cloud of incense to protect him from the glory of the Lord.

There are a couple of reasons for this. First is the obvious level of faith of the brother of Jared. His faith was so strong, that "he had faith no longer, for he knew, nothing doubting" (Ether 3:19). Another reason was the keys of the priesthood. The high priest in Leviticus was of the Aaronic order, but the brother of Jared would have held the same Melchizedek Priesthood as the patriarchs of old did. He was a seer who was given possession of the Urim and Thummim (see Ether 3:23; Joseph Smith—History 1:35). Moroni speaks of the faith of some of the ancient prophets, including the brother of Jared, and also says, "Behold it was by faith that they of old were called after the holy order of God" (see Ether 12:10, 20). We know from the cross-reference of this verse, which is Alma 13:3–4, that this "holy calling" or "holy order" is the Melchizedek Priesthood. "And without the ordinances thereof, and the authority of the [Melchizedek] priesthood, the power of godliness is not manifest unto men in the flesh; For without this no man can see the face of God, even the Father, and live" (D&C 84:21–22).

We can see from these examples that one of the great blessings of true consecration is communion with the Lord. We are eventually brought back into the presence of God through pure consecration.

Let's go back and dig a little deeper. The brother of Jared fills his hands with something perhaps even more precious than the "sweet incense" spoken of in Leviticus. He carries in his hands, small, clear, and white stones—"even as transparent glass" (Ether 3:1)—which are symbolic of our celestial potential.

In D&C 130 it states, "This earth, in its sanctified and immortal state, will be made like unto crystal and will be a Urim and Thummim to the inhabitants who dwell thereon." It further states, "Then the *white stone* mentioned in Revelation 2:17, will become a Urim and Thummim to each individual who receives one, whereby things pertaining to a higher order of kingdoms will be made known; And a *white stone* is given to each of those who come into the celestial kingdom, whereon is a new name written, which no man knoweth save he that receiveth it" (D&C 130:9–11, emphasis added).

John saw the celestial earth and the throne of God and described it by saying, "And before the throne there was a sea of *glass* like unto crystal" (Revelation 4:6, emphasis added). He also writes about the celestial city, "the holy Jerusalem," by saying, "Her light was like unto a stone most precious, even like a jasper stone, *clear* as crystal . . . And the street of the city was pure gold, as it were *transparent glass*" (Revelation 21:10, 11, and 21; emphasis added). These stones, which are white and clear like transparent glass, have ties to the celestial kingdom.

The brother of Jared "did *molten* out of a *rock* sixteen *small stones*" (Ether 3:1, emphasis added). One of the Hebrew roots for *molten* means to pour out or anoint, particularly as a king would be anointed (see *Strong's* #5258). Thus, it becomes a type of Christ—the "King of kings" (Revelation 19:16)—with temple significance. There is a connection with the ordinance of anointing. The word *Messiah* means "anointed one." The same Hebrew word also refers to the king and high priest of Israel, who were also anointed (see *Strong's* #4899; Bible Dictionary, "Messiah"; 1 Kings 1:39; 1 Kings 19:15–16; and Exodus 40:13–15).

There is some Atonement significance as well. Since the Hebrew word for *molten* means to anoint or pour out, it becomes symbolic of the Atonement. In Gethsemane and on Calvary, He "poured out his soul unto death" (Isaiah 53:12).

These small stones were molten out of a rock. Addicts in recovery must build a foundation "upon the rock of our Redeemer, who is Christ." He is the only "sure foundation, a foundation whereon if men build they cannot fall" (Helaman 5:12). This wonderful promise is an addict's assurance of staying clean and sober.

As our lives and characters are molten and shaped to match the image of the Savior, we truly can become "lively stones," being built into a "spiritual house, an holy priesthood, to offer up spiritual sacrifices, acceptable to God by Jesus Christ" (1 Peter 2:5). The only sacrifice acceptable to the Lord is a "broken heart and a contrite spirit" (3 Nephi 9:20).

"Lively stones," as Peter describes, are living stones. It means to have a true life and be blessed endlessly in the kingdom of God (see 1 Peter 2:5, footnote a; *Strong's* #2198). Peter would know. His name means *rock*. The Greek word *petros* means small rock or a stone, and the word *petra* means large rock, bedrock, or cliff (see Matthew 16:18, footnote a; *Strong's* #4074, #4073; and Bible Dictionary, "Cephas"). Christ is the "Stone of Israel" (Genesis 49:24).

It is not surprising that the brother of Jared has this temple-like experience—after all, he is standing upon the top of a mountain. The brother of Jared also received seer stones (see Ether 3:23–28). Thus, he was also a "rock" like unto Peter (see JST, John 1:42).

Then, in some of the most beautiful imagery in all of scripture, "the Lord stretched forth his hand and *touched* the stones *one by one* with his finger." This is the exact point when and where the brother of Jared's understanding of God changed significantly. "The veil was taken from off the eyes of the brother of Jared, and he saw the finger of the Lord" (Ether 3:6). He had a six-dimensional experience.

If Jesus is the true Rock—the Stone of Israel—and we are His "lively stones," created and molten in His image as He vividly shows to the brother of Jared that we are, by saying, "Seest thou that ye are created after mine own image? Yea, even all men were created in the beginning after mine own image" (Ether 3:15), then it follows that we are like small stones—touched by the finger of the Lord!

An Isaiah passage reminds us of our infinite and divine potential, as well as "what we used to be like, what happened, and what we are like now." It states, "Look unto the rock from whence ye are hewn, and to the hole of the pit from whence ye are digged" (2 Nephi 8:1; see also Isaiah 51:1). This verse refers to Abraham and Sarah, but it also applies nicely to the Savior. Each of us is "hewn" out in the image of the Savior, and each is a son or daughter "in the similitude of his Only Begotten" (Moses 1:13). But addicts cannot forget the wreckage from their pasts and the "hole of the pit from whence [they] are digged." Whether they allow the Savior to touch their individual lives, or, in this case, dig them out of the pit, will determine whether they turn out to be plain rocks buried in the dirt or gems that sparkle with the brilliance of His countenance. They must rely on His grace. They are not able to dig themselves out.

As "lively" or living "stones," the Lord touches each of our lives "one by one." He doesn't merely cover all the stones with His hand, lighting them all at once. Rather individual attention is given to each stone as the Light of the World touches them for good (see John 8:12; 3 Nephi 11:11). Each stone is unique in character and brilliance. Some may be harder, darker, rougher, and more jagged than others, yet all are touched and radiate a pure, divine light!

As we "fill the hand," offer our "whole souls as an offering unto him," and surrender our will and our lives to His loving care, we let go and allow Him to touch us (see *Strong's* #4390, #3027; Omni 1:26; and Step Three). When He touches our individual lives "one by one," we become illuminated with His marvelous light and receive a "newness of life" (see Romans 6:4). We become His "peculiar treasure," His "jewels," and a "kingdom of priests," or, in other words, kings and priests as we let go and allow Him to touch our lives (see Exodus 19:5–6; Malachi 3:17). We become spiritually begotten sons and daughters of God and heirs to the kingdom.

As we "turn our will and our lives over to the care of God," and as we pray "for knowledge of His will for us," according to Steps Three and Eleven, we are engaged in an act of consecration, or "filling the hand." Elder Neal A. Maxwell said:

> The submission of one's will is really the only uniquely personal thing we have to place on God's altar. The many other things we 'give,' brothers and sisters, are actually the things He has already given or loaned to us. However, when you and I finally submit ourselves, by letting our individual wills be swallowed up in God's will, then we are really giving some-

thing to Him! It is the only possession which is truly ours to give! Consecration thus constitutes the only unconditional surrender which is also a total victory! (Neal A. Maxwell, "Swallowed Up in the Will of the Father," *Ensign* [November 1995]: 22)

The brother of Jared is able to make such a complete consecration because of his great faith and trust in the Lord. He knows the Lord has "all power" and is able to "show him all things" (Ether 3:4, 26). His "conscious contact," according to Step Eleven, is greatly improved, as he comes face to face with the Lord. Although he had a wonderful understanding of God before, now he has an even greater understanding, realizing that the Lord had a spirit body in similitude of the body of flesh and blood, which He would later take upon Himself. Housed in a mortal body, He would "make intercession for all the children of men" (2 Nephi 2:9).

The brother of Jared now has greater knowledge and power, also according to Step Eleven. His knowledge of the true nature of God is greatly increased, and he now has a power source—stones molten out of a rock to light the vessels. "And thus the Lord caused stones to shine in darkness, to give light unto men, women, and children, that they might not cross the great waters in darkness" (Ether 6:3). The brother of Jared and all those who were with him are now able to carry out God's will and navigate their way to the promised land!

FOR THE BROTHER OF JARED, IT'S AS SIMPLE AS ONE, TWO, THREE

Let's review how the brother of Jared was able to work the steps, allowing him to come into the presence of the Lord upon the mount. He works Step One by admitting his powerlessness and his need for Christ's Atonement. His humility is evident by the following phrases:

"Do not be angry with thy servant because of his weakness before thee" (Ether 3:2).

"We are unworthy before thee; because of the fall our natures have become evil continually" (Ether 3:2).

He works Step Two by coming to believe in the Lord's ability to restore, rescue, and redeem him. His faith and understanding of God are made evident in the following phrases:

> "We know that thou art holy and dwellest in the heavens" (Ether 3:2).
> "From thee we may receive according to our desires" (Ether 3:2).
> "Thou hast been merciful unto us" (Ether 3:3).
> "And I know, O Lord, that thou hast all power, and can do whatsoever thou wilt for the benefit of man" (Ether 3:4).
> "Behold, O Lord, thou canst do this. We know that thou art able to show forth great power" (Ether 3:5).
> "Yea, Lord, I know that thou speakest the truth, for thou art a God of truth, and canst not lie" (Ether 3:12).

He works Step Three by "filling his hands" with the precious stones that represent the seeds of divinity. By "filling the hands," he makes a sacred covenant; and the *place* whereon he *stands* is "holy ground" (see Exodus 3:5). His act of "filling the hand" upon the top of the mount, which is symbolic of the temple, is an act of consecration. He shows his willingness to consecrate all that he has—including his will and his very life. He trusts the outcome to the Lord's loving care, and he is therefore able to "let go and let God!"

We see how thoroughly he has worked Step Three later on in chapter 6 of Ether as the brother of Jared and his family and friends board the barges. "They got aboard of their vessels or barges, and set forth into the sea, commending themselves unto the Lord their God" (Ether 6:4).

Next to the Savior's perfect Step Three in the Garden of Gethsemane, as He said, "not my will, but thine, be done" (Luke 22:42), this may be the second best Step Three ever worked! I can't imagine anything that would require more trust in the Lord than boarding a barge, knowing I would sometimes be "buried in the depths of the sea" (Ether 6:6) and having neither sail nor steering mechanism for guidance. They didn't have motors to propel them through the water, so they needed to rely wholly upon the Lord to provide a "furious wind" (Ether 6:5) and guide back any barges that veered off course.

As we view the brother of Jared upon the mount, we can tell that he has worked a few other steps as well. He has taken an inventory of his character, and he knows he has weaknesses before the Lord. He acknowledges his powerlessness before God and the fact that "because of the fall our *natures* have become evil continually" (see Ether 3:2, emphasis added). His Step Four inventory allows him to admit before God that his very *nature* has become corrupted and changed because of the Fall. Thus, he is able to admit "the exact *nature*" of his wrongs, according to Step Five.

The brother of Jared's willingness to submit his will and to consecrate himself to the Lord displays his desire "to have God remove all these defects of character," according to Step Six, and to also have his shortcomings removed according to Step Seven. As he seeks the Lord's righteousness, he becomes conscious of his weaknesses, which leave him naked before God, and, like Nephi, he is made to "shake at the appearance of sin!" (2 Nephi 4:31) Thus, he would also "shake" at any defects running contrary to God's will.

Like King Lamoni's father, his commitment to surrender can be aptly expressed in the line: "I will give away all my sins to know thee" (Alma 22:18). He knows the staggering price, but he also knows the payout; and with faith and commitment, he comes to know the Lord Jehovah face to face.

Steps Eight and Nine involve making amends to others. While we do not see these steps in his personal interaction with the Savior, we know the brother of Jared has great concern for others. The very stones he brings *down* off the mount will provide "light unto men, women, and children" (Ether 6:3).

Step Ten is a continuous, daily, personal inventory. The brother of Jared has obviously worked this one too, as he acknowledges, "We are unworthy before thee" (Ether 3:2).

"Conscious contact" (Step Eleven) doesn't get any better than this! His knowledge is greatly increased, and he is "endowed with power from on high" (D&C 38:32) on a mount known for its "exceeding height" (Ether 3:1). We see, once again, the relationship between knowledge and power—the two things we pray for in Step Eleven.

Now that the brother of Jared has had a "spiritual awakening," according to Step Twelve, he has become enlightened—much like the small, clear stones that he places in the vessels. Touched by the finger of the Lord, they, and he, can now "shine in darkness, to give light unto men, women, and children" (Ether 6:3). Thus, he can "carry [the] message" (Step Twelve) to others who are groping in the darkness.

Each of us can also become vessels of light. We can light the way for others. Recovering addicts will particularly find that their sobriety is like a testimony. They have to give it away to keep it. They will find great joy in sharing.

SCALE THE MOUNT

For recovering addicts and addicts who want to recover: If you find yourself wanting recovery but standing at the foot of the mount, then I would invite you to make that journey one step at a time. It is worth the sacrifice. Even in sobriety, you may think you are a long way from God, but do not be discouraged. As you make your best effort to climb the mountain, the Lord will come down to your level. He is your Mediator, pleading with the Father, saying, "Spare these my brethren that believe on my name, that they may come unto me and have everlasting life" (D&C 45:5). You may see steep cliffs towering overhead, but keep on clinging to the Rock! He promises that "Whoso . . . climbeth up by me shall never fall" (Moses 7:53).

The brother of Jared climbed to the top of the mount, where he was "redeemed from the fall . . . [and] brought back into [the Lord's] presence" (Ether 3:13) in a temple-like experience. An addict's ascent up the mount is more of a spiritual struggle, but you don't need to climb to the top of the mount to have a temple experience. You are blessed to have temples nearby, where you can enter into covenants with the Lord, which will give you the knowledge and power needed to someday enter into the presence of the Lord.

The brother of Jared brought down precious stones from the mount, giving light to the vessels in which he and his family and friends traveled. When we are able to go to the temple, we receive special knowledge and covenants. In the temple, the Lord can touch our individual lives—similar to those stones. Even though we keep the things of the temple sacred, and, like Paul, "we cannot . . . speak particularly" (Hebrews 9:5) regarding them, we can still take something away from the temple. Like the precious stones that the brother of Jared carried from the mount, the things we receive in the temple will light up our homes, workplaces, and even the rooms of recovery where we share our stories. Like the stones touched by the Savior, the knowledge gained will enrich our lives.

I invite you to fill your hands full and bring the best you have as an offering unto the Lord. Consecrate yourself to Him. Surrender your will and your life to His loving care. You can trust Him. "Yea, come unto him, and offer your whole souls as an offering unto him" (Omni 1:26). As you "fill the hand" and bring it unto the Lord, He will "open you the windows of heaven, and pour you out a blessing, that there shall not be room enough to receive it" (Malachi 3:10).

king benjamin's feast of tents and ammon's twelve-step call

In chapter 14, we looked at the imagery of the Feast of Tabernacles and saw how the Lord brought the children of Israel out of the "house of bondage" (Exodus 20:2) and commanded them to "dwell in booths seven days" (Leviticus 23:42) each year. Then He commanded them to build a tabernacle, and, finally, a temple.

This pattern seems to be a model for recovery for any kind of addiction. The Feast of Tabernacles was simply called "The Feast" and was considered the "greatest and most joyful of all" the feasts. "The events celebrated were the sojourning of the children of Israel in the wilderness (Leviticus 23:43), and the gathering-in of all the fruits of the year" (see Bible Dictionary, "Feasts").

One might not think it would be such a joyous event to wander in the wilderness for forty years, but remember that the children of Israel had been delivered out of Egypt—out of bondage and away from their taskmasters. Even though recovery takes time and is a new experience for all of us, welcome the challenge and celebrate your newfound freedom! For the addict, the Feast of Tabernacles is a symbol of joyous celebration of sobriety and recovery! The Lord Himself makes the connection between coming out of bondage and the Feast of Tabernacles by saying, "That your generations may know that I made the children of Israel to dwell in booths, when I brought them out of the land of Egypt: I am the Lord your God" (Leviticus 23:43).

There is a connection with the number *seven*. It symbolizes completeness or perfection. Recovering addicts know they are not going to be perfect today. They live for today in sobriety, so they prefer "spiritual progress" over "spiritual perfection" (*Big Book of Alcoholics Anonymous*, p. 60). Nevertheless, perfection is the eternal quest of us all no matter what our temptations are, and we are commanded to become perfect (see Matthew 5:48; 3 Nephi 12:48). The Sabbath day, or seventh day, is also symbolic of deliverance from bondage. Deuteronomy 5:15 states, "And remember that thou wast a servant in the land of Egypt, and that the Lord thy God brought thee out thence through a mighty hand and by a stretched out arm: therefore the Lord thy God commanded thee to keep the sabbath day."

As discussed earlier, the Feast of Tabernacles is also called the Ingathering (see Exodus 23:16), and it is similar in nature and timing to our Thanksgiving. It is a gathering-in of the harvest at the end of the year, and it is a time to rejoice and to take a moral inventory of ourselves. It is a time to give thanks for the bounteous harvest and for all the blessings the Lord has given us. At the top of addicts' gratitude list should be sobriety—it is a gift from God.

The Feast of Tabernacles was a celebration for all of Israel, but personally I don't think it applies to any particular group of people quite as well as it does to addicts. They could say that each time they celebrate a sobriety birthday, they are having a mini-feast, and each time they get down on their knees and thank the Lord for being clean and sober, they are having a mini-feast. They are not going to sit under a booth for seven days, but they *do* go to sacrament meeting, where they can partake of the emblems of our Savior's sacrifice, knowing that it was His "precious blood . . . as of a lamb without blemish" (1 Peter 1:19) that delivered them out of the chains of bondage and addiction and rescued them from "the grasp of this awful monster" (2 Nephi 9:10).

KING BENJAMIN'S FEAST OF TENTS AND AMMON'S TWELVE-STEP CALL   213

The performances of the law of Moses are also discussed in the Book of Mormon. The meaning of the law is plainly given. "And behold, this is the whole meaning of the law, every whit pointing to that great and last sacrifice; and that great and last sacrifice will be the Son of God, yea, infinite and eternal" (Alma 34:14).

The role of the king of Israel is important to the law of Moses. In ancient Israel, there was no separation of church and state, as we have today. The duties of the ministry and the political leadership were intermingled. Thus, we have Elijah, who, according to the Lord's commandment, is instructed to anoint Hazael to be king over Syria, to anoint Jehu to be king over Israel, and to anoint Elisha to be "prophet in [his] room" (see 1 Kings 19:13–16). It should be pointed out here that the "king over Israel" in this verse was the king over the northern kingdom. It did not mean king over all twelve tribes at this time, since the kingdom was divided in the days of Rehoboam, son of Solomon. The northern kingdom, or Israel, consisted of the ten tribes, who would become the "lost ten tribes" after being captured and carried away by the Assyrians in 2 Kings 17. The southern kingdom, or Judah, consisted of the tribes of Judah and Benjamin.

The fact that kings in Israel (and now I'm talking about the entire house of Israel) were anointed tells us something about how highly kings were revered. Kings were deified, at least symbolically. Psalms 74:12 reads, "For God is my *King* of old, working salvation in the *midst* of the earth." The word *midst* has temple connotations as well as a connection to kings.

As the priest would enter the tabernacle, he would approach its midst, or center, which was its most holy place. The tabernacle had divisions. There was a door, or screen, between the outer court and the Holy Place. The Holy Place and the Holy of Holies were separated by a veil. The ark of the covenant was inside the Holy of Holies, near the center of the tabernacle, and was covered by the mercy seat. It was considered the "Throne of God" in Israel (see Bible Dictionary, "Mercy seat").

In Exodus, the Lord describes the mercy seat to Moses:

> The cherubims shall stretch forth their wings on high,
> covering the mercy seat [the throne of God] with their wings,

and their faces shall look one to another; toward the mercy
seat shall the faces of the cherubims be. . . . And there I will
meet with thee, and I will commune with thee from above
the mercy seat, from between the two cherubims which are
upon the ark of the testimony, of all things which I will give
thee in commandment unto the children of Israel (Exodus
25:20, 22).

The mercy seat was the place where the Lord would come to meet
with Moses and give him direction on how to govern the people.

The King is our "advocate with the Father, who is pleading [our]
cause before him" (D&C 45:3). The king in Israel was supposed to be
a type of such a mediator. Solomon offered a dedicatory prayer for the
temple and pleaded with the Lord for blessings for his people. He prayed
for those who were carried "away captives unto the land of the enemy."
Addicts could fall into the same category—people carried away captive
by the enemy. Solomon continues:

Yet if they shall bethink themselves in the land whither
they were carried captives, and repent, and make supplication
unto thee . . . and return unto thee with all their heart . . .
and pray unto thee toward their land, which thou gavest unto
their fathers . . . Then hear thou their prayer and their supplication . . . For they be thy people, and thine inheritance,
which thou broughtest forth out of Egypt, from the midst of
the furnace of iron. (1 Kings 8:46–51)

The presence of kings is also evident in the Book of Mormon. Laman and Lemuel became angry with Nephi because he supposedly took
it upon himself to be a ruler and a teacher (see 1 Nephi 16:37). In other
words, he was a ruler, like a king, and a teacher, like a priest. Near the
end of his life, Nephi "anointed a man to be a king and a ruler over his
people now, according to the reigns of the kings" (Jacob 1:9). Jacob and
Joseph, Nephi's younger brothers, were "consecrated priests and teachers . . . by the hand of Nephi" (Jacob 1:18). The fact that kings were
anointed in both the Old Testament and the Book of Mormon speaks
plainly of the reverence given to kings in Israel. The first words in the

Book of Mormon, right under the heading "The First Book of Nephi," are the words, "His Reign and Ministry." In other words, it is his reign as a king and his ministry as a priest.

Like the commandment given to Elijah, Nephi anoints a king to be a political leader. He also consecrates the spiritual leaders, Jacob and Joseph, to teach the people. Later on in the Book of Mormon, " king Mosiah granted unto Alma that he might establish churches throughout all the land of Zarahemla; and gave him power to ordain priests and teachers over every church" (Mosiah 25:19). Mosiah also translated the Jaredite record and had possession of the seer stones (see Mosiah 28). Thus, he was a seer also. Clearly, he held the keys of the kingdom and the keys of the priesthood.

The role of the king in Israel was to lead the people in temporal and spiritual affairs and to be an advocate and defender of his people. Many kings fell short of their callings, and some led the Israelites into wickedness and idolatry. David and Solomon were great kings and did much good for the people, yet their hearts were turned away (see 1 Kings 11:3–9).

There is a king in the Book of Mormon who succeeded in being both a spiritual and political leader. His name is Benjamin. King Benjamin and really all kings of Old Testament times, including Book of Mormon kings, who reigned in righteousness were types of Christ.

King Benjamin, like the Savior, was a king who humbly served others. He poured out his soul in service to others. A central theme of his beautiful and final sermon was the concept of serving God by serving our fellowmen. Perhaps the most quoted verse in his sermon is Mosiah 2:17: "And behold, I tell you these things that ye may learn wisdom; that ye may learn that when ye are in the service of your fellow beings ye are only in the service of your God." Notice the similar language and reference to the King as the Savior teaches the same concept:

> Then shall the *King* say unto them on his right hand, [His covenant hand] Come, ye blessed of my Father, inherit the *kingdom* prepared for you from the foundation of the world:
>
> For I was an hungred, and ye gave me meat: I was thirsty, and ye gave me drink: I was a stranger, and ye took me in:

Naked, and ye clothed me: I was sick, and ye visited me: I was in prison, and ye came unto me.

Then shall the righteous answer him, saying, Lord, when saw we thee an hungred, and fed thee? or thirsty, and gave thee drink?

When saw we thee a stranger, and took thee in? or naked, and clothed thee?

Or when saw we thee sick, or in prison, and came unto thee?

And the *King* shall answer and say unto them, Verily I say unto you, Inasmuch as ye have done it unto one of the least of these my brethren, ye have done it unto me." (Matthew 25:34–40)

King Benjamin said to his people, "And I, even I, whom ye call your king, am no better than ye yourselves are" (Mosiah 2:26). He felt that if he merited any thanks from his people for his faithful service, they really "ought to thank [their] heavenly King!" (Mosiah 2:19). Even though he sees his role as king as being in similitude to Deity or to the Heavenly King, he also realizes that an ordinary, faithful, and humble servant is just as valiant and valuable as a mortal king. He also draws the comparison by pointing out that an ordinary, humble servant can become a mortal king, and that a mortal king can become a Heavenly King. He is a mediator between the common man and God, representing the natural progression from the "dust of the earth," to the "saint," and finally to becoming like the "Lord Omnipotent" (see Mosiah 2:25; 3:19; and 3:5).

Another similarity between King Benjamin and the "King of kings" (Revelation 17:14) has to do with the relationship between the king and his subjects. Both King Benjamin and the Savior take ownership of their respective kingdoms. We wouldn't need to worry about being subject to either of them—especially the Lord, since He makes those in His kingdom "equal in power, and in might, and in dominion" (D&C 76:95). Notice the parallel of ownership. The Book of Mosiah starts out by saying, "And now there was no more contention in all the land of Zarahemla, among all the people who *belonged to king Benjamin*" (Mosiah 1:1, emphasis added). The Lord said in modern revelation, "Yet I will *own* them, and they shall be *mine* in that day when I shall come to make up *my* jewels" (D&C 101:3, emphasis added; see also Malachi 3:17). The Lord will not use us like pawns, so being "owned" here is a good thing. In fact, *we* are the jewels He is seeking. There is nothing more precious in His sight.

This type of Christ becomes more pronounced in the relationship between the father, the son, and the subjects. Benjamin said to his son Mosiah, "For on the morrow I shall proclaim unto this *my people* out of mine own mouth that thou art a king and a ruler over this people, *whom the Lord our God hath given us*" (Mosiah 1:10, emphasis added). Watch the similar language in the Savior's intercessory prayer to the Father:

> I have manifested thy name unto the men which *thou gavest me* out of the world: *thine* they were, and *thou gavest them me*; and they have kept thy word. . . .
>
> I pray for them: I pray not for the world, but for them which *thou hast given me*; for *they are thine*.
>
> And all *mine* are *thine*, and *thine* are *mine*; and I am glorified in them. (John 17:6, 9, 10, emphasis added)

It is almost like a segment of the general population is pulled out from among the people, and they are those who allow themselves to be purchased, refined, and redeemed by the King. They become His "peculiar treasure" (Exodus 19:5). That is an important distinction of being "owned" by the King. It is really our surrender. We submit our wills over to Him. Thus, through His Atonement, He ransoms each of us. He then can take us from the "dust of the earth" and make us equal to Him—in other words, He can make us kings and queens! Once again, Steps Three, Six, Seven, and Eleven are necessary to complete the submission of ourselves over to Him.

A FEAST FIT FOR A KING

The Feast of Tabernacles represents the millennial reign of Christ on earth in addition to the sojourning of the children of Israel in the wilderness and their deliverance from bondage.

Remember, the feast is an ingathering of all the fruits of the earth's seasons. It marked the end of the entire festival season. It was the greatest and the last feast of the harvest year.

In Zenos's beautiful allegory of the tame and wild olive trees, the Lord of the vineyard expresses his sincere desire to "lay up fruit . . . against the season." Variations of this phrase are repeated in nine different verses (see Jacob 5:13, 18, 19, 20, 23, 27, 29, 71, and 76). The Lord speaks of laboring for the last time to gather in the fruit. After the bad branches are cast out of the vineyard, it says that "the Lord had preserved unto himself that the trees had become again the natural fruit; and they became like unto one body; and the fruits were equal; and the Lord of the vineyard had preserved unto himself the natural fruit, which was most precious unto him from the beginning" (Jacob 5:74). In other words, the natural branches of the house of Israel had been gathered together. Israel is finally home. Only then does the Lord of the vineyard and His fellow servants have joy in the harvest (see D&C 86:7). The Feast of Tabernacles is not just about gathering the crops and the food of the harvest; it is also about the gathering and harvesting of the house of Israel. It is a celebration of the greatest millennium of the earth's history—the time when Christ will reign as king on the earth.

In the Book of Revelation, John sees a book with seven seals, each seal representing approximately one thousand years (see Revelation 5–9; D&C 77:6–7). The Millennium begins in the seventh seal. The Feast of Tabernacles occurred in the seventh month, and the children of Israel dwelt in booths for seven days (see Leviticus 23:34, 40–43). The Feast of Tabernacles was the last feast of the festival season and represented the winding up scene before Christ's Second Coming and His millennial reign as King.

The Bible Dictionary states, "To the seven days was added an eighth . . . a day of holy convocation" (Bible Dictionary, "Feasts"). The word *convocation* means a public meeting, an assembly, a reading, or a rehearsal (see *Strong's Exhaustive Concordance of the Bible* #4744). A holy convocation as a reading and a holy convocation as a rehearsal are very significant. At the time of Ezra, a new tradition that has ties to the Feast of Tabernacles began. During the "feast of the seventh month," (the Feast of Tabernacles) Ezra, the priest, read each day from "the book of the law of God" (see Nehemiah 8:14, 18; Bible Dictionary, "Ezra"). This was an open, public reading of the law, and it was not a private and restricted version as was previously used by the priests. It was a true *convocation* because it was a public meeting and the law was read in front of a great assembly of people.

Convocation as a rehearsal is also significant. If you were rehearsing for a play, you would want to practice and prepare and be ready for the opening night. Thus, the Feast of Tabernacles is a great dress rehearsal, preparing us for the Second Coming and pointing us to that marvelous time when "the glory of the Lord shall be revealed, and all flesh shall see it together" (Isaiah 40:5).

"Hosanna: Blessed Is the King"

There is a single word linking the Feast of Tabernacles to the King of kings. The word is *hosanna*, and it means, "save now." The Bible Dictionary states, "The word [hosanna] is taken from Ps. 118: 25, one of the Psalms of the Hallel. The chanting of this psalm was connected at the Feast of Tabernacles with the waving of palm branches; hence the use of the word by the multitudes at our Lord's triumphal entry into Jerusalem" (Bible Dictionary, "Hosanna"; see also *Strong's* #3467, #4994, and #5614). When Jesus made His triumphal entry into Jerusalem, the multitude shouted, "Hosanna: Blessed is the King of Israel that cometh in the name of the Lord" (John 12:13).

The prophet Zechariah uses beautiful imagery to link the Feast of Tabernacles with Christ as a king. He says, "And the Lord shall be king over all the earth: in that day shall there be one Lord, and his name one." The next verse makes reference to the "king's winepresses" (see Zechariah 14:9–10). He can be the King and have power and grace to save us because He has "overcome and . . . trodden the wine-press alone" (D&C 76:107).

Zechariah continues:

> And it shall come to pass, that every one that is left of all the nations which came against Jerusalem shall even go *up* from year to year to worship the *King*, the Lord of hosts, and to keep the *feast of tabernacles*.

> And it shall be, that whoso will not come *up* of all the *families* of the earth unto Jerusalem to worship the *King*, the Lord of hosts, even upon them shall be no rain.
>
> And if the family of Egypt go not *up*, and come not, that have no rain; there shall be the plague, wherewith the Lord will smite the heathen that come not *up* to keep the *feast of tabernacles*.
>
> This shall be the punishment of Egypt, and the punishment of all nations that come not *up* to keep the *feast of tabernacles*.
>
> In that day shall there be upon the bells of the horses, HOLINESS UNTO THE LORD; and the pots in the *Lord's house* shall be like the bowls before the *altar*.
>
> Yea, every pot in Jerusalem and in Judah shall be *holiness unto the Lord* of hosts: and all they that sacrifice shall come and take of them, and seethe therein: and in that day there shall be no more the Canaanite in the *house of the Lord* of hosts. (Zechariah 14:16–21, emphasis added)

The word *up* is a Leitwort (leading theme word) that is symbolic of the temple and the Feast of Tabernacles. Those who go *up* to the Feast of Tabernacles will worship the King. They go *up* in families, similar to King Benjamin's gathering in the Book of Mormon (see Mosiah 2:5). With words and phrases like "altar," "Holiness Unto the Lord," and "house of the Lord," we are reminded of the temple.

The Feast of Tabernacles becomes a type of the king; and the king becomes a type of Christ.

Psalm 118: 25–26 reads: "Save now [meaning 'Hosanna'], I beseech thee, O Lord: O Lord, I beseech thee, send now prosperity. Blessed be he that cometh in the name of the Lord: we have blessed you out of the *house of the Lord* [or temple]."

Notice the links between kings, covenants, and temples in these verses.

The millennial reign will surely be the time when the Savior will return with all His glory, power, and majesty and reign as a king over all the earth.

A Pattern for Kings

King Benjamin and his selfless service are both types of the Savior. King Benjamin is an exemplary king, but the protocol for kings in Israel did not begin with Benjamin. It goes clear back to the patriarchal fathers and begins with Adam. Latter-day revelation says, "And the Lord administered comfort unto Adam, and said unto him: I have set thee to be at the head; a multitude of nations shall come of thee, and thou art a prince over them forever" (D&C 107:55). Melchizedek, after whom the high priesthood was named, was both a king and a priest. The Old Testament states, "And Melchizedek *king* of Salem [meaning 'king of peace,' see *Strong's* #8004) brought forth bread and wine: and he was the *priest* of the most high God." The Joseph Smith Translation adds further meaning: "And this Melchizedek, having thus established righteousness, was called the *king* of heaven by his people, or, in other words, the *King* of peace" (Genesis 14:18; JST, Genesis 14:36, emphasis added).

This pattern becomes important for us if we are to become "redeemed . . . kings and priests" (Revelation 5:9–10).

The pattern becomes more specific for kings in Israel with the law of Moses. Deuteronomy 17 outlines the duties of the king in Israel. The Lord states, "When thou art come unto the *land* which the Lord thy God giveth thee, and shalt possess it, and shalt dwell therein, and shalt say, I will set a king over me, like as all the nations that are about me" (Deuteronomy 17:14, emphasis added). First, the role of king is related to the Abrahamic covenant. The king reigns in the promised land. Two of the main promises of the Abrahamic covenant are that Christ, as King of kings, would come through the lineage of Abraham, and also that lands would be given as an eternal inheritance (see Genesis 17:6–8; Bible Dictionary, "Abraham, Covenant of").

King Benjamin's people were also "brought . . . out of the *land* of Jerusalem, and . . . delivered . . . out of the hands of their enemies," just like the children of Israel at the time of Moses were brought out of the land of Egypt and away from their taskmasters. The Lord then gave them "just men to be their *teachers*, and also a just man to be their *king*, who had established peace [like the king of Salem—Melchizedek] in the *land* of Zarahemla" (Mosiah 2:4).

There is a pattern here. The Lord brought the Nephites out of the land of Jerusalem—a place where they would have been destroyed or taken into bondage by Babylon (see 1 Nephi 1:13; 2 Nephi 25:10). We have Israelites saved from bondage and captivity. Again, they are brought to a promised land; and again, they triumph over their enemies. Then the Lord provides just men to be their teachers (or priests) and a just man to be their king.

Concerning kings in Israel, the Lord also said:

> But he shall not multiply horses to himself, nor cause the people to return to Egypt, to the end that he should multiply horses: forasmuch as the Lord hath said unto you, Ye shall henceforth return no more that way. Neither shall he multiply wives to himself, that his heart turn not away: neither shall he greatly multiply to himself *silver and gold* . . . That his heart be not lifted up above his brethren. (Deuteronomy 17:16, 17, 20, emphasis added)

The message for the addict is clear: Don't relapse and go back out! Don't return to Egypt and the house of bondage! Don't do anything that will turn your heart away from the Lord. Once you have turned something over to the Lord, according to Step Three, let go and let God have it.

Returning to the verses in Deuteronomy, doesn't this sound exactly like King Benjamin? He always made sure his heart was not lifted up above his brethren:

> I have not commanded you to come up hither that ye should fear me, or that ye should think that I of myself am more than a mortal man.
>
> But I am like as yourselves, subject to all manner of infirmities in body and mind; yet I have been chosen by this people, and consecrated by my father, and was suffered by the hand of the Lord that I should be a ruler and a king over this people; and have been kept and preserved by his matchless power, to serve you with all the might, mind and strength which the Lord hath granted unto me. (Mosiah 2:10–11)

King Benjamin had studied well the writings on the brass plates (see Mosiah 1:3), so he did not tax his people for his own gain. He said, "I . . . have not sought *gold nor silver* nor any manner of riches of you" (Mosiah 2:12).

He continues, "Neither have I suffered that ye should be confined in dungeons, nor that ye should make slaves one of another." He is doing everything he can to ensure that his people do not fall victim to bondage or become enslaved to anything addicting. He teaches that they can avoid such bondage by keeping the commandments of the Lord (see Mosiah 2:13).

Kings of Israel had another requirement. "When he sitteth upon the throne of his kingdom . . . [the king] shall write him a copy of this law in a book out of that which is before the priests the Levites: And it shall be with him, and he shall read therein all the days of his life: that he *may learn* to fear the Lord his God, to keep all the words of this law and these statutes, to do them" (Deuteronomy 17:18–19, emphasis added).

King Benjamin said, "And behold, I tell you these things that ye *may learn* wisdom" (Mosiah 2:17, emphasis added). Perhaps it is even more significant that he taught these principles to his sons, so they might also become kings. He was careful that his three sons (one of whom would become king in a mortal sense, but hopefully all three of whom would become kings and priests in a spiritual sense) "should be taught in all the language of his fathers, that thereby they might become men of understanding; and that they might know concerning the prophecies which had been spoken by the mouths of their fathers, which were delivered them by the hand of the Lord" (Mosiah 1:2).

The king in Israel was commanded to study the laws of God daily, and this intense study pattern was to last "all the days of his life," enabling him to learn the words, statutes, and commandments of God (see the chapter heading to Deuteronomy 17; see also Deuteronomy 17:19). King Benjamin told his sons that the brass plates, which contained the law of Moses, were necessary for their education and salvation. Otherwise, they would have "suffered in ignorance . . . not knowing the mysteries of God" (Mosiah 1:3). Benjamin talks about the importance of consistent, daily scripture study, in order that "we might read and understand of his mysteries, and have his commandments *always before our eyes*" (Mosiah 1:5, emphasis added). The phrase, "always before our eyes," does not sound like a once-a-week study pattern we engage in during Gospel Doctrine class on Sunday. Rather, it is a daily feast of the word of God. We would never deprive our bodies by eating only once a week, and we shouldn't treat our spirits that way either.

KING BENJAMIN TEACHES THE TWELVE STEPS

There is strong evidence that King Benjamin gave his speech during the Feast of Tabernacles. It was one of three required feasts according to the law of Moses (see Exodus 23:14–17; Mosiah 2:3). There were also sacrifices and burnt offerings in both events (see Mosiah 2:3; Numbers 29:12–40).

Instead of dwelling in booths, King Benjamin's people dwelt in tents (see Mosiah 2:6). In the Old Testament, *tent* and *tabernacle* are the same word in Hebrew and the words are interchangeable (see *Strong's* #168). Another reason for dwelling in tents would be the seven-day duration of the feast. This reason would not apply to one of the required feasts— the Feast of Weeks. It was a single-day event (see Bible Dictionary, "Feasts").

Both events were a thanksgiving. King Benjamin's people assembled to "give thanks to the Lord their God." They were grateful they had been delivered from destruction or bondage in Jerusalem (see Mosiah 2:4). For them, it was a double celebration.

Perhaps the biggest similarity would be the reading of the "book of the law" by the king in Israel. In ancient Israel only the kings and priests had a copy of the book of the law (see Deuteronomy 17:18; Nehemiah 8:1, 18). In Nehemiah the "book of the law" was read from a pulpit, "above all the people." This occurred during the Feast of Tabernacles. King Benjamin spoke from a tower (see Nehemiah 8:4–5, 14, 18; Mosiah 2:7).

If the Feast of Tabernacles has ties to kings in Israel, and if King Benjamin's speech has ties to this feast, and if the feast has ties to recovery, then we should be able to find the Twelve Steps within King Benjamin's speech.

Please carefully consider Mosiah 4. I will discuss both the Twelve Steps of Alcoholics Anonymous and the Twelve Steps as they are given in *LDS Family Services Addiction Recovery Program—A Guide to Addiction Recovery and Healing.* I will refer to this LDS publication as GTAR (Guide to Addiction Recovery). This new manual is a marvelous tool and a great blessing for the recovering addict! Then, we will look at the corresponding step in Mosiah 4, though I will reference the passages in this chapter by verse only. Unless otherwise noted, any emphasis in the cited scriptures is my own. Finally, I will give some commentary for each step.

Step One

AA: "We admitted we were powerless over alcohol—that our lives had become unmanageable."

GTAR: "Admit that you, of yourself, are powerless to overcome your addictions and that your life has become unmanageable."

GTAR PRINCIPLE: Honesty.

KING BENJAMIN: "And they had viewed themselves in their own carnal state, even *less than the dust of the earth*" (v. 2). "For behold, if the knowledge of the goodness of God at this time has awakened you to a sense of your *nothingness*, and your *worthless* and *fallen state . . .*" (v. 5). "I would that ye should remember, and always retain in remembrance, the greatness of God, and your own *nothingness*, and his goodness and long-suffering towards you, *unworthy creatures*, and *humble yourselves* even in the *depths of humility*" (v. 11).

COMMENTARY: King Benjamin will show his people, and us as readers of his sermon, how the Lord can deliver them with the help of these Twelve Steps, carry them from "the dust of the earth," and eventually "seal [them] his, that [they] may be brought to heaven" (Mosiah 5:15). Remember that the promised land symbolizes exaltation and becoming a king or a queen in the celestial kingdom.

Step Two

AA: "Came to believe that a Power greater than ourselves could restore us to sanity."

GTAR: "Come to believe that the power of God can restore you to complete spiritual health."

GTAR PRINCIPLE: Hope.

KING BENJAMIN: "We *believe* in Jesus Christ, the Son of God, who created heaven and earth, and all things; who shall come down among the children of men" (v. 2). "The Spirit of the Lord came upon them, and they were filled with joy, having received a remission of their sins, and having *peace* of conscience, because of the exceeding *faith* which they had in Jesus Christ" (v. 3). "*Believe* in God; *believe* that he is, and that he created all things, both in heaven and in earth; *believe* that he has all wisdom, and all *power*, both in heaven and in earth; *believe* that man doth not comprehend all the things which the Lord can comprehend" (v. 9). "And now, if you *believe* all these things see that ye do them" (v. 10).

COMMENTARY: King Benjamin teaches that it is absolutely critical for us all to gain a correct understanding of the attributes of God so that we may have faith and trust in Him. We can have peace, joy, and spiritual wholeness as we develop faith in Jesus Christ and His Atonement. The Hebrew word for peace (*shalowm*) means to be whole, complete, and have soundness of body and mind (see *Strong's* #7965). King Benjamin's people had "peace of conscience." We need to know there is not a problem, habit, or addiction that is too tough for the Lord. He has all wisdom and power, and can comprehend things that baffle us! King Benjamin teaches that real faith requires us to *do* something about the things we believe in.

Step Three

AA: "Made a decision to turn our will and our lives over to the care of God as we understood Him."

GTAR: "Decide to turn your will and your life over to the care of God the Eternal Father and His Son, Jesus Christ."

GTAR PRINCIPLE: Trust in God.

KING BENJAMIN: "They were filled with joy, having received a remission of their sins, and having peace of conscience, because of the *exceeding faith* which they had in *Jesus Christ*" (v. 3). "If ye have come to a knowledge of the goodness of God, and his matchless power, and his wisdom, and his patience, and his long-suffering towards the children of men; and also, the atonement which has been prepared from the foundation of the world, that thereby salvation might come to him that should put his *trust in the Lord* . . . I say, that this is the man who receiveth salvation (v. 6–7).

COMMENTARY: King Benjamin makes a smooth transition from Step Two to Step Three by showing us how we can learn to trust God because we have learned a correct view of His character. GTAR summarizes this step as the simple (but not always easy) concept of trusting in the Lord. You cannot turn your will and life over to someone you do not trust! King Benjamin reminds addicts that the Lord did not begin working on their recovery when they entered the rooms of AA or when they decided to get clean and sober. He planned their recoveries from the foundation of the world.

Step Four

AA: "Made a searching and fearless moral inventory of ourselves."

GTAR: "Make a searching and fearless written moral inventory of yourself."

GTAR PRINCIPLE: Truth.

KING BENJAMIN: "And they had *viewed themselves* in their *own carnal state*" (v. 2). "*Watch yourselves*, and *your thoughts*, and *your words*, and *your deeds*" (v. 30).

COMMENTARY: As King Benjamin's people viewed themselves, each of them took his or her own personal moral inventory. It was then that they realized their need for the atoning blood of Jesus Christ to overcome their character defects. King Benjamin teaches that a searching and complete inventory requires that we look at our thoughts, words, and deeds, along with the underlying causes for them.

Step Five

AA: "Admitted to God, to ourselves, and to another human being the exact nature of our wrongs."

GTAR: "Admit to yourself, to your Heavenly Father in the name of Jesus Christ, to proper priesthood authority, and to another person the exact nature of your wrongs."

GTAR PRINCIPLE: Confession.

KING BENJAMIN: "And they *all cried aloud* with one voice, saying: O have mercy, and apply the atoning blood of Christ that we may receive forgiveness of our sins, and our hearts may be purified" (v. 2).

COMMENTARY: This is an open confession of sin made out loud. The people acknowledge their own sins and impurities of heart. They realize that the "exact nature" of sin begins with the heart. They also realize that their carnal nature or "fallen state" (v. 5) stems back to the Fall of Adam, and that the effects of the Fall can only be overcome through the Atonement of Jesus Christ. This confession, made out loud, is made to one's self, to the others in the congregation, and to God. It is a confessional prayer, as they plead for the atoning blood of Christ to purge their sin and purify their hearts. They plead for the atoning power of the King of kings, in the presence of their mortal king, who clearly holds the keys of the priesthood and the keys of the kingdom.

Step Six

AA: "Were entirely ready to have God remove all these defects of character."

GTAR: "Become entirely ready to have God remove all your character weaknesses."

GTAR PRINCIPLE: Change of heart.

KING BENJAMIN: "And they all cried aloud with one voice, saying: O have mercy, and apply the atoning blood of *Christ* that we may receive *forgiveness of our sins*, and our *hearts* may be *purified*" (v. 2). "And again, believe that ye must *repent of your sins and forsake them*" (v. 10).

COMMENTARY: In compliance with this step, King Benjamin's people realize that they cannot get rid of their sins by themselves. They need, and we need, Christ's atoning blood to remove sin. In the process, they receive a change of heart. In the Old Testament, Samuel commands Saul to offer a burnt offering to the Lord. A burnt offering represents a total surrender to God. Thus, the *entire* animal was burnt on the altar. We too should be willing to surrender all our sins to God, sacrificing the whole animal—with all the animalistic and carnal desires—and allowing the animal in us to go up in smoke (see Bible Dictionary, "Sacrifices"). When Saul became willing to surrender and make such an offering, "God gave him another heart" (see 1 Samuel 10:8–9). In Mosiah

5, King Benjamin's people acknowledge that their "hearts are changed through faith on his [Christ's] name" (Mosiah 5:7).

Step Seven

AA: "Humbly asked Him to remove our shortcomings."

GTAR: "Humbly ask Heavenly Father to remove your shortcomings."

GTAR PRINCIPLE: Humility.

KING BENJAMIN: "*Humble* yourselves before *God;* and *ask* in sincerity of heart that he would forgive you; and now, if you believe all these things see that ye *do* them" (v. 10).

COMMENTARY: We all, addicts or not, need to humbly and sincerely ask God to forgive us and to remove our shortcomings. For most of these steps there is a belief, or willingness, step, and then there is an action step. As King Benjamin points out, if we believe that God would take away our character defects, and if we are willing to surrender them, then we need to get down upon our knees and *do* something about them.

Step Eight

AA: "Made a list of all persons we had harmed, and became willing to make amends to them all."

GTAR: "Make a written list of all persons you have harmed and become willing to make restitution to them."

GTAR PRINCIPLE: Seeking forgiveness.

KING BENJAMIN: "And ye will not have a *mind* to *injure* one another" (v. 13).

COMMENTARY: As they seek forgiveness, addicts will begin to experience a change of heart. They'll experience the gift of sobriety and feel within their hearts "the love of God, which sheddeth itself abroad in the hearts of the children of men" (1 Nephi 11:22). They naturally feel love and concern for those they have injured or harmed in any way. In their *minds* they begin to think about and make a mental list of those they have harmed. They will begin to see through the lie of vain imagination and know that in their addictions, they were not just hurting themselves.

Step Nine

AA: "Made direct amends to such people wherever possible, except when to do so would injure them or others."

GTAR: "Whenever possible, make direct restitution to all persons you have harmed."

GTAR PRINCIPLE: Restitution and reconciliation.

KING BENJAMIN: "And ye will not have a mind to *injure one another,* but to *live peaceably,* and to *render to every man* according to that which is *his due*" (v. 13).

COMMENTARY: *Live* is an action verb. No one wants to harm others, and everyone wants to live peaceably. We make peace with each other as we make amends and attempt to make restitution for the wreckage of our past. King Benjamin teaches us that we must render to every man according to that which is his due. If we owe someone an apology, or if we have damaged anyone in any way, we need to pay up.

Step Ten

AA: "Continued to take personal inventory and when we were wrong promptly admitted it."

GTAR: "Continue to take personal inventory, and when you are wrong promptly admit it."

GTAR PRINCIPLE: Daily accountability.

KING BENJAMIN: "*Continue* in the faith [and, for addicts, also in your program] even unto the end" (v. 6). "If ye do not *watch yourselves,* and *your thoughts,* and *your words,* and *your deeds,* and observe the commandments of God, and *continue* in the faith . . . even unto the end of your lives, ye must perish [and probably relapse]. And now, O man, remember, and perish not" (v. 30).

COMMENTARY: If we switched the order of two of the verbs in verse 30, it would read: *Continue* in the faith and *watch yourselves,* and your thoughts, and your words, and your deeds. That would be quite similar to the phrase, "Continue to take personal inventory." King Benjamin adds another dimension to the personal moral inventory. Being wrong is defined as not observing the commandments of God.

Step Eleven

AA: "Sought through prayer and meditation to improve our conscious contact with God as we understood Him, praying only for knowledge of His will for us and the power to carry that out."

GTAR: "Seek through prayer and meditation to know the Lord's will and to have the power to carry it out."

GTAR PRINCIPLE: Personal revelation.

KING BENJAMIN: "Humble yourselves even in the depths of humility, *calling on the name of the Lord daily*" (v. 11). "The *Spirit of the Lord* came upon them, and they were *filled with joy*" (v. 3). "Ye have been *calling on his* [God's] *name*, and begging for a remission of your sins. . . . He has poured out *his Spirit* upon you" (v. 20). "Ye shall *grow* [or improve] in the *knowledge* of the *glory* [or power] of him that created you, or in the *knowledge* of that which is just and true" (v. 12). "As ye have come to the *knowledge* of the *glory* of God, or if ye have *known* of his goodness and have *tasted* [something conscious; a six-dimensional experience] of his love . . . " (v. 11). "If ye have come to a *knowledge* of the goodness of God, and his matchless *power*, and his *wisdom*, and his patience, and his long-suffering towards the children of men . . . " (v. 6). "Believe that he [God] has all *wisdom*, and all *power*" (v. 9).

COMMENTARY: King Benjamin reminds us all that we need to call upon the Lord in prayer every day. As addicts beg for their sobriety and the strength to overcome their addictions, the Lord will pour out His Spirit upon them. The Holy Ghost is a supernal source of power, which will strengthen all of us in our hour of need. For me, the greatest blessing of my recovery is to have a conscious contact with God through the power of the Spirit. Daily prayer, scripture study, and meditation bring me closer to my Heavenly Father. As I seek to do the will of the Father, I pray for knowledge and power. I know God will give you and I both. As you study the scriptures, notice how often the concepts of knowledge and power are taught together. As King Benjamin emphasizes, you will not seek knowledge and power from God unless you truly believe that He is the ultimate source and has all power and all wisdom.

Step Twelve

AA: "Having had a spiritual awakening as the result of these steps, we tried to carry this message to alcoholics, and to practice these principles in all our affairs."

GTAR: "Having had a spiritual awakening as a result of the Atonement of Jesus Christ, share this message with others and practice these principles in all you do."

GTAR PRINCIPLE: Service.

KING BENJAMIN: "For behold, if the knowledge of the goodness of God at this time has *awakened* you . . ." (v. 5). "I say, that this is the man who receiveth salvation [and recovery], through the *atonement* which was prepared from the foundation of the world for all mankind, which ever were since the fall of Adam, or who are, or who ever shall be, even unto the end of the world. And this is the means whereby salvation cometh. And there is none other salvation save this which hath been spoken of; neither are there any conditions whereby man can be saved except the conditions which I have told you" (vv. 7–8). "And also, ye yourselves will succor those that stand in need of your succor; ye will administer of your substance [for addicts, share your recovery] unto him that standeth in need; and ye will not suffer that the beggar [or addict seeking help] putteth up his petition to you in vain, and turn him out to perish. For behold, are we not all beggars? (or, in other words, are we not all addicts?; vv. 16, 19). "And now, if you believe all these things see that ye do them" (v. 10).

COMMENTARY: By working these steps and through the Atonement of Jesus Christ, addicts are reconciled to God, and they experience a spiritual awakening. King Benjamin teaches that the Atonement is universal for all mankind. There is not another means for salvation or recovery. The "conditions" of which King Benjamin speaks can be likened to the steps. There is not an alternate program, nor is there an "easier, softer way." The *Big Book* states, "Here are the steps we took, which are suggested as a program of recovery" (p. 59). Hence, no steps equals no program, and no program equals no recovery. Step Twelve gives us the privilege of carrying the message to others. Under King Benjamin's program of service and sharing, we don't just share our food and clothing. We also share our experience, strength, and hope. We are all beggars before God. Recovery is not something addicts can achieve or merit on their own. Rather it is a gift that comes through the grace of God. When you see an alcoholic or addict relapse or "hit bottom," reach out the hand of fellowship, so he or she is not left to perish. Step Twelve is all about service, and service is a central theme of King Benjamin's speech. King Benjamin teaches, that if we believe in these principles, or steps, we must live them. In other words, "practice these principles in all our affairs."

KING BENJAMIN'S PEOPLE ARE EMPOWERED

Now that King Benjamin's people have been taught principles relating to the Twelve Steps, and now that they have been properly taught concerning the mission and Atonement of Jesus Christ, and now that they are willing and ready to live by these principles, they are ready to enter into a covenant with God. The promised land, or the land of recovery, is a promise of the Abrahamic covenant (see Genesis 17:8). Just as Abraham received a new name (see Genesis 17:5), the people of King Benjamin also receive a new name. They receive the name of their King—"King Immanuel, who hath ordained, before the world was, that which would . . . redeem them out of their prison; for the prisoners shall go free" (D&C 128:22). They receive the name of the "King of Zion, the Rock of Heaven," who said, "Whoso cometh in at the gate and climbeth up by me shall never fall" (Moses 7:53). That is quite a promise for an addict who has not been able to stay clean and sober in times past.

The people have received a sure witness of the truthfulness of King Benjamin's words, and this witness comes because of the "Spirit of the Lord Omnipotent, which has wrought a mighty change" in their hearts. They have "great views" of the future, and thus, they view the world through new glasses (see Mosiah 5:2–3).

The people respond to their king by saying, "And we are willing to enter into a covenant with our God to do his will, and to be obedient to his commandments in all things" (Mosiah 5:5). As their king and mediator and as a type of Jesus Christ, King Benjamin can now pronounce a blessing upon their heads. He says:

> And now, because of the covenant which ye have made ye shall be called the children of Christ, his sons, and his daughters; for behold, this day he hath spiritually begotten you; for ye say that your hearts are changed through faith on his name; therefore, ye are born of him and have become his sons and his daughters. And under this head ye are made free, and there is no other head whereby ye can be made free. (Mosiah 5:7–8)

As spiritually begotten sons and daughters of Christ, the people become heirs to the kingdom. They become joint-heirs with Christ. Paul said, "And if children, then heirs; heirs of God, and joint-heirs with Christ" (Romans 8:17). As we enter into covenants with the Lord and honor those covenants, we receive an inheritance in the kingdom of God. We receive our inheritance from the King. As you make and keep your covenants from the Lord, you receive your King and His servants. You then receive an inheritance of all that the Father hath (see D&C 84:34–38).

We become spiritually begotten sons and daughters of Christ as we make covenants with the Lord. Paul said, "For as many of you as have been baptized into Christ have put on Christ. . . . And if ye be Christ's, then are ye Abraham's seed, and heirs according to the promise" (Galatians 3:27, 29). King Benjamin explains that part of the process of becoming a saint through the Atonement of Christ is to put off the natural man (see Mosiah 3:19). Paul gives us the other half of the equation. We put off the natural man and put on Christ.

King Benjamin ends his address with a beautiful promise. He invites us to be "steadfast and immovable, always abounding in good works, that Christ, the Lord God Omnipotent, may seal you his, that you may be brought to heaven" (Mosiah 5:15)—the ultimate promised land!

AMMON'S TWELVE-STEP CALL

King Benjamin's speech brought real recovery and rescue from bondage. About three years after Benjamin's address, a Nephite named Ammon journeyed to the land of Lehi-Nephi, where he found King Limhi's people in bondage.

Limhi's father was King Noah. Noah was a "wine-bibber," which may have been the politically correct term for alcoholic. He and his priests spent their time in "riotous living." He lived an immoral lifestyle with his wives and concubines and displayed behavior typical of an addict (see Mosiah 11:14–15). His people were eventually brought into bondage by the Lamanites.

Ammon delivers a message of hope, and the king becomes his people's spokesman and advocate. King Limhi tells his people, "Therefore, lift up your heads, and rejoice, and put your trust in God, in that God who was the God of Abraham, and Isaac, and Jacob; and also, that God who brought the children of Israel out of the land of Egypt, and caused that they should walk through the Red Sea on dry ground" (Mosiah 7:19). He goes on to say, "But if ye will turn to the Lord with full purpose of heart, and put your trust in him, and serve him with all diligence of mind, if ye do this, he will, according to his own will and pleasure, deliver you out of bondage" (Mosiah 7:33).

Then Ammon had an opportunity to speak to the audience. He teaches the Twelve Steps. The scripture records, "He also rehearsed unto them the last words which king Benjamin had taught them, and explained them to the people of king Limhi, so that they might understand all the words which he spake" (Mosiah 8:3).

Shortly thereafter, they hold a "group conscience" (see Mosiah 22:1–2) in order to discover a way in which they might be able to escape bondage. Gideon finally puts forth a plan to supply the Lamanite guards with wine, so that the people can depart into the wilderness while their enemies are drunk and asleep. With the Lord's help and this plan, King Limhi's people are finally able to get out of bondage (see Mosiah 22).

BECOMING KINGS AND QUEENS

To addicts, addicts in recovery, and anyone struggling with a trial or temptation, I say if you feel powerless to change your life, if you are in the emptiest, lowest, most hopeless place, and if you think you will never be good enough to make it in God's kingdom, think again. I know He wants you back. The One who has "trodden the wine-press alone" has also "overcome the world" (see D&C 76:107; John 16:33). There cannot be an addiction or temptation or sin beyond His grasp. He descended even into the depths of hell to pull us out, and lift us up, and exalt us on thrones.

The price has been paid. He has purchased for you the finest, most glorious throne that Gethsemane can buy, and He wants you to sit with Him on that throne! He even said, "To him that overcometh will I grant to sit with me in my throne, even as I also overcame, and am set down with my Father in his throne" (Revelation 3:21). But whenever you read this verse, you should always read the one before it: "Behold, I stand at the door, and knock: if *any man* [or *woman*] hear my voice, and open the door, I will come in to him, and will sup with him, and he with me" (Revelation 3:20, emphasis added). The invitation is for everyone. It doesn't say, "If a *perfect* man hear my voice, and open the door," nor does it say, "I stand at the door with an axe and will break down the door, come in, and tie you to the throne I bought for you!"

battling the enemy

Paul said, "For we wrestle not against flesh and blood, but against principalities, against powers, against the rulers of the darkness of this world, against spiritual wickedness in high places" (Ephesians 6:12).

Personally, that makes me feel better and worse. It makes me feel better that I am not merely beating myself up all the time. I sometimes wonder why I am so weak that I can't even win against myself, but maybe the enemy is bigger than I perceive. Perhaps I am battling forces other than my own flesh and blood.

But it makes me feel worse to know that the battle is going to be tougher than I thought. The rulers of darkness have an awfully big empire. Hollywood, entertainment media, advertisements, and the Internet make up a formidable foe. They are well organized and seem to be backed by almost unlimited funding.

There is also another enemy lurking around out there. In the Book of Mormon, Jacob said, "O, my beloved brethren, remember the awfulness in transgressing against that Holy God, and also the awfulness of yielding to the enticings of that cunning one" (2 Nephi 9:39). It's not only alcohol and drugs that are "cunning, baffling, powerful." It's also Satan—the great counterfeiter "who was a liar from the beginning" (D&C 93:25). His enticements sometimes look so attractive. They are always couched in more glitter and glamour and packaged in flashier forms than the *real* blessings that come from the Lord. By now, we all know those alluring temptations are snares lined with an attractive bait, but the devil sometimes whispers to us that we can just flirt with them a little or give them one more try. Sometimes when we are called upon to flee Babylon, we hesitate, taking one more longing look behind. Each time that happens the odds for victory get even smaller.

We live in a society flooded with filth. A few mouse clicks, a few buttons pushed on a cell phone, or a little television surfing with the remote can place us in enemy territory in mere seconds! Such gadgets can make the slippery slide of immorality even more slippery. Then I have a committee inside my head that can excuse, rationalize, and downplay almost any evil presented to it. It's my center of "vain imagination."

Let's take a tally. It's my own natural man, the rulers of darkness in this world, the enticements of the world, the media, the committee inside my head, and Satan all ganged up against me. That's the bad news.

The good news is that it's not *my* battle. It's not yours either. Once again, The *Big Book of Alcoholics Anonymous* and the scriptures agree on this issue. The *Big Book* states, "And we have ceased fighting anything or anyone—even alcohol" (p. 84). The reason we don't have to fight it ourselves is given in modern revelation. The Lord said, "For, as I said in a former commandment, even so will I fulfil—I will fight your battles" (D&C 105:14).

What a wonderful promise! I have experienced the truth of this principle for myself. On those days when it is not a fight, when I am walking in the light of the Spirit (see Galatians 5:25), when I am willing to "let go and let God," my life is manageable and my program seems to just flow naturally. On those days, I feel the Lord's grace—the enabling power that seems to lift me over every temptation and obstacle.

I once read that eagles encounter a midlife crisis. Their talons and feathers become brittle, and they grow tired and lose strength. They sit on the ground and wait for other eagles to fly overhead and drop them down food. Then the helpless eagles are transformed. They are nourished and grow new baby feathers—layer upon layer. Their wings become stronger than ever, and they fly to a newfound freedom.

Isaiah must have been talking about such an eagle when he stated, "But they that wait upon the Lord shall renew their strength; they shall mount up with wings as eagles; they shall run, and not be weary; and they shall walk, and not faint" (Isaiah 40:31). A similar promise is found in the Word of Wisdom—Doctrine and Covenants 89:20.

It is not our battle to fight—at least not on our own. It is not our own righteousness we are seeking to obtain. Lehi said to his son Jacob, "Wherefore, I know that thou art redeemed, because of the *righteousness of thy Redeemer*" (2 Nephi 2:3, emphasis added), and the Savior taught in the Sermon on the Mount: "But seek ye first the kingdom of God, and *his* righteousness; and all these things shall be added unto you" (Matthew 6:33, emphasis added). We seek the Lord's will and *His* righteousness—not our own.

SCOUTING OUT THE ENEMY

One of the best ways to be proactive is to prepare for those "fiery darts of the adversary" (1 Nephi 15:24) well in advance. If you're going to war, you better know something about the enemy, and whether we want to be at war or not, the adversary "maketh war with the saints of God, and encompasseth them round about" (D&C 76:29). He would like to tear down every addict's program of recovery and take away everyone's peace and serenity. He has a slightly different program of destruction for those who have entered into covenants with the Lord.

In Lehi's vision of the tree of life, there were some people who had commenced in the path that led to the tree of life. For those who are merely beginning their journey to find the truth, Satan throws out a little mist of darkness. Many will get confused or lost and will stumble around, perhaps losing their sense of direction and giving up or wandering off in the wrong direction.

But for those who taste the fruit and have entered into covenants with the Lord, Satan has a path or an agenda to lead them carefully away from their covenants and blessings. As a result, some "fell away into forbidden paths and were lost" (see 1 Nephi 8:22, 23, and 28).

If the Lord reserved His "choice spirits" to "come forth in the fullness of times" to perform the great latter-day work, then you can bet Satan is saving his best weapons (like addiction) for the final inning! (See D&C 138:53.) The objective of the adversary has not changed from the beginning. He knows he cannot take away your agency, because the Lord already gave it to you (see Moses 4:3). So he does the next worst thing. He seeks to take away your desire and ability to act righteously upon your agency.

Also keep in mind that your will and your freedom to act are two different things. A person can be in prison, and while his or her will is to get out, he or she is not able to do so.

When I decided to quit drinking, I realized I was not able to act on my righteous desire. I had tried and failed. I used to think my alcoholism had taken away my agency. It felt like I would die if I tried to stop. I really believed that. Those of us who have gone to jail, myself included, did not push on the bars of the cell, thinking we could break them down. Spiritual bars are just as strong.

Addicts know what the adversary did to them while they were practicing their addictions. Let's take a look at what he attempts to do to them in recovery.

Satan's Quiver of Fiery Darts

1. "The evil spirit teacheth not a man to pray, but teacheth him that he must not pray" (2 Nephi 32:8). Satan's rhetoric: "You can't pray to God after all the awful things you've done."
2. "We are strong, we shall not come into bondage, or be taken captive by our enemies" (Mosiah 12:15). Satan's rhetoric: "You can handle it."
3. "Ye have brought us forth into this wilderness, to kill this whole assembly with hunger" (Exodus 16:3). Satan's rhetoric: "*They* (Church leaders) don't always know what's going on."

4. "We remember the fish, which we did eat in Egypt freely; the cucumbers, and the melons, and the leeks, and the onions, and the garlick: But now our soul is dried away: there is nothing at all, beside this manna" (Numbers 11:5–6). Satan's rhetoric: "Remember how much fun it used to be."

5. "Let us make a captain, and let us return into Egypt" (Numbers 14:4). Satan's rhetoric: "You might as well get loaded."

6. "And the mixt multitude that was among them fell a lusting: and the children of Israel also wept again, and said, Who shall give us flesh to eat?" (Numbers 11:4). Satan's rhetoric: "See how good it looks."

7. "After the year was expired, at the time when kings go forth to battle . . . David tarried still at Jerusalem" (2 Samuel 11:1). Satan's rhetoric: "You've got it made. You can let up on your program for a while."

8. "Ye cannot bear all things now" (D&C 50:40; 78:18). Satan's rhetoric: "I told you that you couldn't keep all the commandments."

9. "Amalickiah caused that one of his servants should administer poison by degrees to Lehonti, that he died" (Alma 47:18). Satan's rhetoric: "Come on, it's only PG-13!"

10. "When Amalickiah found that he could not get Lehonti to come down off from the mount, he went up into the mount, nearly to Lehonti's camp; and he sent again the fourth time his message unto Lehonti, desiring that he would come down, and that he would bring his guards with him" (Alma 47:12). Satan's rhetoric: "Lighten up. Everyone else is doing it."

11. "Behold, the servants of the king have stabbed him to the heart, and he has fallen and they have fled; behold, come and see" (Alma 47:26). Satan's rheto-

ric: "Your testimony is not supported by scientific
evidence."

12. "The king took counsel, and made two calves of
gold, and said unto them, It is too much for you
to go up to Jerusalem: behold thy gods, O Israel,
which brought thee up out of the land of Egypt"
(1 Kings 12:28). Satan's rhetoric: "Getting to the
temple is an impossible dream."

The Lies in Satan's Quiver of Fiery Darts

1. **"You can't pray to God after all the awful things
you've done."**

    Nephi warns us that the "evil spirit teacheth
    not a man to pray, but teacheth him that he must
    not pray" (2 Nephi 32:8). This was perhaps the first
    scripture in my recovery to have a profound impact
    upon me. I knew of its truth from my own per-
    sonal experience.

    The adversary will try to tell addicts that they
    are not worthy to pray and are not worthy of God's
    love and divine grace. The reality is that they "must
    pray always" just as Nephi explains.

    The Father is anxiously waiting to hear from
    each of his children. Satan would have us all be-
    lieve that our hearts must be entirely healed for us
    to express our feelings to God. This is not true. I
    find that my most productive and powerful prayers
    come when I am rigorously honest with the Lord.
    No one can hide feelings from Him anyway.

    In the Church we have temple recommends
    to determine temple worthiness. It is important
    that we are prepared to enter into sacred covenants
    with the Lord, but the Church does not issue any
    "prayer recommends." Our Father invites all of His
    children to come unto Him. There is no "worthi-
    ness" requirement.

2. "You can handle it."

King Noah's people said, "And behold, we are strong, we shall not come into bondage, or be taken captive by our enemies" (Mosiah 12:15). Pride poses a major threat to an addict's sobriety and spiritual program.

After a period of sobriety, it is easy for addicts to feel self-sufficient in their programs. They might think they have it made. Then, they tend to forget about God. But if they, myself included, are rigorously honest, they realize that they can take little, if any, credit for their sobriety. They are still powerless without the Lord's help.

One of the central themes of the Book of Mormon is the pride cycle. Whenever the Nephites became prideful, they suffered great loss and were eventually humbled. A great example is given in Helaman: "And because of this their great wickedness, and their boastings in their own strength, they were left in their own strength; therefore they did not prosper, but were afflicted and smitten, and driven before the Lamanites, until they had lost possession of almost all their lands" (Helaman 4:13).

The AA acronym for *ego* is "Edge God Out." When addicts become caught up in self-righteousness, they gradually "edge God out" of their individual programs of recovery. That is very dangerous because without God, they really don't have a program.

One of the saddest things I have observed in recovery is the fact that some people tend to think they are cured and all is well after achieving some time of sobriety. They quit attending meetings and seem to drop off the face of the earth. Sometimes we never see them back in the rooms of recovery, but sometimes we see them again several months

or years later—after they have given their drinking and/or drugging one more try. We see them
starting over with tears in their eyes because they
thought they could make it on their own, and they
found out they were wrong.

Beware of pride.

3. **"They (Church leaders) don't always know what's
   going on."**

Moses really had a difficult job leading the children of Israel through the wilderness. When everything worked out according to plan, they praised
the Lord, and whenever anything went wrong, they
blamed Moses. In Exodus 14 they are delivered out
of bondage. The Lord parts the Red Sea, allowing them to walk through on dry ground. In the
next chapter, they are singing songs of praise to the
Lord: "The Lord is my strength and song, and he is
become my salvation" (Exodus 15:2).

In the next chapter, they get a little hungry, and
they contend with Moses saying, "*Ye* have brought
us forth into this wilderness, to kill this whole assembly with hunger" (Exodus 16:3, emphasis added). Notice that the Lord is now totally out of the
picture. The Israelites tell Moses, "*Ye* have brought
us forth into this wilderness." It is like they are saying, "This is *your* fault, Moses!" They didn't even
recognize the Lord's hand in their situation.

How many times have you heard people talk
about Church leaders by using the word "*they*"?
"*They* are always harping on us about food storage" or "*They* are always telling us to stay out of
debt." They make it sound as if the Brethren just
sit around and dream these things up so they can't
have any fun. They fail to recognize that these are
commandments from God.

The Israelites began to lack faith in the Lord as their food supply began to diminish. They lusted after the "flesh pots" (Exodus 16:3) in Egypt, the place from whence they had been delivered from bondage. The Lord came through, promising "I will rain bread from heaven." He provided manna for them (Exodus 16:4), and they were delivered once more.

In Twelve-Step recovery meetings, one hears about the "God hole"—an empty place inside addicts that they used to try to fill up with alcohol, drugs, and whatever else. They can rest assured that any empty places still vacated within their soul will be entirely filled by "living water" and the "bread of life" (John 4:10; 6:35).

4. **"Remember how much fun it used to be."**

One of an addict's challenges is the infamous committee inside his or her head. It is good at justifying, rationalizing, and reframing bad behavior and character defects. The committee meets often to recall memories from the past. It has a gigantic video tape recorder.

The good news is that this giant video tape recorder has immense storage and superb retrieval capabilities. The bad news is that this giant video tape recorder has immense storage and superb retrieval capabilities. Some of these tapes should be burned, and yet they never will be. Tapes containing pornographic images, resentments, and failures from the past never seem to get erased. Be extremely careful about what goes on those tapes.

Then there are tapes that romanticize the addiction—tapes and stories of "the good old days." The children of Israel had such tapes. They reminisced about those good old days and recounted, "We remember the fish, which we did eat in Egypt freely;

the cucumbers, and the melons, and the leeks, and the onions, and the garlick: But now our soul is dried away: there is nothing at all, beside this manna, before our eyes" (Numbers 11:5–6).

How could this be the same time period as when the Lord said, "I have surely seen the affliction of my people which are in Egypt, and have heard their cry by reason of their taskmasters; for I know their sorrows?" (Exodus 3:7) Wasn't Egypt their "house of bondage?" (Exodus 20:2) If it was so wonderful, why was there such a big celebration when they left Egypt?

For me, there are triggers. I can hear a song from 1972, and the tapes inside my head play back the glory days. I feel a head rush, and relive the party. I recall those as the days when I could quit drinking anytime I wanted to.

But if I am rigorously honest, I see a different scene. I see a drunk wallowing around in his own vomit. I see a distant man in the mirror. The lights are gone out of his eyes. I hear a pack of lies being told to loved ones the day after the party. I see the inside of a jail cell and the cold, steel bars as I look out. I see the disappointed look on my parents' faces, and I hear the sobbing of a spouse. I see a little shrunken and drunken man, trapped inside his bottle, wondering how he ever ended up in this nightmare.

For some of the children of Israel, the batteries went dead, the tape player stopped, and the committee ruled. They said, "Let us make a captain, and let us return into Egypt" (Numbers 14:4).

5. **"You might as well get loaded."**

At one point, the children of Israel organized a "committee" and concluded, "Let us make a captain, and let us return into Egypt" (Numbers 14:4). In essence, they "went back out."

In their new wilderness of sobriety, Addicts learn to feel things again. Sometimes they may have the mistaken notion that life was better back in Egypt (in bondage) when they didn't have to feel anything. Feelings of sorrow, boredom, disappointment, anger, and grief are not pleasant to experience, but we have the bitter to experience the sweet (see 2 Nephi 2:11).

Satan also attacks with perfectionism. Addicts often get excited about their programs and want to do everything just right. Then they make a little error or slip up a bit. They may feel bad and become impatient with their slower spiritual growth. The enemy pounces on them while they are still down and says, "Well, you might as well get loaded."

Amulek counsels us to "improve our time while in this life" (Alma 34:33). In Step Eleven we "improve our conscious contact with God." The direction we are going may be more important than where we are.

6. **"See how good it looks."**

"And the mixt multitude that was among them *fell a lusting*: and the children of Israel also wept again, and said, Who shall give us flesh to eat?" (Numbers 11:4)

Though the children of Israel were lusting after meat to eat, this scripture identifies a much larger temptation in today's society. The problem of lust is greater today with pornography rampant among all forms of the media. We need to stay clear of and run away from the things of the flesh.

The Savior likened the seeds of a sower to the words of God. Some seeds fell among the thorns and were choked. He explained that "the lusts of other things entering in, choke the word" (Mark 4:19). Lust drives away the Spirit. No wonder Alma tells Corianton to "go no more after the lusts of your eyes, but cross yourself in all these things" (Alma 39:9). We need the power of the Spirit to stay clean and sober, and the Spirit will "not dwell in unholy temples" (Alma 7:21).

Alcoholics and drug addicts need to avoid slippery places where drugs might look appealing or where they might get thirsty.

7. **"You've got it made. You can let up on your program for a while."**

"And it came to pass, after the year was expired, at the time when kings go forth to battle, that David sent Joab, and his servants with him, and all Israel; . . . But David tarried still at Jerusalem" (2 Samuel 11:1).

We have considered how kings in Israel are conquerors for their people. Whenever I read 1 Samuel and see all the great things David has done—like slaying Goliath in chapter 17 or sparing the life of Saul, who was a fierce enemy, in chapter 24—I shed a tear or two because I know I am coming to the spot in 2 Samuel 11 when David puts his program on autopilot and "tarries behind in Jerusalem."

I feel confident in saying that David was not reading his scriptures anymore. He must have forgotten his prayers, and he just wasn't doing the basic things required to have the Spirit of the Lord with him. When we are starved spiritually, the appetite of the natural man takes over. One verse later come the lustful glances from the rooftop, and two verses after that, he is ensnared in adultery. But it all started when David quit working his program!

8. **"See, I told you, you couldn't keep all those commandments!"**

"Ye cannot bear all things now; nevertheless, be of good cheer, for I will lead you along. The kingdom is yours and the blessings thereof are yours, and the riches of eternity are yours" (D&C 78:18).

Satan's speech starts out exactly the same. He'll whisper, "You can never keep all those commandments." Later, the message changes directions dramatically. The Lord leads us along, but Satan abandons us, especially when we hit bottom! The seed of King Noah's priests were "scattered abroad and slain, even as a sheep having no shepherd is driven and slain by wild beasts" (see Alma 25:12).

Don't listen to Satan when he whispers these lies. The scripture says, "No unclean thing can dwell with God" (1 Nephi 10:21). It doesn't say, "No *imperfect* thing can dwell with God."

When we make covenants with the Lord, He will lead us along and walk with us. We can "be of good cheer!"

9. **"Come on, it's only PG-13!"**

If you ever want to learn how Satan operates, open up your Book of Mormon and read Alma 47. Amalickiah is a carbon copy of Satan if I ever saw one.

He is a Nephite by birth (Alma 49:25), rebels against the Nephites, is cast out from among them, seeks to destroy the kingdom, is not loyal to anyone, and uses lies and deception to gain control of the Lamanite kingdom.

Amalickiah had a Lamanite army under his command. He sought to take over another army and place himself in command over all the armies of the king. He sends a "secret embassy" to the mount Antipas, where Lehonti commands the other army. Like Satan, Amalickiah is persistent. He sends messages to Lehonti four times to get him to come down off the mount and stage a mock take-over of Amalickiah's own army. Thus, when Amalickiah's troops awaken, they will be startled to see they are surrounded, even though the whole event has been staged.

The troops beg Amalickiah to surrender to Lehonti's army, and Amalickiah becomes second in command. That's not good enough for him or for Satan. He wants to be the number one commander, so he plots to kill Lehonti. He "caused that one of his servants should administer poison by degrees to Lehonti, that he died" (Alma 47:18).

"Poison by degrees." Isn't that how Satan gets us? He starts out by getting us to rationalize just a little sin. We start getting spiritually sick as the doses of poison increase. Left half sick and spiritually half dead, we can't fight back. Then he goes for the spiritually fatal dose that does us in.

He starts out by saying, "It's not that bad. It's only PG-13. It just has a little bit of profanity, a little bit of violence, and maybe just a scene of immorality. But it's only partial nudity." To the potential alcoholic he says, "One beer won't hurt." And we are left the weaker.

Don't let him poison you.

10. "Lighten up! Everyone else is doing it."

When Amalickiah begged Lehonti to "come down off from the mount" and participate in a counterfeit siege of his troops, Lehonti resisted his urges three times.

On the fourth attempt, Amalickiah "went *up into* the mount, nearly to Lehonti's camp" (Alma 47:12). The mount is symbolic of the temple, especially when one goes "into" the mount. Notice that Amalickiah cannot come right into Lehonti's camp. Satan's bounds are set (see D&C 122:9). He cannot overpower you by standing on the top of the mount and knocking you off of it. He must beg that you will stoop down to his lower level and lower standards.

Amalickiah (like Satan) begs Lehonti to "come down, and . . . bring his guards with him" (see Alma 47:12). If we slightly change the wording, it would read, "Let down your guard."

If we "stand . . . in holy places" (D&C 87:8), we are out of reach of Satan's power. If we stand true, making and keeping temple covenants, we are out of reach of the enemy.

The adversary will try to get each and every one of us to rationalize breaking our covenants with the Lord. He may even whisper, "Lighten up. Everyone else is doing it!" Then he administers "poison by degrees."

Don't listen, and don't let down your guard.

11. **"Your testimony is not supported by scientific evidence."**

The Lord uses six-dimensional experiences to increase our testimonies and spiritual growth. He gives us ordinances like baptism, the sacrament, and the laying on of hands, all of which involve physical elements. Hopefully, we experience the sweet feeling of the Holy Ghost as we receive these ordinances. The Holy Ghost bears witness of the Father and Son and testifies of revealed truth.

Satan, on the other hand, uses five-dimensional experiences to blind us.

At the Savior's birth, marvelous signs were given in both the Holy Land and the Americas. But shortly thereafter, the people "began to be less and less astonished at a sign or a wonder from heaven, insomuch that they began to be hard in their hearts, and blind in their minds, and began to disbelieve all which they had *heard* and *seen*" (3 Nephi 2:1, emphasis added).

When the king of the Lamanites came forth to meet Amalickiah and the united army he commanded after Lehonti's death, Amalickiah sent a servant forward who "stabbed the king to the heart." Of course the king's servants immediately fled the scene in fear of their lives. Then Amalickiah's servants "raised a cry, saying: Behold, the servants of the king have stabbed him to the heart, and he has fallen and they have fled; behold, come and see" (Alma 47:25–26). Amalickiah set up another counterfeit scene and used the physical evidence to deceive the people.

In modern times the Lord has said: "For they that are wise and have received the truth, and have taken the Holy Spirit for their guide, and have not been deceived—verily I say unto you, they shall not be hewn down and cast into the fire, but shall abide the day" (D&C 45:57).

In addiction, addicts always bow down to the physical, giving the body exactly what it craves. In recovery, they must take the Holy Spirit for their guide.

12. "Getting to the temple is just an impossible dream."

"Whereupon the king [Jeroboam] took counsel, and made two calves of gold, and said unto them, It is too much for you to go up to Jerusalem: behold thy gods, O Israel, which brought thee up out of the land of Egypt" (1 Kings 12:28).

Jeroboam was king over the northern ten tribes after the kingdom was divided. Rehoboam was king of Judah, the southern kingdom.

Jeroboam was not so concerned about his people getting blisters on their feet from traveling to the temple in Jerusalem. He was worried he would lose the allegiance of his people if they traveled back to the kingdom of Judah, so he set up a counterfeit god and a counterfeit form of worship.

Addicts are awfully good at bowing down to the god of alcohol or the god of drugs or the god of pornography and sexual addiction. They need to be careful in recovery that they don't fashion other gods.

I have heard some share in meetings that they have an understanding of a higher power different from the one they grew up with. That might be good. As a returned missionary I came into the rooms of AA believing in a stern, punishing, and unforgiving god. Today my understanding of God is just the opposite.

Addicts must be careful to not manufacture a god of convenience. They must seek to "come unto Christ" (Omni 1:26) and approach His level instead of asking Him to bend to their own will.

King Jeroboam was subtle in his approach. He strategically placed his own false gods in Bethel and Dan—one on the north border and one on the south border (see 1 Kings 12:29). Thus, he could distract travelers in either direction, but it was a ridiculous excuse for not going the distance to the temple in Jerusalem. Jeroboam established the capital in Shechem. The distance from Shechem to Dan is greater than from Shechem to Jerusalem, and if you went to Bethel, you would be over halfway to Jerusalem (see map 10 in the Bible).

Jeroboam placed one golden calf in Bethel. What a counterfeit perversion! *Bethel* means "house of God" (see *Strong's Exhaustive Concordance of the Bible* #1008).

If you are an addict in recovery, don't settle for Satan's counterfeits or do "half measures" in your program. Make that journey to the true "house of God." Make that journey to the holy temple of the Lord. It is worth any sacrifice, and it is achievable. He will help you back.

Your Shield from the Fiery Darts

The best defense is the word of God. Nephi said the rod of iron represented the word of God, and "whoso would . . . hold fast unto it, they would never perish; neither could the temptations and the fiery darts of the adversary overpower them unto blindness, to lead them away to destruction" (1 Nephi 15:24).

The "word of God" comes in two forms. It is the written words of the prophets, modern and ancient, and it is also the Holy Ghost. Nephi also said, "Angels speak by the power of the Holy Ghost; wherefore, they speak the words of Christ" (2 Nephi 32:3).

As you battle the enemy and put on the "whole armour of God," take up "the sword of the Spirit, which is the word of God" (see Ephesians 6:13–17). It is your only offensive weapon against the adversary. With it, you will be the conqueror.

The stakes are high in this battle. It is for a throne of exaltation in the celestial kingdom of our God.

"a thorn in the flesh"

Early in my sobriety I heard someone say that he was grateful to be an alcoholic. I thought it was absurd. Why would anyone want to be cursed with the disease of alcoholism? Many times since I have heard my sponsor introduce himself as an alcoholic and then add, "I am grateful to know that today."

At first, I thought these people were crazy, but over time, I came to be grateful to know that I am an alcoholic. Today, I am actually grateful to *be* an alcoholic as well. I am *not* grateful for those many years spent drinking and the awful choices I made, but I am grateful that when I hit bottom and gave it my best shot to quit drinking, I failed. That may sound crazy too. And it was awful at the time, but there was a silver lining in the cloud of my despair. I was driven to my knees, and in my own failure, I came to realize and partake of the power of my God. I couldn't, but He could!

Today, I am grateful that He didn't cure me, and I'm grateful that He does heal me.

I can wake up every morning with a thankful heart, knowing that I must rely "wholly upon the merits of him who is mighty to save" (2 Nephi 31:19). That's a pretty sweet deal.

In my heart, I feel a closeness to the Apostle Paul.

Paul speaks of a six-dimensional experience, wherein he was "caught up" to see and hear things pertaining to celestial glory. In the spiritual realm, he is separated from the flesh to such a degree that he cannot tell whether he is in the body or out of the body. Either he was not permitted to tell, or he was so immersed in the things of the Spirit that he did not notice the things of the flesh.

He must have felt free from physical limitations. He was elevated from the "thorns" of life. He would not feel the compulsion of addiction among many other "thorns" in the flesh. He would not suffer from HALT and would not feel hungry, angry, lonely, or tired. What a sublime experience. He was "caught up into paradise, and heard unspeakable words, which [were] not lawful for a man to utter."

Paul chose to glory not in himself but in his infirmities. Yes, even the great Apostle Paul, who once lived contrary to the will of God (much like addicts do), is a model for us in recovery. As his life changes dramatically, he is relegated back to the mortal, mundane, carnal, and limited world of the physical. He feels "a thorn in the flesh." You can tell he is trying to escape and rise above it. He calls it a "thorn in the flesh, the messenger of Satan to buffet me." Then he says, "For this thing I besought the Lord thrice, that it might depart from me."

But then his tone changes as he receives an answer from the Lord. The Lord says to Paul, "My grace is sufficient for thee: for my strength is made perfect in weakness." Then Paul feels an immense attitude of gratitude for this "thorn," and he exclaims, "Most *gladly* therefore will I *rather* glory in my infirmities, that the *power* of Christ may rest upon me."

Paul must have been praying along the lines of Step Eleven. In this step, we pray for "knowledge of [God's] will for us and the *power* to carry that out." What a marvelous blessing it is to feel the power of God in recovery. I knew I didn't get myself clean and sober. Rather, God made me clean and sober. I knew I was not changing my life, but rather I was allowing God to change my heart, and my life was blessed in the process.

I always say, gratitude beats pride. If I ever tried to take credit for my sobriety and recovery, I would be lying.

There was a time when I could only feel sorrow and anger as I thought about my life; I could only feel fear as I thought about where my life was headed. I wanted only to drown my feelings in food and strong drink. To ponder upon life was painful.

Paul recognizes that the "power of Christ" is only half of the Step Eleven equation. We pray for knowledge *and* power. But Paul feels gratitude as he says, "Yea, doubtless, and I count all things but loss for the excellency of the *knowledge* of Christ Jesus my Lord: for whom I have suffered the loss of all things, and do count them but dung, that I may win Christ" (Philippians 3:8). I should be grateful for everything God puts in my path, even if I step in a little dung along the way.

Paul summarizes his philosophy when he states, "Therefore I take pleasure in infirmities, in reproaches, in necessities, in persecutions, in distresses for Christ's sake: for when I am weak, then am I strong" (see 2 Corinthians 12:1–10).

We often quote a similar scripture in the Book of Mormon. It is perhaps the most quoted scripture in the LDS Twelve-Step Recovery Program. It states, "And if men come unto me I will show unto them their weakness. I give unto men weakness that they may be humble; and my grace is sufficient for all men that humble themselves before me; for if they humble themselves before me, and have faith in me, then will I make weak things become strong unto them" (Ether 12:27).

There are two things we gain in weakness. We gain humility, and we gain trust in the Lord. These two traits activate grace. To the suffering addict and alcoholic, the best four words in the English language are "My grace is sufficient."

THE THORN, THE ROSE, AND THE CROWN

At the bottom of the Mount of Olives there was a garden, and in that garden was a "tender plant . . . as a root out of a dry ground." There was a "Stem of Jesse," and on Him was placed a "crown of thorns." There, and upon the cross, the Savior paid for the thorns of life. He bought something else for you and me! Out of the stem and amidst the thorns, there blooms a beautiful rose. It is the rose of recovery that He purchased for you and me! (See Isaiah 53:2; 11:1; D&C 113:1–2; and Matthew 27:29.)

The thorns were made into a crown. He descended below all things to find us and lift us up—so you and I could wear the crown and shout Hosanna to the King. He sees you wearing your crown, and He reveals a prayer for you and me: "That our garments may be pure, that we may be clothed upon with robes of righteousness, with palms in our hands, and crowns of glory upon our heads, and reap eternal joy for all our sufferings" (D&C 109:76).

The thorn was not so bad after all.

a free bird

About two years after I got sober, I would go on long walks on Saturday afternoons. I had to find something to fill the void of those Saturday afternoons and evenings I used to spend in local bars.

One Saturday afternoon, I walked by a large, open field. The ground was freshly plowed, and the earth looked clean with all of the weeds removed. It had a fresh, earthy smell. I had my headphones on. A beautiful new age track came on the radio, and I was on a natural high. The fresh air filled my lungs, and energy filled my being.

I spotted a hawk flying over the open field, and I watched its wings as it glided against the blue-sky backdrop. I was filled with gratitude. What a feeling of freedom! Who was more free—the hawk or me? I watched it circle high above the field and the freshly plowed soil. It almost seemed to be circling over something, ready to descend to the prey below, but I could see nothing but dirt.

I had a peaceful feeling inside as I listened to the beautiful music, and a chill went down my spine. It felt good to be in touch with nature and God's beautiful world. I was soon past the field and the hawk, but the peaceful feeling continued throughout my walk. I thought about how wonderful it was to be sober.

The image of the hawk flying freely over the open field was tucked away in the back of my mind, and the months passed on.

Several months later, my stake president was teaching a scripture class. I loved his excellent talks, and he always motivated me to do better. In those days, the scriptures had not yet come to life for me as they do today. I rarely studied the scriptures, but I liked to be spoon-fed and just sit back and listen.

One night, at the end of class, I followed him to the parking lot with tears of gratitude in my eyes and told him what an impact his lesson had had on me. He then said he had not planned to share that particular passage from the scriptures, but the Spirit prompted him to do so. He felt that someone needed to hear it. I knew the Lord had done something special for me. The lesson he taught has become a favorite of mine. I call it, "A Free Bird."

Turn to Leviticus 14. This is the Mosaic law for cleansing lepers. There is beautiful symbolism here, demonstrating how we are cleansed from sin and addiction. Every time Jesus healed a leper, there was a spiritual type for becoming clean through His Atonement.

The leper was brought to the priest. The priest served as a mediator between the unclean leper and God. A priest was a type of Christ. Paul describes Jesus as the "great high priest" (see Hebrews 4:14–16). Jesus Christ is our mediator and "advocate with the Father." He is pleading our cause (see D&C 45:3). The priest in this rite also represented a modern-day bishop. Bishops hold priesthood keys and can receive revelation to help us in recovery.

The priest would go forth out of the camp and look and see if the plague of leprosy was healed in the leper. Bishops do the same thing. They are shepherds who look after those sheep who have become lost, and who have become entangled in addiction, and have thereby become unclean.

I am grateful for bishops who came calling on me when I thought I was not worth saving. The bishop is our judge in Israel. He determines if we are ready for baptism, worthy to partake of the sacrament, or clean enough to enter the temple.

The priest would take for the person being cleansed, "two birds alive and clean, and cedar wood, and scarlet, and hyssop" (v. 4). The imagery points to the Atonement.

Cedar wood symbolizes the wooden cross upon which our Savior hung. The crucifiers put a scarlet robe on Jesus, and when He was on the cross, they "filled a spunge with vinegar, and put it upon hyssop, and put it to his mouth" (see Matthew 27:28; John 19:29).

As we look at Leviticus 14, we notice in verse 5 that the priest commands one of the birds be killed in "an earthen vessel over running water." After the crucifixion, the body of Jesus was placed in an earthen vessel—the tomb of Joseph of Arimathaea, which he had "hewn out in the rock" (see Matthew 27:57–60).

The prophet Jonah, who, contrary to Step Three, sought after his own will, was an Old Testament type of Christ. Jonah was swallowed up by a great fish and spent "three days and three nights" in the "belly of hell." He relates, "The *earth* with her bars was about me for ever: yet hast thou brought up my life from corruption, O Lord my God." It sounds like Jonah spent a little time in an "*earthen* vessel" too! (See Jonah 1:17–2:6.)

Like Jonah and the remaining bird (in Leviticus 14), addicts too can be rescued from the earthen grave, from the belly of hell, and from those worldly *bars* that used to hold them captive. They too can have their lives brought up from corruption. They too can be delivered from spiritual bondage and physical death. One day we will all be resurrected, and our bodies will come forth out of the grave.

I will never forget those times when I was held captive in the "belly of hell." Earth with her bars (dual meaning here), drugs, immorality, pornography, and addictive substances has held us captive, but Jesus Christ can set us free.

Let's get back to the story of the two birds. One bird was "killed in an earthen vessel over running water." The "running water" is also beautiful symbolism, pointing us to Jesus Christ. The Lord said to the woman at the well, "If thou knewest the gift of God, and who it is that saith to thee, Give me to drink; thou wouldest have asked of him, and he would have given thee *living water.*" He said, "But whosoever drinketh of the water that I shall give him shall never thirst; but the water that I shall give him shall be in him a well of water springing up into everlasting life" (see John 4:10–14). "Running water" is continuous "living water." It is water that never runs dry. It is what addicts thirst after when they try to fill themselves up with booze, drugs, and other stuff. "Living water" fills their souls and springs up into everlasting, eternal life. If we turn to the Lord, we will never dry up in recovery.

The second bird remains alive. "As for the living bird, [the priest] shall take it, and the cedar wood, and the scarlet, and the hyssop, and shall dip them and the living bird in the blood of the bird that was killed over the running water" (v. 6). The blood of the bird killed in the earthen vessel becomes a cleansing, life-giving, purifying agent.

There was a time when I feared to take the sacrament, but today, I have images in my mind of that "precious blood . . . as of a lamb without blemish and without spot," and I know I was not purchased with "silver and gold." (See 1 Peter 1:18–19.) The best things cost the most (see D&C 135:6). I see images of a bird—alive and clean. Sometimes tears of gratitude fill my eyes, as I hear the words of the sacrament prayer: "bless and sanctify this [water] to the souls of all those who drink of it, that they may do it in remembrance of the blood of thy Son, which was shed for them." (D&C 20:79).

My AA sobriety chip helps me to "always remember Him." I carry a red medallion in my pocket. It is the same color as His blood, which He freely spilt for you and me. Like the bird that remains alive, I know I am clean and sober today because of His blood.

When the bread is passed, I think of His "earthen vessel," which housed His immortal spirit, even the spirit of Jehovah, creator of all things. He gave His "earthen vessel"—His own mortal body—for me, so my spirit could soar free from an addicted, compulsive, mortal vessel—an addicted, mortal body.

The story of the unclean leper continues. Leviticus 14:7 states, "And [the priest] shall sprinkle upon him that is to be cleansed from the leprosy seven times, and shall pronounce him clean." The unclean leper is cleansed as the blood of the bird is sprinkled upon him seven times. The number seven represents perfection, completeness, and wholeness. Like the leper, an addict's complete cleansing from addiction and healing can come from only the Atonement—from His precious blood. We all can be cleansed from sin and set free from addiction or temptation as we have the opportunity to partake of the sacrament, which we do on the Sabbath, or *seventh* day of the week (see Exodus 20:10–11).

Our respective bishops, our judges in Israel, can "pronounce us clean," so we can receive saving ordinances. As we make and keep our covenants, we are cleansed from sin and set free from bondage, making the purifying process complete. Even when Jesus cleansed the ten lepers, He commanded them to show themselves unto the priest, so the priest could pronounce them clean. Our bishops serve in a similar capacity. As the ten lepers demonstrated their obedience by going to the priest, they were cleansed (see Luke 17:12–14).

I am grateful for a bishop who helped me get back to the temple, even though it seemed impossible. I was sober at the time, but I assumed that, because of my wreckage of the past, such dreams and blessings had long ago been forfeited. The Lord had other plans for me. I would have missed the best blessings if I had gone with my own will.

I learned that the priest was commanded to "let the living bird loose into the open field" (v. 7), and in my mind's eye, I saw that hawk circling over the open field and flying free. It soared high into the beautiful blue sky.

I thought about my question: Who was more free—the hawk or me? Then I realized, I *was* that hawk. That was really *me* flying over the open field. I could see for miles. I had a clear vision, far into the future. I had a new view and a higher vantage point. Before, I had seen only the dirt and the mud. But now I smelled the richly plowed soil, and I saw the beauty of the earth. Like King Benjamin's people, who had also entered into a covenant, and "through the infinite goodness of God, and the manifestations of his Spirit," I had "great views" too (see Mosiah 5:3). Whenever I look into my daughter's eyes, or see a picture drawn by my son, or get a kiss from my wife, I realize that I am a free bird, and I can have these blessings for eternity, if I will keep my part of the covenant. When I partake of the sacrament, I remember that I am a free bird only because of my Savior. I can soar because I can be cleansed by His blood, which He willingly shed to set me free. I know I will one day stand in His presence, and I have great hopes that He will pronounce me clean.

Any addict can become a free bird. The covenants they make will not yoke them down, but will rather lift them up to a new and everlasting life. Because of the sacrifice of the Savior, they can sing songs of everlasting joy with the Psalmist, who wrote: "Our soul is escaped as a bird out of the snare of the fowlers: the snare is broken, and we are escaped." (Psalms 124:7)

What about the leper who had a new life of cleanness? The scriptures record:

> And he that is to be cleansed shall wash his clothes, and shave off all his hair, and wash himself in water, that he may be clean: and after that he shall come into the camp, and shall tarry abroad out of his tent seven days.
>
> But it shall be on the seventh day, that he shall shave all his hair off his head and his beard and his eyebrows, even all his hair he shall shave off: and he shall wash his clothes, also he shall wash his flesh in water, and he shall be clean. (Leviticus 14:8–9)

You and I can be washed clean in the waters of baptism and each Sunday as we partake of the sacrament. We can put on our "beautiful garments" and prepare to be clothed in the house of the Lord (see Isaiah 52:1). Like the cleansed leper, we can "walk in newness of life" (Romans 6:4).

The cleansed leper shaves his beard, eyebrows, and hair, and he has the appearance of a newborn baby. Like the leper, we can all be born again and begin a wonderful, new life as a covenant son or daughter of Christ.

"consider the lilies of the field"

Many years ago when my family was returning from a camping trip, we drove through a beautiful canyon. As we reached the summit, we saw a lush, green meadow filled with colorful flowers of white, yellow, and purple. The majestic pines provided a scenic contrast to the grassy meadow. We stopped and viewed with awe this magnificent scene and thanked God for such natural beauty. We wondered who planted all the gorgeous flowers, and how they were watered and nourished.

Several years later I was sitting at the bus stop and reading the Sermon on the Mount, when I came across this scripture: "Consider the lilies of the field, how they grow" (Matthew 6:28).

My mind flashed back to that day in the mountains when I saw the beautiful flowers in a green meadow. Something struck me. I went back and read the verse in context: "And why take ye thought for raiment? Consider the lilies of the field, how they grow; they toil not, neither do they spin: And yet I say unto you, That even Solomon in all his glory was not arrayed like one of these" (Matthew 6:28–29).

The unmistakable impression I received from the Spirit was one like Elder Richard G. Scott spoke of in general conference. It was a "response to the mind . . . very specific, like dictated words" (Richard G. Scott, "Using the Supernal Gift of Prayer," *Ensign* [May 2007]: 8). I did not hear any voices, but the impression was specific enough for me to turn to 1 Kings, where Solomon's temple is described. At the time, I had read very little out of the Old Testament, and the scriptures had only begun to come alive for me about two years earlier. I had absolutely no idea what I would find in 1 Kings.

I began reading. I read about how Solomon used the finest materials to build the house of the Lord. The best craftsmen were hired. I read about two pillars in the porch of the temple. The pillars were even given names—Boaz and Jachin. Boaz was a name shared with an ancestor of Christ, an ancestor who was also a kinsman-redeemer to Ruth. The name *Jachin* means, "He will establish" (see Matthew 1:5–16; Ruth 4:17–22; and *Strong's Exhaustive Concordance of the Bible* #3199).

Pillars in the temple are mentioned in the Book of Revelation: "Him that overcometh will I make a pillar in the temple of my God, and he shall *go no more out*: and I will write upon him the name of my God . . . and I will write upon him my new name" (Revelation 3:12, emphasis added).

Interestingly, in Twelve Step recovery, the phrase "go out" means to drink or use drugs after a period of sobriety.

The concept of a "new name," or taking upon one's self the name of Christ, is closely related to covenants. We take the name of Christ upon ourselves when we are baptized and when we partake of the sacrament each Sunday (see D&C 20:77). Our hearts, and indeed our very natures, are changed through His name. King Benjamin's people took upon themselves the name of Christ, and because of the covenant they made, they became spiritually begotten sons and daughters of Christ (see Mosiah 5:7, 9–11).

I continued reading in 1 Kings 7. When I got to verse 22, a light came on, and the sweet peace of the Spirit illuminated my inner being: "And upon the top of the pillars was *lily* work: so was the work of the pillars finished" (emphasis added). God is not finished with us yet. The work and spiritual progress go on.

When I got to verse 26, I saw that the baptismal font was decorated like a giant cup. The font contained about 16,500 gallons of water. "And the brim thereof was wrought like the brim of a cup, with *flowers of lilies*."

Consider the lilies on tops of pillars. "He will establish" them in glory and righteousness. In them is His strength (see Bible Dictionary, "Jachin and Boaz") Consider the wretched alcoholic, once washed up and ruined, now a pillar made strong in the House of the Lord! Consider the addict with a heart of stone, now strengthened and fortified like the pillars in the temple.

There were four elements all tied up in the same chapter of scripture—Solomon, the temple, a baptismal font, and some lilies. When the Savior said that "even Solomon in all his glory was not arrayed like one of these," was He talking about the lilies in Solomon's temple? I pondered this question along with imagery of covenant making that was laced throughout the entire Sermon on the Mount with words like mountain, salt, house, and candlestick. I tried to put this imagery in context.

I backed up to Matthew 6:25: "Therefore I say unto you, Take no thought for your life, what ye shall eat, or what ye shall drink; nor yet for your body, what ye shall put on. Is not the life more than meat, and the body than raiment?" I could almost hear Him saying, "Take no thought for your life—you turned it over to me in Step Three. Don't quit your job or do anything stupid, but trust in me. I will take care of you."

I started to look more carefully at verse 28. I could feel the power of those words, but I would not realize why until a couple of years later when I was studying the once-scary Book of Revelation and came upon the word *clothed*. I learned that the original Greek word for clothed is *enduo* (see *Strong's* #1746). It is the source of the English word *endowment*. The word *enduo* is used in the following contexts in Revelation:

> "And in the midst of the seven candlesticks one like unto the Son of man, *clothed* with a garment down to the foot, and girt about the paps with a golden girdle" (Revelation 1:13, emphasis added).

"And the seven angels came out of the temple, having
the seven plagues, *clothed* in pure and white linen, and having their breasts girded with golden girdles" (Revelation 15:6,
emphasis added).

"And the armies which were in heaven followed [Christ]
upon white horses, *clothed* in fine linen, white and clean"
(Revelation 19:14, emphasis added).

I also discovered the same word translated differently in another
passage. It was translated as *endued* in Luke: "And, behold, I send the
promise of my Father upon you: but tarry ye in the city of Jerusalem,
until ye be *endued* with power from on high" (Luke 24:49, emphasis
added). The Lord commands His disciples to tarry in Jerusalem until
they are endowed with power from on high, and then they will have the
power necessary to preach the gospel to the nations. In our dispensation
the Lord said, "Wherefore, for this cause I gave unto you the commandment that ye should go to the Ohio; and there I will give unto you my
law; and there you shall be *endowed* with power from on high" (D&C
38:32, emphasis added). In Luke 24:53, it is recorded that the disciples
were "continually in the temple," where they were endowed and empowered from on high. There was a temple in Jerusalem and a temple in
Kirtland, Ohio.

When the Lord poses the question, "And why take ye thought for
raiment?" (Matthew 6:28), could He be speaking about something more
than mere clothing? The Greek word *enduo* means to clothe, invest, en-
due, or put on. Is it any wonder the Lord commands us to put off the
"natural man" and "put on" Christ? (See Mosiah 3:19; Galatians 3:27.)

The original Greek word for *raiment* is also a related word: *enduma*
(see *Strong's* #1742). It means clothing, garment, robe, or raiment.

"And why take ye thought for *raiment*? Consider the lilies of the
field, how they grow."

In another context *enduma* is used to represent a wedding garment.
In the parable of the marriage of the king's son, guests are invited to the
wedding feast. Those who are invited make light of it, and the king commands his servants to go out into the highways and to gather as many as
they can find. The king said, "They which were bidden were not worthy."

One guest arrives to the wedding, but he didn't have the wedding garment on. The king said, "Friend, how camest thou in hither not having a wedding garment?" (See Matthew 22:2–12.)

The "wedding garment," translated from the word *enduma*, is clearly a token of the covenant. We enter into a covenant relationship with the Lord, we become yoked to Him, and we are admonished to "be ready at the coming of the Bridegroom" (D&C 33:17).

The guest at the wedding was not properly *clothed*. We can receive our endowment (or *enduo*) and do our very best to keep our covenants, but there is part of our attire that we cannot put on. It is the *kaphar*, and *kaphar* is the Hebrew word for atonement (see *Strong's* #3722). *Kaphar* means to coat, cover, or atone by legal rites.

We must be "clothed with purity, yea, even with the robe of righteousness" (2 Nephi 9:14). We need to "suit up and show up" at the "supper of the Lamb." When the Bridegroom comes again, He will be "clothed in the brightness of his glory, to meet the kingdom of God which is set up on the earth" (see D&C 65:3, 5). We need to be dressed in robes of pure white—like the Lamb.

"Consider the lilies of the field, how they grow; they toil not, neither do they spin: And yet I say unto you, That even Solomon in all his glory was not arrayed like one of these. Wherefore, if God so *clothe* the grass of the field, which to day is, and to morrow is cast into the oven, shall he not much more clothe you, O ye of little faith?" (See Matthew 6:28–30.)

Can you only imagine how He will clothe and empower you?

As I pondered the Sermon on the Mount, the Holy Spirit planted two images in my heart and mind. If God would clothe the grass of the field, which men may consider as weeds to be dug up and burned, how much more will He clothe His own offspring—His own sons and daughters who have His image engraven in their countenances? (See Alma 5:14.) In His loving care, if He would clothe the lilies of the field in pure robes of white, how much more is He anxiously waiting to clothe and endow you? There is a part of the Atonement, or the *kaphar*, that can only be accessed through covenants.

I thought of the lilies on the tops of the pillars and on the baptismal font in Solomon's Temple. Solomon brought in the finest materials. I am sure he called on the best artists and sculptors to carve lilies in the temple. I thought of how beautiful they must have been. The Spirit took me back to the lilies of the field. I reflected back to that scenic drive over a beautiful mountain, and I was certain that those magnificent, carved lilies in Solomon's Temple would not hold a candle to God's own creation. They could not be as breathtaking as the "lilies of the field." The Lord put it best when He said, "Even Solomon in all his glory was not arrayed like one of these" (Matthew 6:29).

If the lilies in the temple do not compare with the Lord's own endowment in a majestic mountain meadow, then how do the temple and its ordinances compare with the eternal world? John the Revelator saw in vision the celestial kingdom. He describes, "The street of the city was pure gold, as it were transparent glass. And I saw *no temple* therein: for the Lord God Almighty and the Lamb are the temple of it. And the city had no need of the sun, neither of the moon, to shine in it: for the glory of God did lighten it, and the Lamb is the light thereof" (Revelation 21:21–23).

My first reaction was how awful it would be to not have a temple. Then I remembered that the purpose of the temple is to prepare to return to the presence of God. Those who return home to His presence to live with Him eternally will have no need of a temple.

As we attend the temple, we see our brothers and sisters standing in holy places, arrayed in spotless white, with smiles on their faces. A warm, peaceful feeling is present. Can you imagine how much more glorious they will appear as they stand in the presence of the Father and the Son? As Their countenances shine upon them? Can you imagine how you will appear as you stand before Him, clothed with eternal life and in "robes of righteousness"? (See D&C 109:76) Can you imagine the gratitude you will feel, knowing your garments have been washed white in the blood of the Lamb? (See Alma 5:21, 24, and 27.)

"Wherefore, if God so clothe the grass of the field, which to day is, and to morrow is cast into the oven, shall he not much more clothe you?"

DEW FROM HEAVEN AND A POT OF GOLD

I've continued my study of the lilies of the field, and just four days ago, I felt impressed to go to Doctrine and Covenants 84 and read more.

I felt a connection between the "lilies of the field" (v. 82) and the section heading where "the Prophet [Joseph Smith] designates it a revelation on priesthood." I knew priesthood covenants would help the lilies of the field to *grow*, as verse 82 promised.

I turned to Hosea and read a related passage:

> "I will be as the dew unto Israel: he shall grow as the lily.
> . . . His branches shall spread, and his beauty shall be as the
> olive tree" (Hosea 14:5–6).

I thought of the Lord's covenant with the house of Israel portrayed beautifully in the Book of Mormon. The house of Israel is likened unto a tame olive tree (see Jacob 5:3). I thought of the Mount of Olives and Gethsemane, the "oil press" (see *Strong's #1068*).

Then my mind turned to the dew that watered the lilies. The Lord said, "I will be as the dew unto Israel." The Lord is the dew, allowing Israel (us) to grow. We can be made beautiful through the Atonement.

My thoughts turned to another modern passage:

> "Let virtue garnish thy thoughts unceasingly; then shall
> thy confidence wax strong in the *presence of God*; and the *doctrine* of the *priesthood* shall distil upon thy soul as the *dews*
> from heaven" (D&C 121:45, emphasis added).

The "doctrine of the priesthood" would water the lilies as the "dews from heaven," and that would bring us back into "the presence of God." To come back into the presence of God is the purpose of the temple, and as in the days of Solomon, the lilies are in the temple again, and you are His "pleasant plant" (Isaiah 5:7).

I remembered from scripture study, that *dew* is mentioned in Deuteronomy:

> "My doctrine [of the priesthood] shall drop as the rain,
> my speech shall distil as the *dew*, as the small rain upon the

tender herb, and as the showers upon the *grass*" (Deuteronomy 32:2, emphasis added).

When the Lord spoke of the lilies of the field, He called them "grass." "Wherefore, if God so *clothe* the *grass* of the field, which to day is, and to morrow is cast into the oven, shall he not much more *clothe* you, O ye of little faith?" (Matthew 6:30)

The grass is watered by the doctrine of the priesthood and its ordinances. The nourishing rain is His speech and His word. If the Lord would clothe (or endow) the lilies with so much glory, can you imagine how He will endow you in His temple?

The doctrine and ordinances of the priesthood "drop as the rain" to water precious lilies in the temple. "Be glad then, ye children of Zion, and rejoice in the Lord your God: for he hath given you the former rain moderately, and he will cause to come down for you the rain, the former rain, and the latter rain in the first month" (Joel 2:23).

It may sound backwards, but it's not. The former rain fell in late fall and early winter to prepare the ground for spring planting. The rain fell right after the sacrifice of water by Israel at the water libation of the Feast of Tabernacles. Then the latter rain fell in the first month, which would be March or April on the Hebrew calendar (see Bible Dictionary, "Rain").

The "latter rain" fell in the latter days, as the heavens opened a new dispensation and poured down rain and restoration. In 1820, the first month on the Hebrew calendar began on March 16 (see Michael J. Radwin, "Jewish Calendar Tools," www.hebcal.com). Joseph Smith retired to the Sacred Grove "early in the spring" of that year (Joseph Smith—History 1:14). The Father and the Son appeared to young Joseph, ushering in the dispensation of the fullness of times, complete with priesthood keys and ordinances necessary to water the lilies of the field.

As the rain is refined from heavy rain to "small rain" (Deuteronomy 32:2) to "dews from heaven" (D&C 121:45), a beautiful rainbow can be seen in the clouds. It is a token of the covenant—a token of God's love for each of us. He said, "I do set my bow in the cloud, and it shall be for a token of a covenant between me and the earth" (Genesis 9:13).

As lilies of the field, we really can't be watered without covenants found in holy places.

A POT OF GOLD AT THE END OF THE RAINBOW

Couched within this beautiful revelation pertaining to priesthood (D&C 84) is a Step Eleven rainbow for the addict. At one end is his or her "wreckage of the past." At the other end is a pot of gold. Section 84 is the rainbow connecting the two. Interestingly, it is called, "the oath and *covenant* of the priesthood" (see v. 39, emphasis added).

Before we arrive at the lilies found in verse 82, we pass the following scriptures:

> And this greater priesthood [Melchizedek Priesthood] administereth the gospel and holdeth the key of the mysteries of the kingdom, even the key of the *knowledge* of God.
>
> Therefore, in the ordinances thereof, the *power* of godliness is manifest.
>
> And without the ordinances thereof, and the authority of the priesthood, the *power* of godliness is not manifest unto men in the flesh;
>
> For without this no man can see the face of God, even the Father, and live." (D&C 84:19–22, emphasis added)

Remember, we are seeking knowledge and power. Without priesthood ordinances we cannot enjoy a full knowledge of God nor can we receive a full manifestation of His power. And just as we could not see His face and live, we also could not live eternally in His presence without priesthood ordinances.

As lilies, we could not be watered or grow or live in the presence of our Father without temple covenants.

The conclusion of this spiritual experience came as I was leaving the bus stop. I heard distinct words in my mind. I did not hear a voice, but the exact words were these, repeated three times: "You must grow in the knowledge of the truth." I knew they sounded familiar, and I soon found similar words in a scripture: "Ye must *grow* in *grace* [an enabling power] and in the *knowledge* of the truth" (D&C 50:40, emphasis added).

WHERE THE LILIES GROW

"Often called the 'white-robed apostles of hope,' lilies were found growing in the Garden of Gethsemane after Christ's agony. Tradition has it that the beautiful white lilies sprung up where drops of Christ's sweat fell to the ground in his final hours of sorrow and deep distress" (Jerry Parsons and Dan Lineberger, "Easter Lily," PLANTanswers, http://plantanswers.tamu.edu/publications/lily/lily.html).

"Consider the lilies of the field, how they grow" (Matthew 6:28). Consider the lilies of the field, where they grow. Consider the lilies in a garden, grown in the rich soil of the earth and sprinkled with drops of blood, sweat, and tears. Consider the lilies of the Garden of Gethsemane, where our Savior knelt in incomprehensible agony and purchased recovery and healing for each of us. We grow in the same way as those lilies.

LIVING WATER TO SWIM IN

The prophet Ezekiel was shown in vision the reconstructed temple of the Lord. In this vision he was brought to the door of the house and "waters issued out from under the threshold of the house eastward" (Ezekiel 47:1). The heavenly ministrant conducting this temple tour had a measuring reed in his hand (see Ezekiel 40:3).

> And when the man that had the line in his hand went forth eastward, he measured a thousand cubits, and he brought me through the waters; the waters were to the ankles.
>
> Again he measured a thousand, and brought me through the waters; the waters were to the knees. Again he measured a thousand, and brought me through; the waters were to the loins.

Afterward he measured a thousand; and it was a river
that I could not pass over: for the waters were risen, waters to
swim in, a river that could not be passed over.

And he said unto me, Son of man, hast thou seen this?
(Ezekiel 47:3–6)

The measuring reed is our standard. We will be measured by our
worthiness to enter the temple and by making and keeping sacred covenants. Our purpose for temple worship is to endow, empower, clothe,
and prepare us to enter into the presence of the Lord.

The temple is the Lord's university. We are continually learning. I
marvel that I am taught new and different things each time I enter the
temple.

I received my endowment when I was twenty years old. I was nervous and bewildered by all the symbolism. I went to the temple several
times before falling away into inactivity.

During my drinking years, I thought I would never return, but in
recovery, I did return to the temple, and for the first time, I began to love
my temple experiences.

Like Ezekiel's vision, the first time I went to the temple, I stuck my
little toe in the water and didn't even get my feet wet. But over time, as I
grew spiritually in recovery, the symbolism and meaning became a little
deeper. After a while, the water was to my ankles—then to my knees.
I could feel the blessings of a refreshing stream as I waded through recovery, but the living waters of temple worship had not entered into my
heart. After a while, that all changed, and I was totally immersed in
deep symbolism and deep gratitude. Precious truth was revealed to me
in that holy house as the Spirit permeated my thoughts and feelings.
Pure, refreshing, healing waters filled my heart and mind! The waters
became deep enough to swim in. When I live righteously, the blessings
of the temple spill over into everyday life. I feel immersed in the Savior's
love.

Ezekiel saw the living waters running eastward. The water gave life
to a parched desert, healed the Dead Sea, and soaked the thirsty land.
I once thirsted after alcohol, and it left me spiritually dead. The living
waters are healing me now. I hunger and thirst for the temple. It fills me,

and, like Ezekiel, I can proclaim (as everyone can), "Every thing shall live whither the river cometh" (Ezekiel 47:9).

Ezekiel concludes his vision of the temple with this verse: "And by the river upon the bank thereof, on this side and on that side, shall grow all trees for meat, whose leaf shall not fade, neither shall the fruit thereof be consumed: it shall bring forth new fruit according to his months, because their waters they issued out of the sanctuary: and the fruit thereof shall be for meat, and the leaf thereof for medicine" (Ezekiel 47:12).

For me, the protective façade of alcoholism faded. It quit working somehow. But where rivers run deep from the Lord's sanctuary, the "leaf shall not fade." I was consumed in my addictions, but the fruit of recovery and the blessings of temple worship shall never be consumed. Neither shall they fade away. They bring new fruit in their seasons. I am spiritually nourished, and the leaf thereof is medicine. You and I can sit side by side in the temple, dressed in white, and you can receive your medicine, and I can receive my medicine, even though our prescriptions may differ. The Lord knows each of us that intimately.

"IF GOD SO CLOTHE THE GRASS OF THE FIELD"

My patriarchal blessing mentions clothing twice. I received my blessing when I was fifteen years old. At that time in my life, clothes were only something to wear to make me fashionable. I only wanted to look good and impress my friends. I wondered why it was in my blessing, since I was not planning on ever wearing the articles of clothing mentioned. In my darkest despair as an alcoholic, there came a time when I wanted to put away forever the last remaining copy of my patriarchal blessing—so I didn't have to be taunted by the impossible dream. Today, I am grateful that I did not follow through with that impulse. Many of the promises in my patriarchal blessing have come to pass. Today, I am clothed, endowed, empowered, and blessed in the covenant. Today, and for altogether different reasons, it matters how I am clothed.

To the addict I plead that if you are like that "certain man" in the parable of the good Samaritan, who made that treacherous descent into Jericho, if you hit a bottom well below sea level, and "fell among thieves," who stripped you of your raiment, wounded you, and left you half dead, and if your drug of choice has taken everything away from you and the evil one, who drove you there, has now abandoned you, and if you think life is over and you cannot climb that mountain, do not give up (see Luke 10:30–37).

There is One who atoned for us all. He will come right to the spot, bind up your wounds, and pour in sacramental wine and the best oil, wrought out in Gethsemane. He will set you on His own beast. He felt your very pain in His mortal body, that He might "know according to the flesh how to succor [you]" (Alma 7:12). He will bring you to the inn—His Church—where He can take care of you. The cost has already been paid for; His grace is sufficient (see Ether 12:27). The best things cost the most!

And after all this, He desires not to make you a servant, but rather, a son or a daughter. In your descent of addiction, you may have been stripped of your raiment, but He can clothe you! Let go and let God. Let Him clothe you, empower you, and endow you, that you may receive the promised blessings of the Abrahamic covenant—even the blessings of exaltation and "a continuation of the seeds forever and ever" (D&C 132:19).

For so many years, I didn't see the mountains or green meadows or beautiful flowers. My heart waxed cold. The icy clutches of addiction had me frozen in my tracks. It was a long winter.

But once in recovery, the following words entered into my mind: Where the snow and ice melt, the lilies of the field will grow.

CHAPTER TWENTY-ONE

a penitent prodigal returns in royal raiment

The Lord is waiting. He is waiting for us to return and come unto Him with "full purpose of heart" so He can heal us (see 3 Nephi 18:32). He is waiting for us to put the Steps into action, to make covenants, and to consecrate our will and our lives to Him. He is waiting for that "pleasant" offering—"an offering made by fire unto the Lord," complete with a "broken heart and a contrite spirit" (see Malachi 3:4; Leviticus 24:7; 3 Nephi 9:20; and D&C 59:8).

"FOR THIS MY SON WAS DEAD, AND IS ALIVE AGAIN"

I love the parable of the prodigal son. The Savior gives three choice parables in a setting where publicans and sinners are drawn near to hear Him, and Pharisees and scribes murmur in the background. You can almost hear them saying, "Why does this Jesus spend so much time hanging out with those sinners, tax collectors, drunks, addicts, and other losers?"

The Savior personally invites each addict back to the real world of healing and recovery—to the life of eternal joy and happiness. He grants addicts license to do their best dreaming, knowing they will fall short and cheat themselves big time. But He still invites them to dare to dream, and to put their own wills and plans on the back burner for now, so He can show them the vision He has for them, which is far too beautiful, far too glorious, far too possible, and far too real for any addict to fathom.

In Luke 15, you'll find the parable of the prodigal son. The parable goes as follows:

"A *certain* man had two sons" (v. 11, emphasis added). Indeed, this father is a *certain* Personage, and, in the story, becomes a type of our Heavenly Father.

The younger son goes to the father and requests the portion of the inheritance that would fall to him. We can already sense that he is likely an addict, since he lacks the faith and patience to wait for the real reward of eternal life. Instead, he goes for instant gratification and seeks the pleasure of the moment—the instant buzz, the cheap thrill, the fleeting pleasure, or the immediate head rush. The father, who is a type of our Heavenly Father, is desirous to share with him "his living" (v. 12). The original Greek word here is *bios* (see *Strong's Exhaustive Concordance of the Bible* #979). It is the source of the English word *biology*. It means life or the course of life. It has implications of eternal life—the only life the Father can give. Jesus said, "For as the Father hath life in himself; so hath he given to the Son to have life in himself" (John 5:26). He also said, "Whoso eateth my flesh, and drinketh my blood, hath eternal life; and I will raise him up at the last day" (John 6:54). In other words, if we make and keep covenants with the Lord, we will inherit exaltation in the celestial kingdom!

When the Father in the parable "divides his living," he is not merely splitting up the assets. The Greek word for *divided* means to share, assign, or distribute (see *Strong's* #1244). In a symbolic sense, the father is sharing eternal life with the son.

Sadly addicts know from painful personal experience that if you offer a practicing alcoholic the choice between eternal life and his next drink, he will probably take the drink. The prodigal takes what he can get his hands on right now and chooses immediate self-gratification.

"Not many days after," the son takes his journey into a "far country." Elder Neal A. Maxwell said, "Like the prodigal son, we too can go to 'a far country,' which may be no further away than a vile rock concert. The distance to 'a far country' is not to be measured by miles but by how far our hearts and minds are from Jesus! (see Mosiah 5:13). Fidelity, not geography, really determines the distance!" (Neal A. Maxwell, "The Tugs and Pulls of the World," *Ensign* [November 2000]: 35).

As addicts, we speak of the former days when we were "out there" in a "far country," far away from our Father. In my own case, I turned and ran and stayed far away for thirteen lonely years.

In this far country the son quickly wastes his substance with "riotous living." The Greek word for *riotous* suggests immoral, lascivious, and lustful behavior (see *Strong's* #811). This behavior is confirmed by his brother, who accuses the prodigal of devouring his living with harlots (Luke 15:30). Perhaps the prodigal son had multiple addictions. We can all relate to the state of being "wasted," as we remember wasting away our lives and our resources.

Indeed, this sounds like a party to rival King Noah in the Book of Mormon—complete with wine, women, and song. But the party always ends and the so-called "glory days" quickly fade away. The pain of a "wasted" life seeps through the alcohol and drugs, and the best we can hope for is numbness or, better yet, extinction of "soul and body" (see Alma 36:15).

The prodigal can't go home anymore, so he joins himself to a citizen of that "far country." He is now a bondman, and his taskmaster stands over him. He is consigned to feed the pigs. It's a sickening life, but he will do anything to survive.

After a while, it seems like the pigs are eating better than he is. All of his friends have passed him up, and it seems that life has passed him by. How did it ever come to this pitiful mess? He likely asked himself, "Where did I go wrong? How did I get off the path, so far away from home?"

There is that wretched hole in the middle of his soul that he can't fill up with alcohol, drugs, sex, food, money, or anything else in the world. "He would fain have filled his belly with the husks that the swine did eat: and no man gave unto him" (Luke 15:16). He has spent all and given all to the god of addiction, and he is famished and in want.

Then, one day, he "came to himself." I imagine his thoughts were something like "I have lost everything. I can only salvage the fragments of a broken life. I have squandered my inheritance, and the promises of the fathers are mythical dreams that have somehow slipped away. I cannot return with honor. I will beg to be a slave—maybe a lowly servant. 'How many hired servants of my father's have bread enough and to spare, and I perish with hunger' (Luke 15: 17).

"'I will arise and go to my father, and will say unto him, Father, I have sinned against heaven, and before thee, And am no more worthy to be called thy son: make me as one of thy hired servants'" (Luke 15:18–19).

Finally, he arises and goes to his father. "But when he was yet *a great way off*, his father saw him, and had compassion, and ran, and fell on his neck, and kissed him" (Luke 15: 20, emphasis added).

Remember that the father in this parable is a type of our Heavenly Father, who is anxiously waiting for the wayward addict to make the slightest move toward heaven. He waits for us to hit bottom—to realize we have lost everything—and then make that slightest turn to Him.

The prodigal son returns to his father to make a deal with him. How oft I played that game with God during my drinking years! But this time the prodigal son is serious about the deal, and he dares to do his best dreaming. He says, "'Father, I have sinned against heaven, and in thy sight, and am no more worthy to be called thy son" (Luke 15:21). "Make me as one of thy hired servants" (Luke 15:19).

The Father flatly rejects the offer. He essentially says, "This is not good enough for my son, whom I love!" Isaiah said it nicely: "I gave Egypt for thy ransom" (Isaiah 43:3). His Only Begotten Son "suffered death in the flesh; wherefore he suffered the pain of all men, that all men might repent and come unto him." Remember the worth of your soul is great in the sight of God (see D&C 18:10–11).

The Father calls his servants (the prodigal son not included) and speaks to them saying, "Bring forth the *best robe*, and put it on him; and put a *ring* on his hand, and *shoes* on his feet: And bring hither the fatted calf, and kill it; and let us eat, and be merry: For this my *son* was dead, and is alive again; he was lost, and is found" (Luke 15:22–24, emphasis added).

The Father wants His son (or daughter) properly clothed in the covenant, so He calls for the *best robe*. The *best robes* this side of the veil are found in the temple. In the Book of Mormon, Jacob declares, "Wherefore, we shall have a perfect knowledge of all our guilt, and our uncleanness, and our nakedness; and the righteous shall have a perfect knowledge of their enjoyment, and their righteousness, being *clothed* with purity, yea, even with the *robe of righteousness*" (2 Nephi 9:14, emphasis added).

I think that the robe the father wants for his son is the robe in which our Heavenly Father wants us to be clothed. It is a robe representing His holy priesthood, and we become *clothed*, or embraced, in the covenant! No wonder Paul tells us to enter into a covenant, become clothed, and "put on Christ!" As we do so, we become Abraham's seed, and "heirs according to the promise" (see Galatians 3:27, 29).

The prodigal son is clearly a son, not a servant. Jesus made this distinction during His mortal ministry, as He said, "And the *servant* abideth not in the house for ever: but the *Son* abideth ever. If the Son therefore shall make you free, ye shall be free indeed" (John 8:35–36, emphasis added). We are only made free from addiction and temptation, in and through Jesus Christ.

We become much more than clean and sober servants. Through covenants we are born of Him and become spiritually begotten sons and daughters of Christ (see Mosiah 5:7). "And if children, then heirs; heirs of God, and joint-heirs with Christ" (Romans 8:17).

The father commands that the son be *clothed, endued,* and *endowed* in the robe, as he says, "Bring forth the *best robe,* and *put it on him*" (Luke 15:22, emphasis added; see also *Strong's* #1746). In a very real sense, he is "putting on Christ!"

Let's look at the other articles of clothing. "The father said to his servants, Bring forth the *best robe,* and put it on him; and put a *ring* on his hand, and *shoes* on his feet" (Luke 15: 22).

The ring signifies the eternal sealing power of the King, or the sealing power of one in authority. Like the robe, a ring would only be given to an heir of the covenant, not a servant. It is placed on the *hand*, and the *hand* is symbolic of covenants, power, and direction. The *right hand* in scripture is the covenant hand. You would use your hand to point or give direction. You would motion for someone to "come unto you" with your hand. It also suggests being led by the Lord, which is an important component of Steps Three and Eleven (and actually all twelve).

The Lord said:

> Behold, the days come, saith the Lord, that I will make a *new covenant* with the house of Israel, and with the house of Judah:
>
> Not according to the *covenant* that I made with their fathers in the day that I took them by the *hand* to bring them out of the land of Egypt [or house of bondage], which my covenant they brake, although I was an husband unto them, saith the Lord:
>
> But this shall be the *covenant* that I will make with the house of Israel; After those days, saith the Lord, I will put my law in their inward parts, and write it in their hearts; and will be their God, and they shall be my people. (Jeremiah 31:31–33, emphasis added)

The Lord took the children of Israel by the *hand* to bring them out of bondage. He continues to lead addicts by the *hand* in recovery. After leading them by the *hand*, He *seals* the law in their hearts, so it becomes permanent and eternal.

The *ring* placed on the hand of the prodigal son is also symbolic.

In the Book of Esther, Mordecai is given the king's ring as a token for him to write the law and "seal it." He is instructed, "Write ye also for the Jews, as it liketh you, in the *king's name*, and *seal it* with the *king's ring*: for the writing which is written in the *king's name*, and *sealed* with the *king's ring*, may no man reverse." Mordecai was given the power, authority, and responsibility to write the law, which no man could reverse. The scripture records, "And [Mordecai] wrote in the king Ahasuerus' name, and sealed it with the king's ring" (Esther 8:8, 10; emphasis added).

Also in the Old Testament, Joseph becomes ruler for all of Egypt:

> And Pharaoh said unto Joseph, Forasmuch as God hath shewed thee all this, there is none so discreet and wise as thou art:
>
> Thou shalt be over my house, and *according unto thy word* shall all my people be ruled: only in the throne will I be greater than thou.
>
> And Pharaoh said unto Joseph, See, I have set thee over all the land of Egypt.
>
> And Pharaoh took off his *ring* from his *hand,* and *put it* upon Joseph's *hand,* and *arrayed* him in vestures of *fine linen,* and put a *gold* chain about his neck;
>
> And he made him to ride in the second chariot which he had; and they cried before him, *Bow the knee:* and he made him ruler over all the land of Egypt. (Genesis 41:39–43, emphasis added)

Joseph is also given power and authority to rule according to his word and seal the law upon the land of Egypt. Again, the symbolic token is to take the ring and put it upon his hand. Then Joseph is arrayed in fine linen. In the Book of Revelation, the armies in heaven, which followed Christ, are also *"clothed in fine linen,* white and clean" (see Revelation 19:14, emphasis added). Again, the word *clothed* is *enduo,* where we get the English word *endowment* (see *Strong's* #1746).

Rings were also used in the construction of the tabernacle—the forerunner to the temple— and rings were placed on the corners of the ark of the covenant (see Exodus 26:23–24; 25:12).

A gold chain was placed on Joseph's neck. Gold represents the very best. The wise men presented their treasures of gold, frankincense, and myrrh to the young Christ child (see Matthew 2:11). As we give our very best to the Lord, He promises us eternal life—"the greatest of all the gifts of God" (D&C 14:7).

As the Egyptians "bow the knee" before Joseph, he becomes a type of Christ, the King of kings. Of this, Paul said, "For it is written, As I live, saith the Lord, every knee shall bow to me, and every tongue shall confess to God" (Romans 14:11).

In ancient times, the ring sealed the deal. In modern times, the sealing power was restored when Elijah appeared and stood before Joseph Smith and Oliver Cowdery in the Kirtland Temple on April 3, 1836. This glorious restoration of priesthood keys occurred on Easter Sunday, which was also during Passover. Thus, Elijah returned at Passover, according to tradition. The restoration of these priesthood keys would "turn the hearts of the fathers to the children," and "plant in the hearts of the children the promises made to the fathers" (see D&C 110:13–16; Malachi 4:5–6; and Joseph Smith—History 1:38–39). The "promises made to the fathers" are the promises and blessings of the patriarchal fathers—Abraham, Isaac, and Jacob—and we refer to these promises as the Abrahamic covenant, which promises lands for an "everlasting possession" and a "continuation of the seeds forever and ever" (see Genesis 17:8; D&C 132:19).

Thus, families can be sealed together for all eternity, and what is bound on earth shall be bound in heaven as sacred ordinances are performed in holy temples (see D&C 128:8).

Families once threatened by addiction can become eternal families. There can be no greater blessing in recovery. How grateful I am to know that our family can be eternal and can continue beyond the grave and beyond this mortal existence. How grateful I am to know that my sweet wife can be mine forever, and that our two wonderful children are sealed to us for all eternity. These sublime blessings can be ours because of sacred ordinances performed in holy temples, and they will come to fruition if we live worthily so that these ordinances are sealed and ratified by the "Holy Spirit of promise" (see D&C 132:19).

The prodigal son was given shoes to complete his apparel. Shoes, like the robe and ring, would not be provided for servants, but rather for an heir to the covenant. Shoes were very expensive in those days and would only be given to a chosen son or daughter.

Paul speaks of "the whole armour of God." He warns us to, "Stand therefore, having your . . . feet shod with the preparation of the gospel of peace" (Ephesians 6:11-15). The peace of the gospel is much more than mere absence of conflict. The "record of heaven" and the "peaceable things of immortal glory" are given through the Holy Ghost—the Comforter. It is given to abide in us, "the truth of all things; that which quickeneth all things, which maketh alive all things; that which *knoweth* all things, and hath all *power*" (Moses 6:61, emphasis added). Notice how much better addicts will be able to work Step Eleven as they seek *knowledge* of God's will for them, and *power* to carry out His will if their feet are shod with the preparation of the gospel of peace.

We must have the proper shoes on our feet, like the prodigal son, because our feet take us where we want to go. My feet, which used to carry me into bars and unwholesome places of entertainment, are the same feet that today carry me to Church and to the temple! My hand, which is capable of clicking a mouse and carrying me into a "far country" to view a pornographic Internet site, is the same hand I use to partake of the sacrament. I know the hands and feet are the same, but I like to think that I have "put on" a new ring and brand new shoes.

While we are on the subject of protective clothing and proven armor, let's not forget to "put on" the girdle of truth to keep our appetites, feelings, and desires in harmony with God's will, the "breastplate of righteousness" to protect the desires of our hearts, the "shield of faith" to "quench all the fiery darts of the wicked," the "helmet of salvation" to keep our thoughts clean, and the "sword of the Spirit," to provide an offensive weapon in recovery (see Ephesians 6:13–17).

Now that the prodigal son is properly clothed, he is ready for the feast. The father calls for the fatted calf to be brought forth and killed, in likeness to both a sacrifice and a feast.

Under the Mosaic law, animal sacrifices were offered as burnt offerings at the great feasts. For seven days during the Feast of Unleavened Bread, for seven days during the Feast of Tabernacles, and on the day of Pentecost, special burnt offerings were offered. The sacrifices were more numerous during the Feast of Tabernacles, "the greatest and most joyful of all" (see Numbers 28–29; Bible Dictionary, "Feasts"). The return of the prodigal son would certainly qualify as a joyous feast of great celebration.

The burnt offerings given at the great feasts represented sacrifice and total surrender to the Lord. The Bible Dictionary states:

> The *burnt offering* got its Hebrew name from the idea of
> the smoke of the sacrifice ascending to heaven. The charac-

teristic rite was the burning of the *whole* animal on the altar
(Lev. 1:9; Deut. 33:10). As the obligation to surrender was
constant on the part of Israel, a burnt offering, called the continual burnt offering, was offered twice daily, morning and
evening. (Bible Dictionary, "Sacrifices," emphasis added)

What better way is there for addicts to work Steps Three, Six, and
Seven, to turn their will and their lives over to God, to become willing
to sacrifice their character defects, and to ask God to remove them than
to burn the whole animal inside, with all of its sins and carnal desires,
allowing their will to go up in smoke?

The fact that there is a feast with the fatted calf in the parable of the
prodigal son symbolically suggests two things. First, the once-wayward
son is now ready to surrender everything and trust God uncondition-
ally. He is ready to "let go and let God." Second, there is cause for great
celebration at his return to feast at the table of the Lord, for as the Lord
Himself said earlier in this chapter, "There is joy in the presence of the
angels of God over one sinner that repenteth" (Luke 15:10).

Addicts do not have to wait until the completion of their journey
home to feel of Heavenly Father's love for them. Even though they may
be "a great way off," as soon as they turn to their Father and their personal Savior, They will come running to embrace them and help them
come home.

A BIRTHDAY WISH AND A PRAYER
FOR THE SUFFERING ADDICT

July 31, 2008, marks nineteen years since my last drink! That represents 6,935 miracles plus a few leap days. Each sober day is a miracle for
an old drunk like me, and each one represents the grace of God. Each
birthday is the end of another year of sobriety, and it is a new beginning.

I have heard it said in AA and now know it to be true that "I still
have another drunk in me, but I don't know if I have another recovery."
I surely don't want to find out either.

Today, I pray for me. I pray for all addicts and for those who love
them, and whose lives are also in turmoil.

I invite everyone to come unto Christ.

"For we have not an high priest which cannot be touched with the feeling of our infirmities; but was in all points tempted like as we are, yet without sin. Let us therefore come *boldly* unto the throne of grace, that we may obtain mercy, and find grace to help in time of need" (Hebrews 4:15–16, emphasis added).

At the dedication of the Kirtland Temple, the revealed prayer came to the Prophet Joseph Smith: "That our garments may be pure, that we may be clothed upon with robes of righteousness, with palms [of victory] in our hands, and crowns of glory upon our heads, and reap eternal joy for all our sufferings" (D&C 109:76).

I share that hope and prayer for the suffering addict!

> Awake, and arise from the dust ... and put on thy beautiful garments.
>
> Yea, come unto Christ, and be perfected in him, and deny yourselves of all ungodliness; and if ye shall deny yourselves of all ungodliness, and love God with all your might, mind and strength, then is his grace sufficient for you, that by his grace ye may be perfect in Christ; and if by the grace of God ye are perfect in Christ, ye can in nowise deny the power of God.
>
> And again, if ye by the grace of God are perfect in Christ, and deny not his power, then are ye sanctified in Christ by the grace of God, through the shedding of the blood of Christ, which is in the covenant of the Father unto the remission of your sins, that ye become holy, without spot. (Moroni 10:31–33)

I end this book the way it began. I think of an old tavern—my old haunt. There was a mighty change in that old tavern. It has been transformed from a bar to a pizza and ice cream restaurant. The walls have received new paint, and the windows have been cleaned. New lights were installed, and the floors and countertops now shine.

But one thing remains in that tavern. My old barstool is still empty! I have earned a seat in the rooms of Alcoholics Anonymous, a seat at the local LDS Twelve-Step meeting, a seat in sacrament meeting, and, as always, a seat in the temple. My name is Brad. And I am *still* an alcoholic and an addict in recovery, and I hope you'll join me if you are an addict seeking solace; there is an empty seat next to me with your name on it.

author biography

Brad Bertelsen is a lifelong resident of Springville, Utah. He graduated from Springville High School and received a bachelor's degree in psychology from Brigham Young University.

He met his wife, Darlene, after he had been sober for four years. They were married in the Jordan River Utah Temple. They are the parents of two children.

Brad is an active member of Alcoholics Anonymous and regularly attends the LDS Twelve-Step meetings. He has been sober from alcohol and drugs for over nineteen years, which he attributes to the grace of God!

He enjoys long walks, good music, attending the temple, and searching the scriptures.